Good Housekeeping

COOKBOOK

Good Housekeeping

AGA

COOKBOOK

Over 150 recipes for Agas and other range ovens

EBURY PRESS
LONDON

First published 1996

1 2 3 4 5 6 7 8 9 10

First published in the United Kingdom in 1996 by Ebury Press,
Random House, 20 Vauxhall Bridge Road, London SW1V 2SA

Random House Australia (Pty) Limited
20 Alfred Street, Milsons Point, Sydney,
New South Wales 2061, Australia

Random House New Zealand Limited
18 Poland Road, Glenfield,
Auckland 10, New Zealand

Random House South Africa (Pty) Limited
PO Box 337, Bergvlei, South Africa

Random House UK Limited Reg. No. 954009

A CIP catalogue record for this book is available from the British Library.

Managing Editor: JANET ILLSLEY
Design: SARA KIDD
Recipe Testing: SARAH NOPS, MIRANDA HALL, KATE FRYER
Illustrations: MADELEINE DAVID
Photographs: GRAHAM KIRK; except pages 27, 71, 87, 91, 99, and 103: GUS FILGATE; pages 35, 55, 101, 115 and 139: JAMES MURPHY; pages 15 and 59: HARRY CORY-WRIGHT; page 51: LAURIE EVANS; page 107: MICHELLE GARRETT.

ISBN 0 09 181 438 3

Typeset in Helvetica
Colour Separations by Colorlito, Rigogliosi – Milano
Printed and bound in Portugal by Printer Portuguesa L.d.a.

CONTENTS

INTRODUCTION

4

SOUPS AND STARTERS

12

FISH AND SHELLFISH

25

POULTRY AND GAME

37

MEAT DISHES

50

VEGETARIAN DISHES

72

SUPPER DISHES

85

ACCOMPANIMENTS

93

DESSERTS

100

CAKES, BISCUITS AND BREADS

120

PRESERVES

138

INDEX

142

COOKERY NOTES

•Both metric and imperial measures are given for the recipes. Follow one set of measures throughout as they are not interchangeable.

•All spoon measures are level unless otherwise stated. Sets of measuring spoons are available in metric and imperial for accurate measurement of small quantities.

•These recipes have been tested in both 2-oven and 4-oven Aga cookers. Where the cooking instructions differ for a recipe, both are given. The following symbols apply:-

■ ■ for a 2-oven Aga

■ ■ ■ ■ for a 4-oven Aga

•Where a stage is specified for freezing, the dish should be frozen at the end of that stage.

•Size 2 eggs should be used except where otherwise specified. Free-range eggs are recommended.

•Use freshly ground black pepper and sea salt unless otherwise specified.

•Use fresh rather than dried herbs unless dried herbs are suggested in the recipe.

•Stocks should be freshly made if possible. Alternatively buy ready-made stocks or use good quality stock cubes.

INTRODUCTION

The Aga is a cast-iron heat storage cooker which was invented in 1922 by the Swedish physicist, Dr Gustaf Dalen. It was introduced into England in 1929, and has become so popular that 'Aga' is now an established household name.

An Aga may be expensive to buy but it is an excellent investment, as it serves many purposes and will last a lifetime if properly used and maintained. Its timeless, classic design has changed little over the years, although you can now choose from a range of vitreous enamel colours to co-ordinate or contrast the cooker with the rest of your kitchen.

You will find that the Aga becomes the focus of the kitchen, creating a special, all-year-round warm atmosphere. Ensure your cooker is positioned to take full advantage of this, especially if you eat in the kitchen – which you will almost certainly want to do once your Aga is installed! During hot weather simply open the windows to maintain a comfortable temperature.

How an Aga Works

The fuel for your Aga may be natural gas, propane, solid fuel, oil or off-peak electricity but, whatever the heat source, all Agas basically function in the same way. The heat is generated in the burner unit and conducted around the walls of the cast-iron ovens and hot plates. The cast-iron surfaces store heat and release it as radiant heat at a steady rate when needed. As you cook, the heat lost is automatically restored because the Aga is thermostatically controlled. Different areas of the cooker are maintained at different temperatures to provide a range of cooking options. Food smells and vapours are conveniently ducted away from the ovens to the external flue.

Two-oven and Four-oven Agas

Agas are available in two sizes: two-oven and four-oven models. The two-oven Aga has a roasting oven and a simmering oven. In addition to these, the four-oven has a warming oven and a baking oven. These ovens are deceptively large, with a capacity in excess of 30 cu cm (1 cu ft), and every part of the ovens can be used. On top, both appliances have a fast boiling plate and a gentle simmering plate, protected by chrome insulated lids. The four-oven cooker also has a gentle warming plate. Again, the hot plates are large, each allowing room for up to four pans. The most popular model in this country is the two-oven cooker.

Some Aga models will provide domestic hot water. Your choice of model will obviously depend on your individual requirements. Unlike domestic cookers, Agas are assembled in your own home by the manufacturer's engineers.

Differences Between Using an Aga and a Conventional Cooker

▶ The Aga is a constant source of heat: there's no need to wait for the oven or hob to heat up.

▶ The Aga operates on the principle of heat storage and is surprisingly efficient to run.

▶ The Aga has no dials or knobs to adjust for a change in temperature. Once you are used to your Aga, you will find this simplification an advantage.

▶ The Aga does not have a separate grill, but grilling takes place at the top of the roasting oven, or in a grill pan on the boiling plate.

▶ Because most Aga cooking takes place in the large, versatile ovens rather than on the hot plates, condensation and cleaning are minimised.

▶ The Aga is vented through a flue, so there are virtually no cooking smells from the ovens.

▶ Because the cast-iron walls of the Aga ovens retain heat so well, you don't need to worry about losing heat as you open the door, to peep at a soufflé or cake for example. With a conventional oven, this can cause such a drop in temperature that a soufflé or cake may collapse.

Conserving Heat in the Aga

The secret to success with an Aga is to cook inside, rather than on the top with the lids up, whenever possible – this way you conserve heat. Few foods need to be cooked entirely on the hot plates and those which do, such as stir-fries and green vegetables, cook quickly. Many dishes which would be cooked on the top of a conventional cooker, such as soups and stews, are started off on the hot plates, then transferred to the appropriate oven. The following tips on conserving heat may help:-

▶ Always keep the hot plate lids shut unless they are in use.

When using the hot plates, cover as much of the surface area as possible, with one large pan or several smaller ones.

Allow chilled items to stand at room temperature (for 1-2 hours) before placing in the ovens, especially turkeys, joints, casseroles, soups, etc.

Thaw frozen food before cooking. Ideally leave in the refrigerator overnight, then at room temperature for 1-2 hours.

Plan your menu carefully when you are entertaining or cooking for large family gatherings to avoid trying to cook several dishes at the same time which all need a very hot oven. This is particularly important if you have a 2-oven Aga. Of course, many dishes can be cooked in advance and reheated to serve.

If you are batch baking, bread for example, at a high temperature, allow up to 2 hours for your oven to return to temperature if you need maximum heat for your next batch of cooking. Alternatively, take advantage of the slightly cooler oven to bake cakes and biscuits.

When there is going to be a heavy demand on your cooker, turn up the Aga heat dial slightly, about an hour in advance, remembering to return it to the normal setting before going to bed.

The Heat Indicator

The gauge on the front of your cooker indicates whether your Aga has the correct amount of heat stored.

When the heat indicator is on the thin black line, your Aga has the right amount of heat stored and is operating at its optimum.

If the indicator is towards the black shaded area, there is less heat stored and cooking will therefore take longer.

If the mercury reaches the red area, there is more than the required amount of heat stored and it is possible that there may be something wrong. Before calling your local approved Aga engineer, check that the control dial hasn't been altered.

During cooking, the temperature will fluctuate a little, but should soon return to its normal setting. If you've been using the hot plates extensively, the cooker may take 2-3 hours to recuperate.

Getting to Know Your Own Aga

Each Aga is slightly different from the next: its position in the kitchen, whether situated between units or free-standing, on an inside or outside wall; the type of fuel used, and whether or not your Aga also supplies the hot water; these factors will all add to its individuality. You may find it takes a little time to get to know and love your Aga with its own personality!

Basic Principles of Aga Cooking

As different areas of the Aga are kept at different temperatures, you simply need to choose the right position for the dish you are cooking, depending upon whether it requires a low, moderate or high temperature, fast or slow cooking.

Each oven presents a range of options, because the temperature varies slightly within each oven, from top to bottom, front to back, and side to side. The top is the hottest part; the back will be a little hotter than the front; the side nearest the burner unit will be hotter than the opposite side.

The Roasting Oven

Apart from roasting and baking, this versatile hot oven is used for shallow-frying, grilling, steaming and simmering. The oven has four shelf positions; the floor of the oven, and the grid shelf placed on the floor of the oven give two more cooking positions.

THE COLD PLAIN SHELF supplied with the Aga allows you to use the roasting oven for baking items which require a more moderate temperature. You simply slide in the cold shelf, usually two sets of runners above the food being cooked, to deflect the top heat and create a moderate heat below. With the 2-oven Aga, this is an important function. (Other uses – see page 10.) If your cold plain shelf is already in use, the large Aga roasting tin can fulfil the same function; to maintain the lower temperature throughout cooking, half-fill the tin with cold water after 20-30 minutes.

Cooking in the Roasting Oven

The recommended shelf positions for the recipes in this book are, of course, provided, but you may wish to adapt conventional recipes from elsewhere. You can, of course, purchase an oven thermometer to check the operational temperature of the different positions within your oven, if you wish. As a rough guide, the roasting oven shelf positions are used as follows:

TOP (OR FIRST) RUNNERS
Grilling (on oiled preheated rack over roasting tin)
SECOND RUNNERS
Browning dishes, gratins, roast potatoes, scones
THIRD RUNNERS
Fast-roasting, bread-baking, jacket potatoes
BOTTOM (FOURTH) RUNNERS
Medium-roasting, pastry
GRID SHELF ON OVEN FLOOR
Slower-roasting (eg pork, poultry)

THE TWO-OVEN AGA

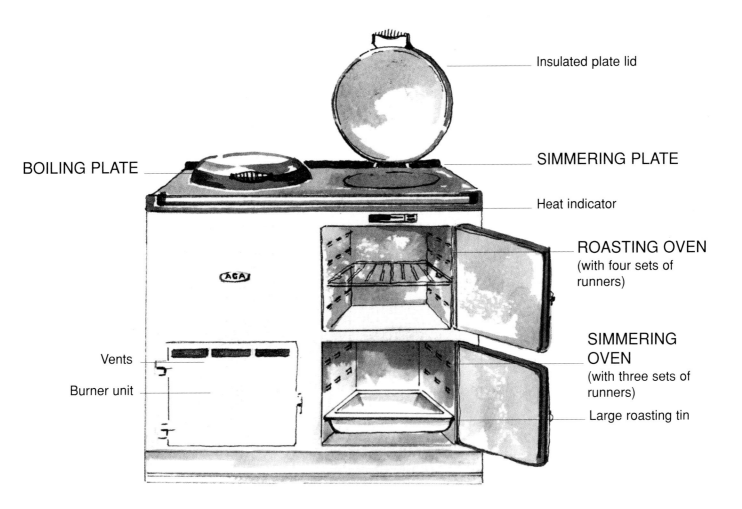

Insulated plate lid

BOILING PLATE

SIMMERING PLATE

Heat indicator

ROASTING OVEN
(with four sets of
runners)

SIMMERING
OVEN
(with three sets of
runners)

Large roasting tin

Vents

Burner unit

OVEN FLOOR
Crisp pastry bases (flans, etc); to crisp roast potatoes, frying, fast reduction of sauces, preheating griddles and frying pans
GRID SHELF ON OVEN FLOOR
WITH COLD PLAIN SHELF ABOVE
(in a 2-oven Aga)
Baking fish, biscuits and cakes

The Simmering Oven

This oven has a minimum of three cooking positions: the floor, the grid shelf on the floor of the oven, and the middle runners which take the cold plain shelf and the Aga roasting tins, as well as the grid shelf. In addition, the 2-oven Aga has a further 2 sets of runners. The temperature of the oven can vary, but is generally around 100°C (212°F), within an ideal range for slow, gentle cooking. Almost all dishes need to be started off at a higher temperature (on one of the hot plates or other ovens), then transferred to the simmering oven to complete cooking.

The main uses of this oven are as follows:-

▶ ROOT VEGETABLES Place in a saucepan, cover with cold water, put the lid on the pan and bring to the boil on the boiling plate. Cook for 3-5 minutes, then drain off all but about 1 cm (½ inch) water. Salt lightly, recover and transfer to the simmering oven to steam until tender, about 20-30 minutes. Potatoes, in particular, benefit from being cooked in this way: they will be soft through to the centre without falling apart.

▶ STOCKS Bring to the boil in a covered pan on the boiling plate, then transfer to the floor of the simmering oven. In this way, you will be able to make flavoursome, jellied stocks, without the unpleasant cooking smells usually associated with boiling stocks.

▶ CASEROLES These cook superbly in the gentle heat of this oven. First bring to a simmer on one of the hot plates, then place in the simmering oven to cook slowly. To speed up cooking, you can place the casserole on the grid shelf on the floor of the roasting oven for 15-20 minutes of each hour.

▶ MERINGUES Perfect light, crisp meringues can be cooked entirely in the simmering oven; the floor is the ideal position.

▶ Porridge can be cooked overnight in this oven.

▶ CAKES With a 2-oven Aga, the simmering oven is often used to complete the cooking of cakes which have been part-baked in the roasting oven. Large rich fruit cakes can be cooked overnight on the grid shelf on the floor of the simmering oven without being started off elsewhere – to delicious effect.

▶ KEEPING FOODS HOT/REHEATING The temperature of the simmering oven is perfect for keeping foods warm, without spoiling.

▶ RESTING MEAT If you have a 2-oven Aga, this oven is most useful for resting roasted poultry and joints of meat.

The Four-oven Aga Baking Oven

This is situated below the roasting oven and has the same number of runners and corresponding versatile cooking positions. The temperature in the middle of this oven averages 180°C (350°F) – ideal for many baking purposes.

▶ The top of the oven is used for baking biscuits, small cakes, roulades, etc.

▶ The middle is used for sandwich cakes, crumbles, poaching and baking fish.

▶ The bottom of the oven with the grid shelf in position is used for casseroles, deep cakes, and poaching ham.

The Four-oven Aga Warming Oven

This is maintained at approximately 70°C (160°F) and is very temperate.

▶ It is the ideal place to warm plates and serving dishes, and to keep foods warm without spoiling, including delicate sauces.

▶ Allow roasts to rest in this oven for 20 minutes before carving.

▶ Meringues and porridge can be cook overnight in this oven.

The Boiling Plate

The main function of this hot plate is to bring foods up to a fast boil, before continuing to cook elsewhere in, or on the Aga. It is also used for quick frying, stir-frying, cooking green vegetables and making toast (with the special Aga toaster).

The Simmering Plate

This is used for bringing foods up to a gentle simmer; slow-frying, including sweating vegetables; foods which require gentle cooking with constant attention, such as delicate sauces.

▶ The hot plate also doubles up as an excellent griddle: simply lightly oil or butter the clean surface and cook drop scones, crumpets, etc, directly on it.

The Four-oven Aga Warming Plate

This is a useful extra warm surface – ideal for holding dishes taken out of an oven, and warming the teapot.

▶ It is also suitable for melting chocolate, butter, etc.

▶ Bread dough can be risen on this hot plate: place the bowl on a folded towel to avoid direct contact.

▶ Note that the area at the back of an Aga is also a good source of warmth.

Aga Equipment

The following items are supplied with your Aga:-

GRID SHELF This has non-tilt runners, so it can be drawn out to the full extent without danger of tipping.

COLD PLAIN SHELF This is used as a shelf, a full-size baking sheet, and to lower the temperature in the roasting oven (see page 8). When not in use, the cold plain shelf should be stored outside the cooker. A second one of these is most useful.

AGA ROASTING TINS These have many uses and two are supplied: the full-size tin and a half-size roasting tin, both of which can be hung from the runners in the ovens. Apart from the obvious functions, the roasting tins can be used for grilling, with the rack in position; traybakes, such as flapjacks; bain-maries, for custards etc. The large roasting tin can also be used as an alternative cold shelf (see page 8).

THE AGA TOASTER This is used to toast bread, crumpets, etc of any thickness on the boiling plate.

Other items of equipment which you will find useful:-

SPLATTER GUARD This is most useful for covering pans during frying, to protect the Aga surface.

THE AGA GRILL PAN This ridged cast-iron non-stick pan is excellent for cooking steaks, chops, etc. It is first preheated on the floor of the roasting oven for 5-10 minutes, then used on the boiling plate. (A similar ovenproof ridged cast-iron skillet can be used.)

THE AGA CAKE BAKER A non-essential item, but one that you will find most useful if you are a 2-oven Aga owner and often bake large cakes that take longer than 45 minutes to cook, such as Madeira, rich fruit cakes, etc.

Pans and Cookware

Although it isn't essential to buy a whole new range of pots and pans when you become an Aga owner, it is important to make sure that the bases of your existing pans are perfectly flat, to ensure good contact with the hot plate. Good quality pans with thick ground bases which conduct heat well should really be used. (Ask the Aga shop or cooker centre in your area for advice on the suitability of your pans.)

All of your saucepans should be suitable for use in the simmering oven (with handles and lids heat resistant to the temperature range of this oven), as well as on the hot plates. For the recipes in this book, it is assumed that this is the case.

Ovenproof is used in these recipes to denote that the pan (or casserole) must be suitable for use in the roasting oven.

Hard anodised aluminium, stainless steel and cast-iron pans are the most suitable choices. Aga manufacture their own ranges of cookware in these materials, so you may prefer to choose from these if you are buying new cookware. The pans are designed with flat lids, so that they can be stacked on top of each other to save space in the oven if required.

Cast-iron cookware is particularly efficient to use with an Aga, and is most attractive. You may, however, find that the very large pans are heavy to lift in and out of the ovens.

If you are buying new pans, consider the following basic selection:-

- 4 saucepans, ranging from 2-4 litre (3½-7 pint) capacity
- 1 large 25-30 cm (10-12 inch) ovenproof frying pan
- 1 omelette pan (which can also be used as a crêpe pan)
- 2-3 casseroles, ranging from 2-4 litre (3 ½-7 pint) capacity – suitable for use on the hot plates)
- The Aga grill pan (or other ridged skillet)

Note: The largest pan which will fit into the oven has a 13 litre (22 pint) capacity. This is useful for preserves and cooking for crowds!

Cleaning the Aga

This is an easy task because most of the cooking takes place in the ovens and you therefore have very little grease to contend with.

The hot plates, roasting oven and 4-oven Aga baking oven are largely self-cleaning. Any thing which is spilt will carbonise and can be brushed away easily with the wire brush provided.

The other areas of the cooker do not become as dirty, due to the type of cooking they are used for. Simply wipe down with warm soapy water, then polish with a soft, dry cloth.

Clean the enamel and chrome areas regularly with a cream cleaner, such as *Astonish*.

Wipe away any spills as soon as they occur. This is particularly important for spilled milk, fruit juice, preserves and other acidic foods which might otherwise damage the enamel with prolonged contact.

Spring Cleaning your Aga

Aim to give your Aga a thorough clean to coincide with its recommended regular service:-

Carefully lift off the oven doors and lay, enamel-side down, on a cloth. Clean the inside of the doors with a cream cleanser, or soap-filled wire pad if necessary. Wipe over the seal but do not allow it to become wet.

Clean the chrome shelves and the inside of the hot plate covers with a cream cleanser. Brush out the ovens.

Clean the rest of the enamel and chrome areas with a cream cleaner, such as *Astonish*. For best results, polish this off with a soft, dry cloth.

The Aga isn't just a Cooker...

Your Aga will make your kitchen an efficient drying and airing room.

Damp washing can be hung over the chrome rail as long as it does not obstruct the vents of the burner unit.

Dry, folded sheets and clothes may be stacked in a neat pile on top of the simmering plate cover to air.

An old-fashioned clothes airer can be suspended from a high kitchen ceiling to provide plenty of additional drying space. Traditional cast-iron and pine ones are available, and these are an attractive feature in any kitchen, without any running costs. You may even find that your tumble dryer becomes obsolete!

Herbs, flowers and petals for pot pouri can be hung near the cooker to dry in the gentle warmth.

On a bitterly cold night, always remember to leave the kitchen door ajar. You will find that the warmth from the Aga will take the chill off the house.

SOUPS AND STARTERS

MINESTRONE ALLA MILANESE

■ SERVES 6-8 ■ PREPARATION 40 MINUTES ■ COOKING ABOUT 1¾ HOURS
■ FREEZING SUITABLE: STAGE 3 ■ 345-260 CALS PER SERVING

Each region of Italy has its own minestrone featuring local produce, but the Milanese version is believed to be the original. You can add almost any vegetable to a minestrone, but you must have onions, celery, carrots, beans, potatoes and tomatoes. If possible, make it the day before serving, to allow the flavours to develop.

50 g (2 oz) butter
125 g (4 oz) pancetta or streaky bacon, derinded and diced
450 g (1 lb) onions, peeled and diced
175 g (6 oz) carrots, peeled and diced
175 g (6 oz) swede or turnip, peeled and diced
125 g (4 oz) celery, diced
125 g (4 oz) courgettes, diced
75 g (3 oz) French beans, finely chopped
175 g (6 oz) potatoes, peeled and diced
75 g (3 oz) Savoy cabbage, cored and finely shredded
1.7 litres (3 pints) beef or vegetable stock
400 g (14 oz) can chopped tomatoes
salt and freshly ground black pepper
400 g (14 oz) can cannellini or borlotti beans, drained and rinsed
50 g (2 oz) Parmesan cheese, freshly grated

1 Melt the butter in a large casserole on the SIMMERING PLATE. Add the pancetta and onions and sauté for 5 minutes or until soft, stirring frequently. Stir in the carrots, swede or turnip and celery, and sauté for 5 minutes.

2 Add the courgettes, French beans and potatoes. Cook, stirring, for about 5 minutes or until all the vegetables are coated in butter, then add the cabbage.

3 Move the casserole to the BOILING PLATE. Add the stock, chopped tomatoes and seasoning. Bring to the boil, then cover and transfer to the floor of the SIMMERING OVEN. Cook for 1 hour, then add the beans and cook for a further 30 minutes.

4 Stir in half of the Parmesan cheese. Ladle the soup into warmed bowls and serve accompanied by the remaining cheese, to be sprinkled over the minestrone to taste.

COOK'S TIP *Pancetta is similar to bacon and is available in Italian delicatessens. As an alternative, use thick-cut, rindless streaky bacon.*

CARROT AND GINGER SOUP

■ SERVES 6 ■ PREPARATION 10 MINUTES, PLUS RESTING
■ COOKING ABOUT 1½ HOURS ■ FREEZING SUITABLE: STAGE 4
■ 160 CALS PER SERVING

If you are short of oven space, omit the pastry and simply serve the hot soup in bowls, garnished with a generous spoonful of crème fraîche.

50 g (2 oz) butter
275 g (10 oz) onions, peeled and roughly chopped
900 g (2 lb) carrots, peeled and roughly chopped
7.5 cm (3 inch) piece fresh root ginger, peeled and grated
2 cloves garlic, peeled and crushed
250 ml (8 fl oz) white wine
1.2 litres (2 pints) vegetable stock
salt and freshly ground black pepper
450 g (1 lb) ready-made shortcrust pastry
beaten egg, to glaze

1 Melt the butter in a large casserole on the SIMMERING PLATE. Stir in the onions, carrots, ginger and crushed garlic, and cook, stirring, for 4-5 minutes.

2 Move the casserole to the BOILING PLATE. Add the wine and stock and bring to the boil.

3 Cover the casserole and transfer to the floor of the SIMMERING OVEN. Cook for about 1 hour until the vegetables are tender. Allow to cool slightly.

4 Transfer the soup to a food processor or blender and process until smooth. Check the seasoning; allow to cool.

5 Fill 6 ovenproof soup bowls with the cold soup.

6 Roll out the pastry thinly on a lightly floured surface and cut out 6 rounds, to fit over the tops of the bowls; set aside. Cut 6 strips of pastry 5 mm (1/4 inch) wide and long enough to fit around the rim of each bowl. Lightly dampen the rim of each bowl with water. Apply the pastry strips and press gently to adhere. Brush the edges with a little of the egg glaze. Position the pastry lids on top of the bowls, pressing the edges together to seal.

7 Brush the pastry lids with egg glaze and season with pepper. Chill in the refrigerator for 10-15 minutes before cooking.

8 Stand the soup bowls in a large roasting tin. With the grid shelf on the third set of runners, cook in the ROASTING OVEN for 6-8 minutes until golden. Slide the cold plain shelf onto the first set of runners and cook for a further 10 minutes or until the pastry is crisp and deep golden brown. Serve at once.

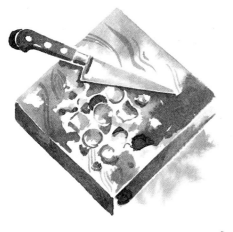

BAKED CHEDDAR AND ONION SOUP

■ SERVES 8 ■ PREPARATION 15 MINUTES ■ COOKING ABOUT 1½ HOURS
■ FREEZING SUITABLE: STAGE 3 ■ 505 CALS PER SERVING

75 g (3 oz) butter
700 g (1½ lb) red onions, peeled and thinly sliced
3 garlic cloves, peeled and crushed
45 ml (3 tbsp) plain flour
600 ml (1 pint) cider or apple juice
1.2 litres (2 pints) vegetable stock
200 ml (7 fl oz) double cream
5 ml (1 tsp) chopped fresh thyme or 2.5 ml (1/2 tsp) dried
2 bay leaves
salt and freshly ground black pepper
1 bunch spring onions, trimmed and roughly chopped
175 g (6 oz) Cheddar cheese, grated
16 thin slices focaccia or ciabatta bread
chopped thyme leaves, to garnish

1 Melt the butter in a large casserole on the SIMMERING PLATE. Add the red onions and garlic and cook, stirring, for 10-15 minutes or until soft and golden and beginning to caramelise. Transfer to the BOILING PLATE, sprinkle with the flour and cook, stirring, for 2 minutes.

2 Remove from the heat and whisk in the cider or apple juice, vegetable stock and cream. Bring to the boil on the BOILING PLATE and add the thyme, bay leaves and seasoning. Boil steadily, uncovered, for 5 minutes.

3 Cover and transfer to the floor of the SIMMERING OVEN. Cook for about 1 hour until the red onions are very soft. Discard the bay leaves. If a smooth soup is preferred, purée the soup in a blender or food processor at this point.

4 Ladle the warm soup into ovenproof bowls. Sprinkle with half of the spring onions and half of the cheese. Float the slices of bread on the soup, then sprinkle with the remaining spring onions and cheese.

5 Place the bowls in a large roasting tin and with the grid shelf on the second set of runners, cook in the ROASTING OVEN for 8-10 minutes, or until bubbling and golden.

6 Serve immediately, garnished with a few chopped thyme leaves as a starter, or lunch or supper dish.

Bacon and Celeriac Soup

■ SERVES 4 ■ PREPARATION 20 MINUTES ■ COOKING ABOUT 45 MINUTES
■ FREEZING SUITABLE: STAGE 5 ■ 190 CALS PER SERVING

Celeriac is a versatile root vegetable with a mild flavour, reminiscent of celery. In appearance, it most closely resembles a turnip. Here it forms the basis of a sustaining soup which is surprisingly low in calories.

350 g (12 oz) lean smoked bacon, derinded
15 ml (1 tbsp) vegetable oil
1 large onion, peeled and finely chopped
1 garlic clove, peeled and finely chopped
350 g (12 oz) celeriac, peeled and sliced
900 ml (1½ pints) vegetable or chicken stock
salt and freshly ground black pepper
thyme sprigs, to garnish

1 Trim any fat off the bacon; set aside 4 rashers and finely chop the remainder.

2 Heat the oil in a large saucepan on the SIMMERING PLATE. Add the onion and garlic and fry gently for 7 minutes or until the onion is beginning to soften.

3 Add the chopped bacon and cook for 5 minutes. Stir in the celeriac and continue to cook for a further 5 minutes.

4 Move the pan to the BOILING PLATE. Add the stock and seasoning and bring to the boil. Let bubble for 2-3 minutes, then cover and transfer to the SIMMERING OVEN. Cook gently for 20-30 minutes or until the celeriac is very tender. Allow to cool slightly.

5 Transfer the soup to a blender or food processor and work until smooth.

6 Place the reserved bacon on a rack in the small roasting tin. Hang the tin on the first set of runners in the ROASTING OVEN and cook the bacon for 3-4 minutes each side, until crisp. Return the soup to the saucepan and reheat on the SIMMERING PLATE. Adjust the seasoning. Serve garnished with the crispy bacon and thyme sprigs.

Seafood Pesto Chowder

■ SERVES 8 ■ PREPARATION 15 MINUTES ■ COOKING 50 MINUTES
■ FREEZING SUITABLE: STAGE 3 ■ 330 CALS PER SERVING

Serve this hearty potage as a substantial starter followed by a light main course, or as a tasty lunch or supper with plenty of warm crusty bread.

50 g (2 oz) butter
225 g (8 oz) onion, peeled and roughly chopped
30 ml (2 tbsp) plain flour
450 ml (¾ pint) fish stock
150 ml (¼ pint) white wine
150 ml (¼ pint) double cream
50 g (2 oz) Parmesan cheese, freshly grated
salt and freshly ground black pepper
125 g (4 oz) shelled scallops, cleaned
275 g (10 oz) salmon fillet
275 g (10 oz) skinned smoked haddock fillet
350 g (12 oz) tomatoes
50 g (2 oz) chopped fresh basil or parsley
125 g (4 oz) cooked peeled prawns

1 Melt the butter in a large heavy-based casserole on the SIMMERING PLATE. Stir in the onion and cook for 10 minutes or until soft and golden. Add the flour and cook, stirring, for 1 minute.

2 Transfer to the BOILING PLATE. Gradually stir in the stock, wine and cream, then whisk continuously until the mixture comes to the boil and is smooth.

3 Transfer to the SIMMERING OVEN and cook gently for 10 minutes. Remove from the oven, stir in the Parmesan cheese and season well.

4 Rinse the scallops well under cold, running water; pat dry. If the scallops are large, cut them in half horizontally.

5 Cut the salmon and haddock into 5 cm (2 inch) strips. Place in a large ovenproof dish in a single layer and pour over the stock mixture. Cover the dish loosely with foil.

6 ■ ■ Cook on the grid shelf on the floor of the ROASTING OVEN with the cold plain shelf on the runners just above for 25-30 minutes, adding the scallops to the sauce halfway through the cooking time.

■ ■ ■ ■ Cook on the grid shelf on the fourth set of runners in the BAKING OVEN for 20-30 minutes, adding the scallops halfway through the cooking time.

7 Meanwhile, immerse the tomatoes in a bowl of boiling water for 30 seconds. Drain, then peel away the skins. Halve the tomatoes, de-seed, then cut the flesh into strips.

8 Stir the basil or parsley, tomatoes and prawns into the chowder. Check the seasoning and warm through in the SIMMERING OVEN for 5 minutes. Serve immediately.

COOK'S TIP *If using frozen scallops and/or prawns, make sure you defrost them thoroughly and drain well before adding to the soup.*

15

MUSHROOM AND ARTICHOKE SOUP WITH WALNUTS

■ SERVES 4 ■ PREPARATION 20 MINUTES, PLUS SOAKING ■ COOKING 1¾ HOURS
■ FREEZING SUITABLE: STAGE 5 ■ 250 CALS PER SERVING

Jerusalem artichokes might be mistaken for a funny looking potato, but these knobbly and often hairy root vegetables have a distinctive flavour of their own. Here an intensely flavoured mushroom stock combines beautifully with the artichokes, and toasted walnuts add texture to the soup.

15 g (½ oz) dried ceps
150 ml (¼ pint) boiling water
25 g (1 oz) butter
1 small onion, peeled and chopped
15 ml (1 tbsp) chopped fresh thyme
450 g (1 lb) chestnut mushrooms, chopped
90 ml (3 fl oz) dry sherry
1 litre (1¾ pints) vegetable stock
450 g (1 lb) Jerusalem artichokes
30 ml (2 tbsp) walnut oil
1 garlic clove, peeled and chopped
salt and freshly ground black pepper
TO SERVE
25 g (1 oz) walnuts, chopped and toasted
extra walnut oil
thyme sprigs, to garnish

1 Put the dried ceps into a bowl, pour over the boiling water and let soak for 30 minutes. Drain, reserving the liquid.

2 Melt the butter in a large casserole on the SIMMERING PLATE. Add the onion and thyme and fry for 10 minutes until soft but not browned. Move to the BOILING PLATE, add the chestnut mushrooms and ceps and stir-fry for 2 minutes. Add the sherry and boil rapidly until well reduced.

3 Add the vegetable stock and reserved cep soaking liquid and bring to the boil. Cover and cook gently in the SIMMER-ING OVEN for 30-40 minutes until the stock is rich tasting and the mushrooms have lost all their flavour.

4 Meanwhile, scrub the artichokes and cut away the knobbly bits. Peel, then dice the flesh. Heat the oil in a large pan on the BOILING PLATE. Add the artichokes and garlic and fry for 8-10 minutes, stirring, until evenly browned.

5 Strain the mushroom stock through a fine sieve. Return to the casserole, add the artichokes and bring to the boil. Cover and cook on the floor of the SIMMERING OVEN for 45 minutes until the artichokes are cooked. Allow to cool slightly, then transfer to a blender or food processor and purée until very smooth.

6 Return the soup to the pan and heat gently on the SIMMERING PLATE for 5 minutes. Season with salt and pepper to taste and spoon into warmed soup bowls. Scatter the toasted nuts over the soup and drizzle with walnut oil. Serve at once, garnished with thyme.

COOK'S TIP *To toast walnuts, spread on a baking sheet and with the grid shelf on the top set of runners, cook in the* ROASTING OVEN *for 2-3 minutes.*

VARIATION To enrich the soup, stir 150 ml (¼ pint) single cream into the puréed artichokes at the end of stage 5. Finish as above.

VICHYSSOISE WITH LEMON GRASS

■ SERVES 6 ■ PREPARATION 15 MINUTES ■ COOKING ABOUT 1 HOUR
■ FREEZING SUITABLE: STAGE 3 ■ 225 CALS PER SERVING

This creamy, velvety soup is based on a popular classic – but with the added fragrance of oriental lemon grass. If possible, use fresh lemon grass, though you will find that dried is more readily available. To ensure a really smooth texture, it is important to liquidise and sieve the soup before serving, either hot or chilled.

75 g (3 oz) butter
2 onions, peeled and thinly sliced
450 g (1 lb) trimmed leeks (white part only), sliced
175 g (6 oz) floury potatoes, peeled and diced
1 lemon grass stalk (preferably fresh), bruised
1.3 litres (2¼ pints) chicken stock
300 ml (½ pint) milk
150 ml (¼ pint) crème fraîche
salt and freshly ground white pepper
TO SERVE
extra crème fraîche
chives, to garnish

1 Melt the butter in a large saucepan on the SIMMERING PLATE and add the onions and leeks. Stir well, add 45 ml (3 tbsp) water, cover tightly and cook for 15-20 minutes in the SIMMERING OVEN until soft and golden.

2 Stir in the potatoes, lemon grass, chicken stock and milk. Bring to the boil on the BOILING PLATE, allow to bubble for 2-3 minutes, then cover and cook in the SIMMERING OVEN for 30-40 minutes until the potatoes are tender.

3 Discard the lemon grass. Allow the soup to cool slightly, then transfer to a blender or food processor and work until smooth. Pass through a sieve and return to the pan if serving hot.

4 Stir in the crème fraîche and seasoning to taste. If serving cold, cool and chill thoroughly (in this case season liberally) or reheat on the SIMMERING PLATE and pour into warmed soup bowls. Serve topped with a dollop of chilled crème fraîche and chives, to garnish.

COOK'S TIP *Fresh lemon grass is sold in the herb section of some supermarkets. It will freeze, but turns brown, which won't impair the flavour. Dried lemon grass is good too, as long as it isn't too old!*

VARIATION Replace the leeks with a bunch of spring onions, and add a bunch of trimmed and chopped watercress to the soup just before liquidising. The soup will be beautifully green, with a wonderful fresh taste.

TOASTED BACON AND GOATS' CHEESE SALAD

■ SERVES 6 ■ PREPARATION 15 MINUTES ■ COOKING 6 MINUTES
■ FREEZING NOT SUITABLE ■ 320 CALS PER SERVING

about 350 g (12 oz) soft, rindless goats' cheese
2 bunches fresh chives, finely chopped
salt and freshly ground black pepper
350 g (12 oz) thin-cut, rindless streaky bacon
25 g (1 oz) walnut pieces, toasted and roughly chopped
60 ml (4 tbsp) walnut oil
10 ml (2 tsp) balsamic or red wine vinegar
1.25 ml (¼ tsp) sugar
75 g (3 oz) mixed green salad leaves, such as lamb's lettuce,
frisée and rocket
toasted ciabatta, to serve

1 With moistened hands, shape the goats' cheese into 6 patties. Carefully roll the patties in the chopped chives to coat and season with pepper only. Chill in the refrigerator until needed.

2 Stretch the rashers of bacon by running the back of a round-bladed knife along each piece. Carefully wrap each patty in bacon, making sure the cheese is totally enclosed and the ends of bacon are tucked underneath; you'll need 3-4 rashers per patty. Cover and chill until required.

3 Mix the walnuts with the walnut oil, vinegar, sugar and seasoning to taste. Combine the salad leaves in a bowl.

4 Preheat an ovenproof frying pan on the floor of the ROASTING OVEN for 5-7 minutes. Lift onto the BOILING PLATE and place the patties in the pan. Cook for 2 minutes until golden underneath, then turn the patties over. Replace the pan on the floor of the ROASTING OVEN for 4 minutes to cook the base and sides of the patties.

5 Toss the salad leaves with the dressing and arrange on individual serving plates. Top each one with a warm cheese patty. (If any cheese has oozed out, scoop it on to the mixed salad leaves to serve.) Serve immediately, with toasted ciabatta.

COOK'S TIP *To toast walnuts, spread on a baking tray and with the grid shelf on the top set of runners, cook in the* ROASTING OVEN *for 2-3 minutes.*

17

BABA GANOUSH

■ SERVES 4 ■ PREPARATION 10 MINUTES, PLUS COOLING

■ COOKING 30-40 MINUTES ■ FREEZING NOT SUITABLE

■ 100 CALS PER SERVING

Baba Ganoush is a tasty mixture of garlicky aubergine and olives which appears on almost every Greek taverna menu. Serve it with warm pitta bread and a bowl of olives as a light starter.

700 g (1½ lb) aubergines
1 garlic clove, peeled and crushed
2.5 ml (½ tsp) salt
30 ml (2 tbsp) lemon juice
30 ml (2 tbsp) olive oil
15 ml (1 tbsp) chopped fresh flat-leaf parsley
30 ml (2 tbsp) roughly chopped black olives
warm pitta bread, to serve

1 Prick the skin of the aubergines with a fork. Place in a roasting tin on the fourth set of runners in the ROASTING OVEN. Cook for 30-40 minutes until very tender.

2 Place the aubergines in a colander and slit lengthwise. Let the bitter juices drain out and leave until cool.

3 Scoop out the aubergine flesh into a bowl, discarding the skins. Add the garlic, salt, lemon juice, olive oil and parsley. Beat with a fork until almost smooth, then add the chopped olives. Serve with warm pitta bread.

COOK'S TIP *Baba Ganoush can be prepared ahead and kept covered in the refrigerator overnight.*

ONION TARTLETS WITH TOMATO AND CAPER SALSA

■ SERVES 4 ■ PREPARATION 25 MINUTES ■ COOKING ABOUT 30 MINUTES

■ FREEZING NOT SUITABLE ■ 490 CALS PER SERVING

Sweet caramelised onions, fresh basil and toasted pine nuts make a delicious filling for these simple tartlets. They are complemented by a piquant sauce of fresh and sun-dried tomatoes flavoured with chilli and capers.

30 ml (2 tbsp) olive or sunflower oil
450 g (1 lb) onions, peeled and sliced
about 300 g (10 oz) puff pastry, fresh or frozen and thawed
25 g (1 oz) pine nuts, toasted
12 fresh basil leaves, shredded
salt and freshly ground black pepper
a little milk, to glaze
SALSA
1 tomato, halved, seeded and finely chopped
1 red chilli, halved and seeded
25 g (1 oz) sun-dried tomatoes in oil, drained
25 g (1 oz) capers
15 ml (1 tbsp) olive oil

1 Heat the oil in a flameproof casserole. Add the onions and cook on the floor of the ROASTING OVEN, stirring occasionally, for about 15-20 minutes until golden brown and caramelised.

2 Meanwhile, roll out the puff pastry on a lightly floured surface to a 3-5 mm (⅛-¼ inch) thickness. Using a saucepan lid or small plate as a guide, cut four 15 cm (6 inch) circles. Knock up the edges using a round-bladed knife and flute them decoratively. Place the pastry discs on a baking sheet and prick with a fork.

3 Add the pine nuts and basil to the caramelised onions and season with salt and pepper to taste. Divide the mixture between the pastry discs, leaving a 2.5 cm (½ inch) clear margin around the edges.

4 Brush the pastry edges with a little milk to glaze. Bake in the ROASTING OVEN with the grid shelf on the second set of runners for about 8-10 minutes until well risen, crisp and golden brown, turning them around halfway through to ensure even cooking if necessary.

5 While the tarts are baking, prepare the salsa. Put the chopped tomato in a small bowl. Chop the chilli, sun-dried tomatoes and capers together on a board and add to the tomato with the olive oil. Mix well, seasoning with salt and pepper to taste.

6 Serve the tartlets hot or warm, accompanied by the tomato and caper salsa.

COOK'S TIP *To toast pine nuts, spread on a baking sheet and with the grid shelf on the top set of runners, cook in the* ROASTING OVEN *for 1-2 minutes.*

VARIATION Replace the capers with roasted peppers in oil, drained and cut into bite-sized pieces.

CRISPY CRAB CAKES WITH SWEET GINGER DIP

■ SERVES 8 ■ PREPARATION 35 MINUTES ■ COOKING 20-25 MINUTES
■ FREEZING SUITABLE: STAGE 3 ■ 255 CALS PER SERVING

These luxury fish cakes may be a little time-consuming to prepare, but they are well worth the effort. An oriental-style dip is the perfect complement.

CRAB CAKES
700 g (1½ lb) old potatoes, peeled and quartered
salt and freshly ground black pepper
450 g (1 lb) white crabmeat, thawed (see cook's tip)
6 spring onions, trimmed and roughly chopped
3 garlic cloves, peeled and finely chopped
5 cm (2 inch) piece fresh root ginger, peeled and finely chopped
2 small red chillies, seeded and chopped
50 g (2 oz) can anchovy fillets, drained and chopped
finely grated zest of 1 lime
45 ml (3 tbsp) chopped fresh parsley
45 ml (3 tbsp) chopped fresh coriander
125 g (4 oz) fresh white breadcrumbs
30 ml (2 tbsp) black or white sesame seeds
seasonal flour, for coating
2 eggs, beaten
50 g (2 oz) unsalted butter, melted
SWEET GINGER DIP
2 spring onions, trimmed and finely chopped
2.5 cm (1 inch) piece fresh root ginger, peeled and grated
30 ml (2 tbsp) dark soy sauce
90 ml (6 tbsp) rice vinegar, or cider vinegar
10 ml (2 tsp) sugar
TO GARNISH
lime slices

1 Cook the potatoes in a pan of boiling salted water on the SIMMERING PLATE for 3-4 minutes. Drain off most of the water, cover and cook in the SIMMERING OVEN for 15-20 minutes or until tender. Drain, then mash with a fork and allow to cool.

2 Flake the crabmeat into a bowl. Add the spring onions, garlic, ginger, chillies, anchovy fillets, lime zest and herbs. Season generously with salt and pepper. Gently stir in the mashed potato.

3 With floured hands, shape the crabmeat mixture into 16 patties. Place on a board, cover and chill in the refrigerator for 10-15 minutes.

4 Mix the breadcrumbs with the sesame seeds. Dip the crab cakes, one at a time, in seasoned flour, then in beaten egg and finally in the breadcrumbs to coat.

5 Brush the crab cakes all over with the melted butter and place in the large roasting tin. Hang the tin from the second set of runners in the ROASTING OVEN and cook for 20-25 minutes until golden brown and hot through, turning the crab cakes halfway through cooking.

6 Meanwhile, prepare the dip. Whisk all the ingredients together in a bowl, then transfer to a shallow serving bowl.

7 Drain the crab cakes on kitchen paper. Serve immediately, with the ginger dip.

COOK'S TIPS
▶ Fresh dressed crabmeat is available from fishmongers and fresh fish counters of larger supermarkets. Alternatively use frozen, rather than canned meat.
▶ Rice vinegar is available from oriental food shops.
▶ For convenience, the crab cakes can be prepared ahead to the end of stage 3, then refrigerated for up to 4 hours before cooking.

MUSSELS WITH GINGER, CHILLI AND CORIANDER

■ SERVES 4 ■ PREPARATION 20 MINUTES ■ COOKING 10 MINUTES
FREEZING NOT SUITABLE ■ 175 CALS PER SERVING

A deliciously spicy alternative to moules marinières, which uses the same method of cooking. If you prefer a creamy sauce, opt for one of the variations.

1 kg (2¼ lb) mussels
15 g (½ oz) fresh coriander sprigs
1 bunch of spring onions, trimmed and shredded
2 garlic cloves, peeled and finely chopped
25 g (1 oz) piece fresh root ginger, peeled and shredded
1 small red chilli, seeded and finely shredded
150 ml (¼ pint) white wine
40 g (1½ oz) butter
coriander sprigs, to garnish

1 Wash the mussels thoroughly in several changes of cold water, then scrub with a stiff brush under cold running water, pulling away the beards from the sides of the shells. Discard mussels with damaged shells, or any that refuse to close when tapped with the back of a knife. Put the mussels in a colander and set aside.

2 Strip the leaves from the coriander and set aside; reserve the stalks.

3 Put the spring onions, garlic, ginger, chilli and coriander stalks in a pan which is large enough to hold the mussels. Add the wine and 150 ml (¼ pint) water. Bring to the boil on the BOILING PLATE and simmer for 2 minutes.

4 Add the mussels to the pan and cover with a tight-fitting lid. Cook on the SIMMERING PLATE, shaking the pan occasionally, until the shells open; this will take about 5 minutes. Turn the mussels into a colander set over a bowl. Discard the coriander stalks and any unopened mussels.

5 Pour the liquid from the bowl back into the pan and place on the SIMMERING PLATE. Whisk in the butter, a piece at a time. Lastly, add the coriander leaves.

6 Transfer the mussels to warmed individual serving dishes and pour over the sauce. Serve immediately, garnished with coriander sprigs.

VARIATIONS
▶ At stage 5, stir in 60-75 ml (4-5 tbsp) crème fraîche instead of the butter.
▶ Replace the wine with 150 ml (¼ pint) coconut milk.

KING PRAWNS WITH A SPICY TOMATO AND PEPPER SAUCE

■ SERVES 4 ■ PREPARATION 20 MINUTES ■ COOKING 40 MINUTES
■ FREEZING NOT SUITABLE ■ 315 CALS PER SERVING

24 raw king prawns in shell
30-45 ml (2-3 tbsp) olive oil
SAUCE
2 ripe plum tomatoes
60 ml (4 tbsp) olive oil
1 onion, peeled and chopped
4 garlic cloves, peeled and chopped
1 canned pimiento, drained and chopped
2.5 ml (½ tsp) dried chilli flakes
75 ml (5 tbsp) fish stock
30 ml (2 tbsp) white wine
10 blanched almonds, toasted
15 ml (1 tbsp) red wine vinegar
salt
TO GARNISH
flat-leaf parsley sprigs

1 To make the sauce, immerse the tomatoes in a bowl of boiling water for 30 seconds, then refresh in cold water. Drain, peel and roughly chop the tomato flesh.

2 Heat 30 ml (2 tbsp) of the oil in a pan on the SIMMERING PLATE. Add the onion and 3 chopped garlic cloves; cook gently until softened. Add the chopped tomatoes and pimiento, chilli flakes, stock and wine. Bring to the boil, cover and cook in the SIMMERING OVEN for 30 minutes.

3 Coarsely grind the toasted almonds in a food processor or blender. Add the remaining oil and garlic, vinegar and salt to taste. Work until evenly combined. Add the tomato sauce and blend until smooth. Reheat if necessary.

4 Remove the heads from the prawns and, using a sharp knife, slit each one down the back and remove the black vein. Rinse in cold water, and dry on kitchen paper.

5 Toss the prawns in olive oil, then place in the large roasting tin in a single layer. Cook on the floor of the ROASTING OVEN for 2-3 minutes on each side, until the shells have turned pink, turning the prawns once only. Arrange the prawns on a serving platter, garnish with parsley and serve at once, with the warm tomato sauce.

ROASTED TOMATO AND SHALLOT SALAD

■ SERVES 6 ■ PREPARATION 15 MINUTES ■ COOKING 15-20 MINUTES
■ FREEZING NOT SUITABLE ■ 300 CALS PER SERVING

Roasting softens tomatoes and enhances their natural sweetness to delicious effect. Make sure you buy full-flavoured tomatoes – vine-ripened ones are ideal – or, better still, use homegrown ones when available.

15 small tomatoes
salt and freshly ground black pepper
10-15 ml (2-3 tsp) caster sugar
15 ml (1 tbsp) chopped fresh thyme
130 ml (4 fl oz) olive oil
45 ml (3 tbsp) freshly squeezed orange juice
5 ml (1 tsp) Dijon mustard
5 ml (1 tsp) white wine vinegar
15 small shallots or spring onions, peeled and halved
(see cook's tip)
TO GARNISH
chopped chives
thyme sprigs

1 Immerse the tomatoes in a bowl of boiling water for 15-30 seconds, depending on ripeness, to loosen the skins, then plunge into cold water. Remove and peel away the skins. Halve the tomatoes and scoop out the seeds if you wish. Place the tomatoes, cut-side up, on the oiled base of the large roasting tin. Sprinkle with salt, pepper, the sugar and thyme.

2 ■ ■ With the cold plain shelf on the second set of runners, hang the roasting tin on the third set of runners in the ROASTING OVEN. Cook for 8-10 minutes.
■ ■ ■ ■ Hang the roasting tin on the third set of runners in the BAKING OVEN and cook for 10-15 minutes or until the tomatoes are tender but still retain their shape.

3 For the dressing, whisk 100 ml (3½ fl oz) of the olive oil with the orange juice, mustard and vinegar.

4 Heat 30 ml (2 tbsp) oil in a frying pan on the SIMMERING PLATE. Add the shallots or spring onions and fry for 6-8 minutes, until golden and tender. Take off the heat, then pour in the dressing to warm through.

5 Arrange 5 tomato halves on each serving plate. Top with the shallot halves. Spoon over the dressing and sprinkle with chopped chives and thyme sprigs to serve.

COOK'S TIP *To make it easier to peel shallots, first plunge them into a bowl of boiling water and leave for a few minutes to loosen the skins, then drain and peel.*

ROASTED ASPARAGUS SALAD

■ SERVES 4-6 ■ PREPARATION 10 MINUTES ■ COOKING ABOUT 10-12 MINUTES
■ FREEZING NOT SUITABLE ■ 275-180 CALS PER SERVING

Roasting is a great way to cook asparagus.
There is no water added so the true flavour of the vegetable is not 'diluted', and the asparagus remains crisp.
The cooking time applies to stalks of medium thickness.
Plump asparagus stems should be cooked for longer, and their stalks may require peeling.

700 g (1½ lb) asparagus spears
90 ml (6 tbsp) olive oil
45 ml (3 tbsp) lemon juice
coarse sea salt and freshly ground black pepper
TO SERVE
rocket leaves
lemon wedges
Parmesan cheese shavings (optional)

1 Trim the woody ends from the asparagus spears, then lay the asparagus in the large roasting tin. Spoon over 60 ml (4 tbsp) of the olive oil and shake lightly to mix.

2 Hang the roasting tin from the second set of runners in the ROASTING OVEN and cook for 10-12 minutes, or until the asparagus is just tender, shaking gently halfway through cooking. Allow to cool.

3 To serve, spoon the remaining olive oil over the asparagus and sprinkle with the lemon juice. Season with coarse sea salt and freshly ground black pepper and toss lightly. Serve with rocket leaves and lemon wedges. Sprinkle with finely pared shavings of Parmesan, if liked.

SALMON TERRINE

■ SERVES 8-10 ■ PREPARATION 45 MINUTES, PLUS CHILLING
■ COOKING 50 MINUTES-1 HOUR ■ FREEZING SUITABLE: SEE COOK'S TIPS
■ 435-540 CALS PER SERVING

This sumptuous terrine is perfect for entertaining, as it can be made 2-3 days in advance. Serve accompanied by thin slices of wholemeal or granary bread.

625 g (1 lb 6 oz) skinned salmon fillet
175 g (6 oz) skinned plaice fillets
3 eggs
7.5 ml (1½ tsp) salt
freshly ground black pepper
350 ml (12 fl oz) double cream
15 ml (1 tbsp) chopped fresh parsley
15 ml (1 tbsp) chopped fresh chives, or spring-onion tops
60 ml (4 tbsp) mayonnaise
two 125 g (4 oz) packs gravadlax with mustard and dill sauce
(see cook's tips)
lemon wedges, to serve

1 Roughly chop 400 g (14 oz) of the salmon and all of the plaice fillets. Put the chopped salmon in a blender or food processor and work until smooth. With the machine still running, add 2 eggs, one at a time, through the feeder tube, processing until evenly mixed. Transfer the mixture to a bowl, then beat in 5 ml (1 tsp) each salt and pepper.

2 Wash out the blender or processor goblet and repeat this process using the plaice fillets, remaining egg, 2.5 ml (½ tsp) each salt and pepper. Cover both bowls and chill in the refrigerator for 30 minutes.

3 Gradually beat 200 ml (7 fl oz) cream into the salmon mixture by hand, one tablespoonful at a time. Beat the remaining cream into the plaice mixture, in the same way, then fold in the chopped herbs.

4 Thinly slice the remaining salmon fillet diagonally into escalopes, then place between two sheets of cling film and flatten gently with a rolling pin until almost transparent.

5 Base-line a 1.4 litre (2½ pint) terrine with greaseproof paper. Spoon half the salmon mixture into the terrine and spread evenly to cover base. Lay half the salmon escalopes on top in a thin, even layer to completely cover the salmon

mixture, trimming them to fit as necessary. Spread half the plaice and herb mixture evenly over the salmon. Lay the remaining salmon escalopes on top, then cover with the remaining plaice and herb mixture. Top with the remaining salmon mixture. Cover the whole terrine with foil and chill for 30 minutes.

6 Stand the covered terrine in the small roasting tin containing enough boiling water to come halfway up the sides.

7 ■■ Cook on the grid shelf on the floor of the ROASTING OVEN with the cold plain shelf on the runners just above for 40 minutes. Transfer to the SIMMERING OVEN with the grid shelf on the second set of runners and cook for a further 10-20 minutes, or until a skewer inserted in the centre comes out clean and hot.
■■■■ Cook on the grid shelf on the floor of the BAKING OVEN for 50-60 minutes, or until a skewer inserted into the centre comes out clean and hot.

8 Take the terrine out of the water, remove the foil and leave to cool completely. Cover with cling film and refrigerate for at least 4 hours.

9 Stir the mayonnaise into the mustard and dill sauce from the gravadlax. Unmould the terrine, remove the greaseproof paper and spread a little of the dill sauce all over the top and sides. Cover the terrine with slices of gravadlax. Cover with cling film and chill again until ready to serve.

10 To serve, slice the terrine and arrange on individual plates. Serve with lemon wedges and the remaining mustard and dill sauce.

COOK'S TIPS

▶ *Most supermarkets sell packs of gravadlax with mustard and dill sauce. If you can't find it, use smoked salmon and make a mustard and dill sauce by blending 5 ml (1 tsp) each white wine vinegar and sugar with 15 ml (1 tbsp) mild American mustard, 7.5 ml (1½ tsp) chopped fresh dill and 50 ml (2 fl oz) oil.*

▶ *For convenience, the terrine can be prepared 2-3 days ahead and stored in the refrigerator. If you wish to freeze the terrine, place in the freezer covered with cling film as at stage 8. When ready to use, thaw overnight in the refrigerator.*

FISH AND SHELLFISH

MUSSELS IN SAFFRON CIDER BROTH

■ SERVES 4-6 ■ PREPARATION 15 MINUTES ■ COOKING 25 MINUTES
■ FREEZING NOT SUITABLE ■ 630-420 CALS PER SERVING

This delicious alternative to moules marinières will serve 4 as a main course, or 6 as a starter. Accompany with plenty of crusty bread to mop up the delectable juices.

3 kg (6$\frac{1}{2}$ lb) mussels
50 g (2 oz) butter
225 g (8 oz) onion, peeled and chopped
2 garlic cloves, peeled and crushed
300 ml ($\frac{1}{2}$ pint) cider
large pinch of saffron strands
300 ml ($\frac{1}{2}$ pint) double cream
30 ml (2 tbsp) chopped fresh herbs, such as parsley, dill or chives

1 Wash the mussels thoroughly in several changes of cold water, then scrub under cold running water pulling away the beards from the sides of the shells. Discard mussels with damaged shells, or any that refuse to open, when tapped with the back of a knife.

2 Melt the butter in a large saucepan on the SIMMERING PLATE. Add the onion and garlic, and cook, stirring, for 10 minutes, or until soft. Add the cider and saffron strands.

3 Transfer to the BOILING PLATE. Bring to the boil, then add the mussels and bubble vigorously for 3-5 minutes, or until the shells open, shaking the pan from time to time.

4 Drain the mussels in a colander over a large bowl, reserving the liquid. Strain the liquid through a fine sieve, then return to the saucepan. Add the cream and bring to the boil on the BOILING PLATE. Allow to bubble for 10 minutes or until reduced and syrupy.

5 Meanwhile, discard any mussels that have not opened. Add the cooked mussels to the sauce and reheat for 30 seconds. Serve immediately, garnished with herbs.

SEAFOOD RISOTTO

■ SERVES 4 ■ PREPARATION 15 MINUTES ■ COOKING 30 MINUTES
■ FREEZING NOT SUITABLE ■ 615 CALS PER SERVING

A wonderfully aromatic risotto, this makes a perfect dish for an informal supper, piled high with steaming mussels.

50 g (2 oz) butter
175 g (6 oz) onion, peeled and finely chopped
225 g (8 oz) Arborio (risotto) rice
4 garlic cloves, peeled and crushed
450 ml ($\frac{3}{4}$ pint) white wine
450 ml ($\frac{3}{4}$ pint) hot fish or vegetable stock
45 ml (3 tbsp) pesto sauce
50 g (2 oz) Parmesan cheese, freshly grated
60 ml (4 tbsp) chopped fresh parsley
salt and freshly ground black pepper
1.4 kg (3 lb) mussels in their shells, cleaned (see left)

1 Melt 25 g (1 oz) butter in a large saucepan on the SIMMERING PLATE. Stir in the onion and fry for about 5 minutes or until soft but not coloured. Add the rice with half of the garlic and stir well.

2 Add 300 ml ($\frac{1}{2}$ pint) of the wine and the hot fish stock, a ladleful at a time, allowing each addition to be absorbed before adding the next. This should take about 25 minutes; the rice is ready when it is tender and creamy but retains some bite; it may not be necessary to add all of the stock.

3 Stir in the pesto, Parmesan cheese and 30 ml (2 tbsp) parsley. Check the seasoning. Keep warm.

4 Place the mussels in a large saucepan with the remaining 25 g (1 oz) butter, crushed garlic and 150 ml ($\frac{1}{4}$ pint) wine. Cover with a tight-fitting lid and cook on the SIMMERING PLATE for 3-5 minutes shaking the pan frequently, until the shells open; discard any that do not.

5 Spoon the risotto onto warmed serving plates. Pile the mussels on top, allowing the cooking juices to seep into the risotto. Sprinkle with the remaining chopped parsley and serve at once.

FISH FILLETS WITH SPICY TOMATO SAUCE

■ SERVES 6 ■ PREPARATION 20 MINUTES, PLUS MARINATING
■ COOKING ABOUT 12 MINUTES ■ FREEZING NOT SUITABLE
■ 180 CALS PER SERVING

4 garlic cloves, peeled and crushed
5 ml (1 tsp) ground ginger
5 ml (1 tsp) ground coriander
2.5 ml (½ tsp) chilli powder
60 ml (4 tbsp) white wine vinegar
700 g (1½ lb) fish fillets, such as cod, haddock or salmon
30 ml (2 tbsp) oil
175 g (6 oz) shallots or onions, peeled and sliced
1 large red chilli, seeded and thinly sliced
2.5 ml (½ tsp) ground turmeric
30 ml (2 tbsp) soft brown sugar
5 ml (1 tsp) mustard
15 ml (1 tbsp) lemon juice
15 ml (1 tbsp) tomato purée
450 g (1 lb) tomatoes
125 g (4 oz) spring onions, trimmed and sliced

1 For the marinade, mix half the garlic with half the ginger, the coriander, chilli powder and half the vinegar. Arrange the fish in a shallow dish and pour over the marinade. Cover and leave to marinate for 1 hour, turning occasionally.

2 Meanwhile make the sauce. Heat the oil in a saucepan on the BOILING PLATE. Add the shallots, sliced chilli, remaining garlic and ginger, and the turmeric. Stir well, cover and cook in the SIMMERING OVEN for 5 minutes.

3 Return the pan to the BOILING PLATE. Stir in remaining vinegar, sugar, mustard, lemon juice, tomato purée and 120 ml (4 fl oz) water. Bring to the boil and bubble for 1-2 minutes.

4 Meanwhile, immerse the tomatoes in boiling water for 30 seconds; remove and peel. Halve, deseed and roughly chop the tomatoes. Add to the sauce with the spring onions. Heat through, then keep warm on the back of the cooker.

5 Remove the fish from the marinade and place in a single layer in an oiled large, shallow baking tray. Cook in the ROASTING OVEN with the grid shelf on the fourth set of runners for 5 minutes until the flesh is opaque and the fish is just cooked. Serve at once, with the hot spicy tomato sauce.

SEARED SCALLOPS WITH ROASTED PLUM TOMATOES

■ SERVES 4 ■ PREPARATION 15 MINUTES ■ COOKING 30-35 MINUTES
■ FREEZING NOT SUITABLE ■ 350 CALS PER SERVING

16 large fresh scallops, cleaned (see cook's tip)
90 ml (6 tbsp) extra-virgin olive oil
2 garlic cloves, peeled
coarse sea salt and freshly ground black pepper
30 ml (2 tbsp) chopped fresh thyme or parsley
6 large plum tomatoes (or other flavourful tomatoes)
3 rosemary sprigs

1 Rinse the scallops and pat dry with kitchen paper. Place in a bowl and spoon over 45 ml (3 tbsp) of the olive oil. Crush the garlic cloves to a paste on a chopping board with a little coarse sea salt. Add to the scallops with the chopped thyme or parsley. Season with pepper and mix well. Cover and refrigerate while preparing the tomatoes.

2 Cut the tomatoes lengthwise in half. Place them in one layer, cut-side up, in a shallow baking tin. Add the rosemary and season liberally with sea salt. Drizzle over the remaining olive oil. Roast on the grid shelf in the middle of the ROASTING OVEN for about 30-35 minutes, until tender but still holding their shape.

3 About 15 minutes before the tomatoes will be ready, pre-heat a large cast-iron ridged skillet or ovenproof heavy-based frying pan on the floor of the ROASTING OVEN for about 10 minutes, then oil lightly and set on the BOILING PLATE.

4 Add the scallops to the hot skillet in a single layer. Allow to sizzle undisturbed for 1½ minutes, then turn each scallop and cook the other side for 1½ minutes.

5 To serve, lift the tomatoes onto a warmed serving platter; add the scallops and rosemary sprigs. Tip the oil from the tomatoes onto the hot skillet and add the lemon juice to deglaze. Trickle the juices over the scallops and roasted plum tomatoes. Serve at once.

COOK'S TIP To prepare scallops, shell if necessary, by prising open with a strong knife and severing the muscle, then carefully loosen the scallop. Cut away the beard-like fringe and tough muscle at the side. Rinse well.

BAKED HERRING WITH AN OATMEAL, MUSHROOM AND PARSLEY STUFFING

■ SERVES 4 ■ PREPARATION 20 MINUTES ■ COOKING 20-25 MINUTES
■ FREEZING NOT SUITABLE ■ 500 CALS PER SERVING

Fresh herring are delicious pan-fried in oatmeal, or, as in this recipe, baked with an oatmeal stuffing. Oatmeal has a perfect affinity with herring, the nutty taste and texture contrasting with the oiliness of the fish. Serve the herring with boiled new potatoes and a green vegetable, such as broccoli or courgettes.

30 ml (2 tbsp) oil
1 small onion, peeled and finely chopped
90 ml (3 tbsp) oatmeal
125 g (4 oz) brown cap mushrooms, roughly chopped
45 ml (3 tbsp) chopped fresh parsley
juice of ½ lemon (approximately)
salt and freshly ground black pepper
1 egg yolk
25 g (1 oz) butter
4 herrings, each about 225-300 g (8-10 oz), cleaned
(see cook's tip)
60 ml (4 tbsp) milk
TO SERVE
lemon wedges

1 Heat the oil in a pan on the SIMMERING PLATE. Add the onion, cover and cook for about 5 minutes until softened but not coloured.

2 Add 30 ml (2 tbsp) of the oatmeal and cook, stirring, for a further 3-4 minutes on the BOILING PLATE until the oatmeal turns slightly golden. Add the mushrooms and cook for 2-3 minutes.

3 Remove from the heat and stir in the parsley and lemon juice to taste. Season with salt and pepper. Stir in the egg yolk to bind the mixture together.

4 Use a little of the butter to grease an ovenproof dish. Spoon the stuffing into the herring cavities. Brush the herring with milk and roll in the remaining oatmeal to coat. Lay the fish in the greased dish and dot with the remaining

butter. Bake in the ROASTING OVEN with the grid shelf on the second set of runners for 10-15 minutes until the oatmeal is golden brown and the herring flesh is just firm. Serve immediately.

COOK'S TIP *To prepare the herrings, trim away the fins and tails, using strong scissors. Scrape off the scales from tail to head, using a fish scaler or back of a knife, rinsing frequently. Slit along the belly and remove the intestines; rinse thoroughly. Carefully bone out the backbone (if time permits).*

VARIATION Use the stuffing to fill mackerel instead of herring. Increase the baking time by about 5 minutes.

PINK TROUT WITH ALMOND AND HERB PURÉE

■ SERVES 4 ■ PREPARATION 20 MINUTES ■ COOKING 10 MINUTES
■ FREEZING NOT SUITABLE ■ 745 CALS PER SERVING

A sophisticated version of trout with almonds! Fresh pink trout is basted with paprika butter and baked until crisp and russet coloured. The accompanying purée of toasted almonds, parsley, garlic, Parmesan and olive oil has a superb earthy flavour.

4 pink-fleshed trout, each about 225-300 g (8-10 oz), cleaned
(see cook's tip)
75 g (3 oz) blanched whole almonds
50 g (2 oz) butter
10 ml (2 tsp) paprika
1 garlic clove, peeled
30 ml (2 tbsp) freshly grated Parmesan cheese
50 g (2 oz) fresh parsley sprigs
150 ml (¼ pint) light olive oil
30 ml (2 tbsp) fromage frais
salt and freshly ground black pepper
30 ml (2 tbsp) lemon juice
TO GARNISH
parsley sprigs

1 Rinse the trout and pat dry. With a sharp knife, make shallow diagonal slashes on both sides of each trout.

2 Spread the almonds on a baking sheet and, with the grid shelf on the fourth set of runners, cook in the ROASTING

OVEN for 5-7 minutes, turning frequently until toasted and golden. Allow to cool.

3 Place the butter and paprika in a small heatproof bowl on the back of the cooker until the butter is melted. Line a large roasting tin with foil, place a rack on top and slide onto the top set of runners in the ROASTING OVEN to preheat for 5 minutes.

4 Meanwhile, put the toasted almonds in a blender or food processor and process briefly until roughly chopped; remove one third of them and set aside. Add the garlic, Parmesan, parsley, olive oil, fromage frais, salt and pepper to the blender or processor and work to a smooth purée.

5 Season the trout with salt and pepper and brush with the paprika butter. Lay on the preheated rack over the roasting tin and bake for 5 minutes on each side or until the flesh is opaque and cooked through, basting from time to time with the paprika butter.

6 Transfer the trout to warmed serving plates. Add the lemon juice to the juices in the roasting tin, stir well, then spoon over the trout. Put a generous spoonful of toasted almond and herb purée onto each plate and scatter over the remaining toasted almonds. Garnish with sprigs of parsley and serve immediately.

COOK'S TIP *Pink-fleshed trout has the colour of salmon, but a much more delicate taste. To prepare the trout yourself, trim away the fins and tails, with strong scissors. Scrape off the scales from tail to head, using a fish scaler or back of a knife, rinsing frequently. Slit along the belly and remove the intestines; rinse thoroughly.*

MEDITERRANEAN FISH CASSEROLE

■ SERVES 4-6 ■ PREPARATION 10 MINUTES ■ COOKING 30 MINUTES
■ FREEZING NOT SUITABLE ■ 330-220 CALS PER SERVING

This richly flavoured fish stew is surprisingly low in calories. Serve it with rice or crusty bread to mop up the tasty juices.

700 g (1½ lb) skinless firm white fish fillets, such as cod, haddock or halibut
30 ml (2 tbsp) olive oil
2 large garlic cloves, peeled and finely chopped
2 red onions, peeled and sliced
2.5 ml (½ tsp) paprika
1 large red pepper, cored, seeded and cut into strips
100 ml (3½ fl oz) dry white wine
two 400 g (14 oz) cans chopped tomatoes
15 ml (1 tbsp) sun-dried tomato paste
salt and freshly ground black pepper
75 g (3 oz) pitted black olives, halved
thyme sprigs, to garnish

1 Cut the fish into 4 cm (1½ inch) pieces and place in a shallow 2 litre (3½ pint) ovenproof dish; set aside.

2 Heat the oil in a shallow flameproof casserole on the BOILING PLATE. Stir in the garlic and onions, cover and cook in the SIMMERING OVEN for about 15 minutes. Add the paprika and red pepper. Cook, stirring, on the BOILING PLATE for 1 minute and let bubble to reduce by half.

3 Add the tomatoes, sun-dried tomato paste and seasoning. Bring to the boil and place, uncovered, on the floor of the ROASTING OVEN for 15-20 minutes, until thick and pulpy.

4 Spoon the sauce over the fish and place on the grid shelf on the floor of the ROASTING OVEN for 10-15 minutes or until the fish is just firm and opaque. Scatter over the olives and garnish with thyme. Serve with rice and/or crusty bread.

ROASTED FISH WITH COURGETTES, TOMATOES AND GARLIC-HERB CRUMBS

■ SERVES 6 ■ PREPARATION 20 MINUTES ■ COOKING 20-30 MINUTES
■ FREEZING NOT SUITABLE ■ 430 CALS PER SERVING

900 g (2 lb) firm-textured, chunky filleted white fish, such as
monkfish or cod, skinned
125 g (4 oz) fresh breadcrumbs
3 garlic cloves, peeled and crushed
175 g (6 oz) butter
275 g (10 oz) courgettes, preferably baby ones, thickly sliced
salt and freshly ground black pepper
juice of 1 lemon
15 ml (1 tbsp) chopped fresh thyme, or 5 ml (1 tsp) dried
6 medium plum tomatoes, about 700 g (1½ lb), thickly sliced
30 ml (2 tbsp) chopped fresh parsley
30 ml (2 tbsp) chopped fresh basil
lemon wedges, to garnish

1 Cut the fish into large steaks.

2 Mix the breadcrumbs and garlic together and scatter
evenly in a small baking tin. Dot with a third of the butter in
flakes and bake on the floor of the ROASTING OVEN for 4-6
minutes until beginning to brown and crisp. Stir and finish
cooking in the SIMMERING OVEN for 10-20 minutes.

3 Meanwhile, cook the courgettes in boiling salted water
for 3-4 minutes until just tender; drain thoroughly.

4 In the meantime, melt the remaining butter in the small
roasting tin in the SIMMERING OVEN. Toss the fish in the
melted butter, with the lemon juice, seasoning and thyme.
Arrange in a single layer in the tin. Cover and place on the
grid shelf on the second set of runners in the ROASTING
OVEN and bake for 10-15 minutes (see cook's tip).

5 Uncover the fish and scatter the courgettes and tomatoes
around it. Season well and baste the vegetables with the
fish juices. Cook, uncovered, in the ROASTING OVEN for a
further 10 minutes. Stir the herbs into the garlic crumbs and
scatter over the fish. Garnish with lemon wedges to serve.

COOK'S TIP *Monkfish requires about 5 minutes longer
cooking than flakier fish, such as cod or haddock.*

COD FILLET WRAPPED IN FILO PASTRY WITH ROCKET

■ SERVES 6 ■ PREPARATION 20 MINUTES ■ COOKING 10-13 MINUTES
■ FREEZING SUITABLE: STAGE 4 ■ 335 CALS PER SERVING

6 thick cod fillets, each about 125 g (4 oz)
salt and freshly ground black pepper
50 g (2 oz) rocket leaves, roughly chopped
50 g (2 oz) ricotta cheese
40 g (1½ oz) Parmesan cheese, freshly grated
1 garlic clove, peeled and crushed
30 ml (2 tbsp) chopped mixed herbs, such as parsley and dill
grated rind and juice of ½ lemon
90 ml (6 tbsp) olive oil
12 small sheets filo pastry
beaten egg, for brushing

1 Wash and dry the cod fillets and season well on both
sides.

2 Place the rocket leaves in a blender or food processor
with the ricotta cheese, 25 g (1 oz) of the Parmesan, the
garlic, herbs, lemon rind and juice, and 30 ml (2 tbsp) of the
olive oil. Purée until fairly smooth and season with salt and
pepper to taste.

3 Lay one sheet of filo pastry on the work surface. Brush
with a little oil and top with a second filo sheet; brush with a
little more oil. Place a cod fillet in the middle of the pastry
and spread with some of the rocket paste. Wrap the filo

pastry over and around the fish and press the edges together to seal. Place on a greased baking sheet, seam-side down.

4 Repeat with the remaining filo pastry and cod fillets to make 6 parcels in total.

5 Brush all the parcels with a little more oil and bake on the floor of the ROASTING OVEN for 7-8 minutes. Brush with egg, then sprinkle with the remaining grated Parmesan and bake for a further 3-5 minutes until the pastry is crisp and golden, and a skewer inserted into the centre of the fish comes out hot.

6 Carefully transfer the fish parcels to warmed serving plates and serve immediately, accompanied by new potatoes and baby carrots.

COOK'S TIPS
▶ *Make sure you buy thick fillets of cod from the head end of the fish.*
▶ *Keep the filo pastry sheets covered with a damp tea-towel until ready to use to prevent them drying out.*

VARIATIONS
▶ Use watercress instead of rocket leaves.
▶ Use salmon fillets in place of cod.

SALMON ESCALOPES WITH CUCUMBER AND DILL SALSA

■ SERVES 4 ■ PREPARATION 20 MINUTES ■ COOKING 4-8 MINUTES
■ FREEZING NOT SUITABLE ■ 460 CALS PER SERVING

Salmon escalopes are basted with a tangy sun-dried tomato flavoured butter during cooking, then served with a piquant salsa. New potatoes and mangetouts would be suitable accompaniments.

4 salmon escalopes, each about 175 g (6 oz)
salt and freshly ground black pepper
15 ml (1 tbsp) oil
FLAVOURED BUTTER
50 g (2 oz) butter
20 ml (4 tsp) sun-dried tomato paste
10 ml (2 tsp) lemon juice
CUCUMBER AND DILL SALSA
275 g (10 oz) cucumber
175 g (6 oz) red onion, peeled and roughly chopped
30 ml (2 tbsp) capers
30 ml (2 tbsp) chopped fresh dill
30 ml (2 tbsp) dill mustard sauce (see cook's tip)

1 To prepare the flavoured butter, put the butter, sun-dried tomato paste, lemon juice and seasoning in a small heat-proof bowl and melt in the SIMMERING OVEN.

2 Season the salmon with pepper. Place a ridged grill pan or skillet on the floor of the ROASTING OVEN for 10 minutes to preheat (see alternative method).

3 Meanwhile make the salsa. Peel the cucumber and halve lengthwise. Scrape out the seeds using a teaspoon, then finely chop the flesh and place in a bowl. Add the onion, capers, dill and dill mustard sauce. Mix well and season with salt and pepper to taste.

4 Transfer the preheated grill pan or skillet to the BOILING PLATE and brush with the oil. Brush the salmon escalopes with the flavoured butter and add to the pan. Cook for 2-3 minutes on each side, turning once and brushing occasionally with the melted butter.

5 To serve, transfer the salmon escalopes with the pan juices and any remaining butter to warmed serving plates.

Serve the salmon escalopes with the cucumber and dill salsa, and seasonal vegetables.

COOK'S TIPS

▶ *Dill mustard sauce is available in jars from larger supermarkets and delicatessens. If you can't find it, make your own version by blending 5 ml (1 tsp) each white wine vinegar and sugar with 15 ml (1 tbsp) mild American mustard, 7.5 ml (1½ tsp) chopped fresh dill and 50 ml (2 fl oz) oil.*
▶ *The salsa can be prepared ahead and kept covered in the refrigerator overnight.*

ALTERNATIVE METHOD Preheat a rack in the large roasting tin in the ROASTING OVEN. Brush the rack with the melted butter, then lay the salmon on the grid. Hang the tin from the top set of runners in the ROASTING OVEN and cook for 3-4 minutes each side, turning once and basting with the butter.

SALMON WITH HOLLANDAISE SAUCE

■ SERVES 8 ■ PREPARATION 20-30 MINUTES ■ COOKING 20-30 MINUTES
■ FREEZING NOT SUITABLE ■ 570 CALS PER SERVING

A whole baked salmon is a splendid centrepiece for a special occasion. Farmed salmon is wonderfully moist and oily, so it responds well to this method of cooking. A classic hollandaise is the perfect complement. If possible, ask your fishmonger to clean and scale the fish for you.

1.6 kg (3½ lb) tail end piece of salmon, or 1 small whole
salmon, weighing about 1.8 kg (4 lb), cleaned (see cook's tip)
coarse sea salt and freshly ground black pepper
2-3 fresh dill sprigs
oil, for basting
HOLLANDAISE SAUCE
225 g (8 oz) unsalted butter, diced
1 shallot, peeled and finely diced
6 peppercorns
45 ml (3 tbsp) wine vinegar
2 eggs
5-10 ml (1-2 tsp) lemon juice
30 ml (2 tbsp) chopped fresh dill or parsley
TO GARNISH
dill sprigs

1 Melt the butter for the sauce in a heatproof bowl in the SIMMERING OVEN, then skim off any foam from the surface.

2 Rinse the fish thoroughly, inside and out, making sure there are no blood clots left in the cavity. Season the salmon cavity with salt and pepper and tuck in 2-3 sprigs of dill. Rub the skin with oil and sprinkle generously with coarse sea salt. Lay the fish in the foil-lined roasting tin.

3 Slide the roasting tin onto the fourth set of runners in the ROASTING OVEN: If cooking a tail-end piece of salmon, ensure the thickest part is to the left hand side of the oven; for a whole fish, position the head end to the back of the oven. Cook for 20-30 minutes or until the flesh just feels firm and will come away from the bone.

4 Meanwhile, prepare the sauce. Put the shallot, peppercorns and vinegar in a shallow heavy-based saucepan, about 18 cm (7 inch) in diameter. Bring to the boil on the SIMMERING PLATE, and let bubble until reduced to 15 ml (1 tbsp). Allow to cool.

5 Place the saucepan containing the reduced vinegar on the top of the cooker, near the edge of the SIMMERING PLATE. Gradually add the eggs, whisking constantly. Whisk in the warm, melted butter in a thin, steady stream until the mixture is creamy and just thickened. Remove the pan from the heat and continue to whisk as the mixture cools, until it is the thickness of thick double cream. Immediately strain into a cold bowl. Season with salt and pepper and flavour with lemon juice to taste. Add the chopped herbs just before serving.

6 Carefully lift the salmon out of the roasting tin, using the foil, and place on a warmed serving platter. Garnish with dill and serve immediately, with the warm hollandaise.

COOK'S TIPS

▶ To clean the fish yourself, cut off the fins and trim the tail into a neat v-shape, using strong scissors.

▶ The sauce can be prepared 1-2 hours ahead if required; place in a heatproof jug and set aside. Stand the jug in a bain-marie (or bowl of hot water) and warm through in the SIMMERING OVEN for 20-30 minutes before serving.

WARNING The young, elderly, pregnant women and anyone suffering from an immune deficiency disease should avoid eating hollandaise, owing to the possible risk of salmonella from lightly cooked eggs.

ROAST SALMON IN MUSTARD BUTTER

■ SERVES 6 ■ PREPARATION 10 MINUTES ■ COOKING 20 MINUTES
■ FREEZING NOT SUITABLE ■ 560 CALS PER SERVING

This elegant, yet quick and easy main course is perfect for a dinner party. A chilled oak-aged white wine is the ideal partner.

1.1 kg (2¹/₂ lb) piece boned middle cut of salmon, cleaned (see cook's tip)
175 g (6 oz) butter, melted
45 ml (3 tbsp) wholegrain mustard
20 ml (4 tsp) dried dill
salt and freshly ground black pepper
300 g (10 oz) fresh young spinach, rocket or mixed salad leaves

1 Open out the salmon like a book until almost flat by pressing along the backbone area. Place skin-side up in a shallow ovenproof dish just large enough to hold it.

2 Mix together the butter, mustard, dill and seasoning. Pour over the salmon. Cook towards the back of the ROASTING OVEN with the grid shelf on the third set of runners for about 20 minutes, or until just cooked in the thickest part of the fish.

3 Toss the salad leaves together and season well. Place on large serving plates.

4 Cut the salmon into thick slices and place on top of the salad leaves. Serve at once, with the mustard butter spooned over. Accompany with vegetables of your choice.

COOK'S TIP Your fishmonger will probably scale and bone the salmon. To do this yourself, trim away the fins. Scrape off the scales from tail to head end, using a fish scaler or back of a knife, rinsing frequently. Open out the fish and carefully cut the rib bones free from the flesh, working through to the backbone, then pull the backbone out. Remove any residual bones from the flesh with tweezers.

BRAISED MONKFISH WRAPPED IN PARMA HAM

■ SERVES 4-6 ■ PREPARATION 15 MINUTES, PLUS MARINATING
■ COOKING 45 MINUTES ■ FREEZING NOT SUITABLE
■ 550-365 CALS PER SERVING

Monkfish is a firm-fleshed fish, which can withstand cooking methods that are more suited to meat. Here the fish is wrapped in delicate thin slices of Parma ham, pan-fried until golden, then gently braised on a bed of Puy lentils.

1 kg (2¼ lb) monkfish tail (whole)
1 small lemon
15 ml (1 tbsp) chopped fresh marjoram
salt and freshly ground black pepper
4-6 thin slices Parma ham
45 ml (3 tbsp) olive oil
1 small onion, peeled and finely diced
1 carrot, peeled and finely diced
1 celery stick, finely diced
1 garlic clove, peeled and finely chopped
350 g (12 oz) Puy lentils
150 ml (¼ pint) red wine
30 ml (2 tbsp) chopped fresh coriander or parsley

1 Fillet the monkfish by cutting down either side of the central bone. Peel the lemon, removing all the white pith, then cut into thin slices. Lay the fish, cut-side up, on a board and sprinkle with the marjoram. Season with salt and pepper. Lay the lemon slices over one piece of fish, then sandwich together with the other monkfish fillet.

2 Wrap the fish in the Parma ham, making sure that it is completely covered. Tie at 5 cm (2 inch) intervals with fine string. Cover and leave in a cool place for 1-2 hours to allow the flavours to develop.

3 Heat 30 ml (2 tbsp) olive oil in a saucepan on the SIMMERING PLATE. Add the vegetables and garlic and cook, stirring, for about 5 minutes until golden. Stir in the lentils and wine. Add sufficient water to cover by 1 cm (½ inch). Bring to the boil on the BOILING PLATE, then transfer to the SIMMERING OVEN and cook for 20 minutes.

4 Preheat a large heavy-based frying pan on the floor of the ROASTING OVEN. Brush with the remaining oil and place on the BOILING PLATE. Add the monkfish parcel and fry, turning, until the Parma ham is browned all over. Carefully remove the fish parcel and spread the lentils in the frying pan. Replace the fish on top, burying it into the lentils slightly. Cover the pan and transfer to the SIMMERING OVEN for about 20 minutes, until the lentils are cooked and the juices from the fish run clear, when tested with a knife.

5 Remove the string from the fish, then cut into thick slices. Pile the lentils onto warmed serving plates and sprinkle with the chopped coriander or parsley. Arrange the fish on top and serve immediately.

COOK'S TIP *If a large monkfish is not available, use 2 smaller ones instead. Lay the fillets side by side, overlapping them slightly.*

MIXED SEAFOOD GRATIN

■ SERVES 4 ■ PREPARATION 10 MINUTES ■ COOKING 20-25 MINUTES
■ FREEZING NOT SUITABLE ■ 800 CALS PER SERVING

A crunchy crushed tortilla and breadcrumb topping is the perfect foil for this creamy seafood gratin. Shredded leeks make an excellent accompaniment.

50 g (2 oz) butter
50 g (2 oz) onion, peeled and roughly chopped
2 garlic cloves, peeled and crushed
15 ml (1 tbsp) plain flour
125 ml (4 fl oz) white wine
50 ml (2 fl oz) milk
225 g (8 oz) cod or haddock fillet, skinned and cut into cubes
175 g (6 oz) Emmental cheese, grated
150 ml (¼ pint) double cream
225 g (8 oz) packet cooked mixed seafood (see cook's tip)
125 g (4 oz) watercress, finely chopped
salt and freshly ground black pepper
50 g (2 oz) fresh breadcrumbs
125 g (4 oz) plain tortilla chips, crumbled

1 Melt the butter in a large saucepan on the SIMMERING PLATE. Add the onion and garlic and sauté for 2-3 minutes. Add the flour and cook, stirring, for 1 minute. Pour in the wine and milk, and bring to the boil, stirring all the time.

2 Add the cod and bring to simmering point. Cover and cook in the SIMMERING OVEN for 5-6 minutes.

3 Stir in 125 g (4 oz) of the grated cheese, the cream, mixed seafood and watercress. Season with salt and pepper to taste. Spoon into a shallow, ovenproof dish.

4 Mix the breadcrumbs, remaining cheese and tortilla chips together and sprinkle over the fish. Bake in the ROASTING OVEN with the grid shelf on the second set of runners for 10-15 minutes until golden and bubbling, and heated through. Serve immediately with leeks or other vegetables of your choice.

COOK'S TIP *Packets of ready-prepared mixed seafood are available from most supermarkets. If frozen, defrost thoroughly and drain well before use.*

SEARED TUNA STEAKS WITH CORN SALSA

■ SERVES 4 ■ PREPARATION 25 MINUTES, PLUS MARINATING

■ COOKING 6 MINUTES ■ FREEZING NOT SUITABLE ■ 270 CALS PER SERVING

4 tuna steaks, each about 125-150 g (4-5 oz) (see cook's tip)

salt and freshly ground black pepper

MARINADE

1 green chilli, seeded and finely chopped

1 cm (½ inch) piece fresh root ginger, peeled and finely chopped

30 ml (2 tbsp) chopped fresh basil

30 ml (2 tbsp) chopped fresh coriander

30 ml (2 tbsp) chopped fresh mint

2 garlic cloves, peeled and crushed

15 ml (1 tbsp) Thai fish sauce (nam pla)

15 ml (1 tbsp) sesame oil

50 ml (2 fl oz) lime juice

CORN SALSA

50 g (2 oz) baby corn cobs

50 g (2 oz) carrot, peeled and finely chopped

50 g (2 oz) fennel, finely chopped

5 mm (¼ inch) piece fresh root ginger, peeled and finely chopped

50 g (2 oz) red pepper, seeded and finely chopped

30 ml (2 tbsp) chopped fresh basil

30 ml (2 tbsp) chopped fresh coriander

30 ml (2 tbsp) chopped fresh mint

1 garlic clove, peeled and crushed

60 ml (4 tbsp) orange juice

15 ml (1 tbsp) soy sauce

TO GARNISH

lime halves

mint sprigs

1 For the marinade, mix together the chilli, ginger, herbs, garlic, fish sauce, sesame oil, lime juice and a little pepper in a small bowl. Lay the tuna steaks in a non-metallic dish and spoon over the marinade. Cover and leave to marinate in a cool place for at least 1 hour, or overnight if possible, turning the fish occasionally

2 Remove the tuna steaks from the dish, reserving the marinade, and season with salt. Preheat a ridged skillet or ovenproof frying pan on the floor of the ROASTING OVEN for 10 minutes, then place on the BOILING PLATE.

3 Meanwhile, make the corn salsa. Cook the baby corn in a pan of boiling water on the SIMMERING PLATE for 2-3 minutes until tender. Plunge into cold water and leave until cool, then drain and chop finely. Mix with the carrot, fennel, ginger, red pepper, herbs, garlic, orange juice, soy sauce and seasoning.

4 Add the tuna steaks to the hot skillet or frying pan and cook for 3 minutes on each side, basting with the marinade and turning once.

5 To serve, lift the tuna steaks onto warmed serving plates. Spoon over the corn salsa and garnish with lime halves and mint sprigs. Serve at once.

COOK'S TIPS

▶ *Tuna loin steaks are available from good fishmongers and larger supermarkets. Swordfish and shark steaks can be cooked in the same way.*

▶ *The corn salsa can be prepared a day in advance and kept covered in the refrigerator overnight.*

Poultry and Game

Traditional Roast Chicken with Apple Gravy

■ SERVES 4-6 ■ PREPARATION 20 MINUTES ■ COOKING ABOUT 1¼ HOURS
FREEZING NOT SUITABLE ■ 440-295 CALS PER SERVING

1.4 kg (3 lb) oven-ready chicken
SAGE AND ONION STUFFING
15 ml (1 tbsp) oil
75 g (3 oz) onion, peeled and roughly chopped
125 g (4 oz) pork sausagemeat
15 ml (1 tbsp) finely chopped fresh sage or 5 ml (1 tsp) dried
FOR THE ROAST
275 g (10 oz) shallots or button onions, peeled
450 g (1 lb) cooking apples
25 g (1 oz) butter, softened
salt and freshly ground black pepper
25 g (1 oz) raisins
1 cinnamon stick
450 ml (¾ pint) medium cider
30 ml (2 tbsp) sherry vinegar or white wine vinegar
150 ml (¼ pint) sherry
TO GARNISH
sage sprigs

1 First prepare the stuffing. Heat the oil in a pan on the SIMMERING PLATE. Add the onion and fry for 7-10 minutes until soft. Allow to cool, then mix with the sausagemeat, sage and seasoning. Fill the neck end of the chicken with the stuffing and secure with fine skewers or truss with string.

2 For the roast, roughly chop 50 g (2 oz) of the shallots. Peel, core and roughly chop the apples. Place 50 g (2 oz) inside the chicken cavity with 50 g (2 oz) of the chopped shallots.

3 Spread the butter all over the bird. Season well. Place the chicken, lying on one breast, in the small roasting tin. Add the remaining whole shallots, chopped apples, raisins, cinnamon stick, cider and vinegar to the tin.

4 Cook on the grid shelf on the floor of the ROASTING OVEN with the legs towards the back of the oven for about 1¼ hours, basting occasionally. After 20 minutes, turn the chicken on to the other breast, cook for 20 minutes, then place the chicken on to its back for the remainder of the cooking time. Cover the breast with foil if it shows signs of over-browning, or position the cold plain shelf on the runners above the chicken. The chicken is cooked if the juices run clear when the thickest part of the thigh is pierced with a skewer.

5 Transfer the chicken to a warmed serving platter. Add the apples and shallots from the cavity to the roasting tin with the sherry. Cover the chicken with foil and place in the SIMMERING OVEN to keep warm. Place the roasting tin on the SIMMERING PLATE and simmer for 10 minutes or until the cooking juices are syrupy. Adjust the seasoning. Serve the chicken garnished with sage, and accompanied by the apple gravy and vegetables of your choice.

CHICKEN HOTPOT WITH LEEKS

■ SERVES 4 ■ PREPARATION 15 MINUTES ■ COOKING 1-1½ HOURS
■ FREEZING NOT SUITABLE ■ 465 CALS PER SERVING

30 ml (2 tbsp) oil
1 large garlic clove, peeled and crushed
700 g (1½ lb) trimmed leeks, cleaned and thickly sliced
275 g (10 oz) potatoes
200 g (7 oz) soft cheese with garlic and herbs
90 ml (3 fl oz) white wine
150 ml (¼ pint) chicken stock
10 ml (2 tsp) cornflour
8 skinless, boneless chicken thighs, about
700 g (1½ lb) total weight
salt and freshly ground black pepper

1 Heat the oil in a flameproof casserole on the BOILING PLATE. Add the garlic and leeks, cover and cook on the SIMMERING PLATE (or in the SIMMERING OVEN) for about 5 minutes or until just beginning to soften.

2 Meanwhile, do not peel the potatoes but slice them as thinly as possible.

3 Place the cheese, wine, stock and cornflour in a blender or food processor and blend for about 30 seconds or until smooth.

4 Season the chicken thighs with salt and pepper and arrange on top of the leeks. Pour the cheese mixture over and layer the potatoes on top. Place a lightly oiled sheet of greaseproof paper on top of the potatoes, then place the lid on the casserole.

5 ■■ Place on the floor of the ROASTING OVEN for 5-10 minutes. Transfer to the SIMMERING OVEN and cook for a further 1-1¼ hours or until the chicken is just cooked. Uncover and transfer to the ROASTING OVEN with the grid shelf on the fourth set of runners for 15-20 minutes or until the potatoes are golden brown.
■■■ Cook on the grid shelf on the fourth set of runners in the BAKING OVEN for 45 minutes or until the chicken is just cooked. Uncover and place in the ROASTING OVEN with the grid shelf on the fourth set of runners for 15-20 minutes or until the potatoes are golden brown.
Serve with a green vegetable, such as broccoli.

DEVILLED ROAST CHICKEN

■ SERVES 4-6 ■ PREPARATION 15 MINUTES ■ COOKING ABOUT 1½ HOURS
■ FREEZING NOT SUITABLE ■ 675-450 CALS PER SERVING

Ring the changes with this tasty variation of the universally popular roast. Here chicken is roasted with chunks of corn and chick peas in a spicy devilled sauce – which helps to keep the meat moist during cooking.

30 ml (2 tbsp) olive oil
125 g (4 oz) onion, peeled and roughly chopped
2 red peppers, cored, seeded and roughly chopped
2 garlic cloves, peeled and crushed
15 ml (1 tbsp) Worcestershire sauce
15 ml (1 tbsp) cider vinegar
5 ml (1 tsp) dried marjoram
5 ml (1 tsp) dried thyme
30 ml (2 tbsp) soft dark brown sugar
300 ml (½ pint) lager
700 g (1½ lb) corn-on-the-cob
400 g (14 oz) can chick peas, drained and rinsed
50 g (2 oz) butter, softened
10 ml (2 tsp) paprika
salt and freshly ground black pepper
1.4 kg (3 lb) oven-ready chicken
TO SERVE
Crispy Potato Skins (see page 96)

1 Heat the olive oil in a large roasting tin. Add the onion, peppers and garlic. Cook on the floor of the ROASTING OVEN for about 10 minutes, until golden. Add the Worcestershire sauce, cider vinegar, marjoram, thyme, brown sugar and lager. Return to the floor of the ROASTING OVEN for 10 minutes.

2 Add the corn-on-the-cob to a pan of boiling water and cook on the BOILING PLATE for 5-7 minutes. Drain and thickly slice, reserving 300 ml (½ pint) cooking liquid. Add the corn to the roasting tin with the drained chick peas.

3 Mix the butter with the paprika and seasoning and spread all over the chicken. Place the chicken in the roasting tin, lying it on one breast, and spoon over the corn and chick pea mixture.

4 Place the roasting tin on the grid shelf on the floor of the ROASTING OVEN and cook for about 1¼ hours: After

20 minutes cooking time, turn the chicken on to the other breast, cook for 20 minutes, then turn on to its back for the remainder of the cooking time. Cover the breast with foil if it shows signs of over-browning. The chicken is cooked if the juices run clear when the thickest part of the thigh is pierced with a skewer.

5 When cooked, lift the chicken on to a warmed serving platter, cover with foil and keep warm in the SIMMERING OVEN. Pour off the excess fat from the roasting tin and add the reserved corn cooking liquid. Bring to the boil on the

BOILING PLATE and let bubble for 3-4 minutes. Adjust the seasoning.

6 Carve the chicken and arrange on warmed serving plates. Serve accompanied by the devilled corn and chick pea mixture, and crispy potato skins.

VARIATION Use 4-6 chicken breasts or suprêmes instead of a whole chicken. Cook on the grid shelf on the floor of the ROASTING OVEN for 20-25 minutes or until golden and tender. Finish as above.

LEMON CHICKEN WITH SAFFRON RISOTTO

■ SERVES 4 ■ PREPARATION 20 MINUTES ■ COOKING 30 MINUTES
■ FREEZING NOT SUITABLE ■ 885 CALS PER SERVING

grated zest and juice of 1 lemon
small handful of fresh parsley sprigs
25 g (1 oz) blanched almonds
15 ml (1 tbsp) dried thyme
1 garlic clove, peeled and chopped
90 ml (3 fl oz) olive oil
salt and freshly ground black pepper
4 chicken breast fillets, with skin
50 g (2 oz) butter
225 g (8 oz) onion, peeled and finely chopped
small pinch of saffron strands
225 g (8 oz) arborio (risotto) rice
125 ml (4 fl oz) white wine
450 ml (3/4 pint) hot chicken stock
50 g (2 oz) Parmesan cheese, freshly grated
thyme sprigs, to garnish

1 Put the lemon zest, parsley, almonds, thyme and garlic in a blender or food processor and process for a few seconds; slowly add the oil and process until evenly combined. Season with salt and pepper. Spread this mixture under the skin of each chicken breast fillet and place in a roasting tin.

2 Melt the butter in a medium saucepan on the SIMMERING PLATE and brush half over the chicken; pour on the lemon juice. Cook on the grid shelf on the floor of the ROASTING OVEN for 25 minutes, basting occasionally.

3 Meanwhile, heat the butter remaining in the saucepan on the SIMMERING PLATE, add the onion and fry for about 5 minutes until softened. Stir in the saffron and rice and stir well to coat with the butter.

4 Add the wine and hot stock a ladleful at a time, allowing each addition to be absorbed before adding the next. The risotto is ready when the rice is tender and creamy. This will take about 25 minutes; it may not be necessary to add all of the stock.

5 Remove the risotto from the heat, and stir in the Parmesan. Serve the risotto with the chicken, pouring over any juices from the roasting tin. Garnish with thyme.

PROVENÇAL CHICKEN BAKE

■ SERVES 8 ■ PREPARATION 30 MINUTES ■ COOKING 1³/₄ HOURS
■ FREEZING SUITABLE: SEE COOK'S TIP ■ 515 CALS PER SERVING

This tasty creamy chicken and pasta bake can be prepared ahead, making it perfect for a midweek supper. If you are cooking for 4 people, simply freeze half for another occasion.

45 ml (3 tbsp) olive oil
225 g (8 oz) onions, peeled and roughly chopped
2 garlic cloves, peeled and crushed
pinch of saffron strands (optional)
15 ml (1 tbsp) dried thyme
150 ml (1/4 pint) dry white vermouth or white wine
two 400 g (14 oz) cans chopped tomatoes
500 g (1 lb) passata or creamed tomatoes
salt and freshly ground black pepper
15 ml (1 tbsp) caster sugar
225 g (8 oz) dried pasta shells
700 g (1¹/₂ lb) skinless chicken breast fillets or
boned chicken thighs
25 g (1 oz) butter
25 g (1 oz) plain white flour
450 ml (3/4 pint) milk
200 g (7 oz) full-fat soft cheese
50 g (2 oz) stoned black olives
75 ml (5 tbsp) pesto
basil sprigs, to garnish

1 Heat 15 ml (1 tbsp) olive oil in a large saucepan on the BOILING PLATE. Add the onions, garlic, saffron if using, and thyme. Cook for 1-2 minutes, then pour in the dry vermouth or wine and allow to bubble for 2-3 minutes. Add the tomatoes, passata, seasoning and sugar. Bring to the boil and cook on the floor of the ROASTING OVEN for 20-30 minutes, or until reduced by one third.

2 Meanwhile, add the pasta to a large saucepan of boiling salted water and cook in the SIMMERING OVEN for 10-12 minutes, or until al dente. Drain, refresh under cold running water and set aside.

3 Cut the chicken into chunks and place in a roasting tin. Drizzle over the remaining olive oil and season with salt and pepper. Cover with foil and cook on the grid shelf on the floor of the ROASTING OVEN for 10-15 minutes or until just tender; do not overcook.

4 Melt the butter in a heavy-based saucepan on the SIMMERING PLATE. Stir in the flour and cook, stirring, for 1 minute, then gradually add the milk, whisking until smooth. Bring to the boil and simmer for a further 5-10 minutes, stirring occasionally, or place in the SIMMERING OVEN for 10-15 minutes. Remove from the heat and whisk in the full-fat cheese; season with salt and pepper to taste.

5 Mix together the chicken, pasta, olives and tomato sauce. Spoon into a 3.4 litre (6 pint) ovenproof dish, which is about 4 cm (1½ inches) deep. Lightly stir the pesto into the white sauce, to create a marbled effect. Spoon the white sauce over the chicken mixture.

6 Bake on the grid shelf on the floor of the ROASTING OVEN for 30-35 minutes or until golden and heated through. Serve immediately, garnished with basil sprigs.

COOK'S TIP *This dish may be frozen at the end of stage 5. To use, thaw overnight at cool room temperature, then cook as in stage 6 for 45-50 minutes.*

GOLDEN CHICKEN LASAGNE

■ SERVES 6 ■ PREPARATION 40 MINUTES ■ COOKING ABOUT 2 HOURS
■ FREEZING SUITABLE: SEE COOK'S TIP ■ 870 CALS PER SERVING

This is an ideal dish to prepare ahead and freeze
for impromptu entertaining.

1.4 kg (3 lb) oven-ready chicken (see variation)
300 ml (½ pint) white wine
1 onion, peeled
handful of leek trimmings
1 celery stick
1 bay leaf
6 peppercorns
salt and freshly ground black pepper
125 g (4 oz) butter
1 garlic clove, peeled and crushed
450 g (1 lb) trimmed leeks, thickly sliced
75 g (3 oz) plain flour
50 g (2 oz) Cheddar cheese, grated
125 g (4 oz) Gruyère cheese, grated
150 ml (¼ pint) single cream
60 ml (4 tbsp) freshly grated Parmesan cheese
200 g (7 oz) no-need-to-precook lasagne
45 ml (3 tbsp) pine nuts

1 Put the chicken in a saucepan in which it fits snugly. Add half the wine, the onion, leek trimmings, celery, bay leaf, peppercorns and 5 ml (1 tsp) salt. Pour on sufficient cold water to cover and bring to the boil on the BOILING PLATE. Cover and cook on the grid shelf on the floor of the ROASTING OVEN for 45 minutes to 1 hour until tender. Leave until cool enough to handle.

2 Remove the chicken from the stock and cut into bite-sized pieces, discarding the skin and bones. Reduce the stock by boiling if necessary to about 1 litre (1¾ pints). Strain the stock and skim off the fat.

3 Heat 25 g (1 oz) butter in a saucepan on the SIMMERING PLATE. Add the garlic and leeks and fry for about 10 minutes; remove with a slotted spoon.

4 Add the remaining butter to the pan and heat until melted. Stir in the flour and cook, stirring, for 1 minute. Off the heat, whisk in the reserved 1 litre (1¾ pints) stock and remaining wine. Bring to the boil and cook, stirring, for 4-5 minutes. Off the heat, stir in the Cheddar cheese and two thirds of the Gruyère. Stir in the cream and season liberally with salt and pepper.

5 Spoon a little of the sauce over the base of a 3 litre (5¼ pint) shallow ovenproof dish. Top with a layer of pasta, followed by the chicken, leeks, a sprinkling of Parmesan and a little sauce. Continue layering in this way, finishing with pasta and sauce. Sprinkle over the remaining Gruyère, and Parmesan and pine nuts.

6 Stand the dish in the large roasting tin and bake in the middle of the ROASTING OVEN for 45-50 minutes. Leave to stand at room temperature or in the SIMMERING OVEN for 10 minutes before serving.

COOK'S TIP *The lasagne can be frozen at the end of stage 5. To use, thaw overnight at cool room temperature, then cook as in stage 6 for 1 hour or until piping hot.*

VARIATION Alternatively, you can use 450 g (1 lb) cooked boneless chicken or turkey. Make the sauce with the wine and chicken stock.

THAI GREEN CURRY

■ SERVES 6 ■ PREPARATION 10 MINUTES ■ COOKING 12 MINUTES
■ FREEZING ■ 360 CALS PER SERVING

This delicious creamy Thai curry is perfect for a dinner party. Serve it with fluffy Thai fragrant rice, which is available from most larger supermarkets.

350 g (12 oz) skinless chicken fillets
1 lemon grass stalk (see cook's tip)
60 ml (4 tbsp) oil
1 green chilli, seeded and finely chopped
4 cm (1½ inch) piece fresh root ginger, peeled and grated
225 g (8 oz) brown-cap or oyster mushrooms, thickly sliced
15-30 ml (1-2 tbsp) Thai green curry paste or tandoori paste
300 ml (½ pint) thick coconut milk
150 ml (¼ pint) chicken stock
15 ml (1 tbsp) Thai fish sauce (nam pla)
5 ml (1 tsp) light soy sauce
350 g (12 oz) cooked, peeled king prawns
salt and freshly ground black pepper
30 ml (2 tbsp) chopped fresh coriander

1 Cut the chicken into bite-sized pieces. Cut the lemon grass into 3 pieces.

2 Heat 30 ml (2 tbsp) oil in a large non-stick frying pan on the BOILING PLATE and stir-fry the chicken in batches for 2-3 minutes. Transfer to an ovenproof dish and keep warm in the SIMMERING OVEN.

3 Add the remaining oil to the pan and stir-fry the chilli, ginger, lemon grass and mushrooms together for about 3 minutes, until the mushrooms begin to turn golden. Add the curry paste and fry for a further 30 seconds.

4 Pour in the coconut milk, stock, fish sauce and soy sauce. Bring to the boil and let bubble for 2-3 minutes. Stir in the chicken and bring to the boil. Add the prawns and seasoning, then cover and cook in the SIMMERING OVEN for 5 minutes or until the prawns are heated through. Garnish with chopped coriander and serve immediately, with Thai fragrant rice.

COOK'S TIP *Fragrant lemon grass, with its sour-sweet lemony flavour, looks rather like a pale, woody spring onion. It imparts a wonderful flavour and aroma to a Thai curry but needs to be removed before serving.*

CHICKEN AND PEPPER CASSEROLE

■ SERVES 4 ■ PREPARATION 20 MINUTES ■ COOKING ABOUT 1 HOUR
■ FREEZING SUITABLE: STAGE 5 ■ 670 CALS PER SERVING

For this Spanish-style casserole, buy the spiciest chorizo sausage you can find – to impart a rich flavour and colour. Serve with rice or potatoes, a crisp salad and a glass of red wine.

8 small chicken joints, or 1 chicken, about
1.6 kg (3½ lb), jointed
salt and freshly ground black pepper
45 ml (3 tbsp) olive oil
1 onion, peeled and chopped
4 large or 8 small shallots, peeled
2 garlic cloves, peeled and sliced
225 g (8 oz) chorizo sausage, sliced
150 ml (¼ pint) dry white wine
two 400 g (14 oz) cans plum tomatoes in tomato juice
30 ml (2 tbsp) chopped fresh parsley
2 fresh rosemary sprigs
1 strip of orange peel
2 red peppers, or 1 red and 1 yellow pepper
TO GARNISH
rosemary sprigs

1 Season the chicken joints with salt and pepper. Heat the oil in a large heavy-based sauté pan (which has a lid) on the BOILING PLATE. Add the chicken pieces, skin-side down, and brown well. Turn and lightly brown the other side. Transfer to a plate, cover and keep warm in the SIMMERING OVEN.

2 Move the sauté pan to the SIMMERING PLATE. Add the onion and shallots and cook, stirring frequently, for 1-2 minutes. Cover and transfer to the SIMMERING OVEN for 5 minutes until the onion is soft and golden and the shallots are lightly browned.

3 Return pan to the SIMMERING PLATE. Stir in the garlic and chorizo and cook for 3-4 minutes until the juices begin to run from the chorizo. Add the wine and bring to the boil on the BOILING PLATE. Allow to bubble hard for 1-2 minutes.

4 Meanwhile, drain and roughly chop the tomatoes,

reserving the juice. Add the tomatoes and juice to the pan together with the parsley, rosemary sprigs and orange peel. Bring to the boil, then return the chicken to the pan. Cover and cook in the SIMMERING OVEN for 40-45 minutes or until the chicken is tender.

5 Meanwhile, halve and deseed the peppers then place, skin-side up, on a lightly oiled baking sheet. With the grid shelf on the top set of runners in the ROASTING OVEN, cook for 15-20 minutes or until the skins are blistered and beginning to blacken. Place in a bowl, cover and allow to

cool slightly, then peel away the skins. Cut the flesh into thin strips. Add to the chicken about 5 minutes before the end of the cooking time.

6 Lift the chicken pieces out of the pan, using a slotted spoon. Place in an ovenproof dish and keep warm in the SIMMERING OVEN. Discard the orange peel and rosemary. Bring the sauce to the boil on the BOILING PLATE and let bubble hard for 5-6 minutes until well reduced and syrupy. Return the chicken to the pan and check the seasoning. Serve garnished with rosemary.

TURKEY WITH ROAST ONIONS AND MADEIRA GRAVY

■ SERVES 10-15 ■ PREPARATION 40 MINUTES
■ COOKING 3¼-3½ HOURS, PLUS RESTING ■ FREEZING SUITABLE: LEFTOVERS
■ 850-570 CALS PER SERVING

4.5 kg (10 lb) oven-ready turkey
salt and freshly ground black pepper
SAUSAGE AND CHESTNUT STUFFING
125 g (4 oz) dried pears or apricots, roughly chopped
12 pitted prunes
450 g (1 lb) coarse pork sausages
25 g (1 oz) butter
1 small onion or 2 shallots, peeled and chopped
grated zest of 1 lemon
50 ml (2 fl oz) lemon juice
30 ml (2 tbsp) chopped flat-leaf parsley
225 g (8 oz) cooked chestnuts, preferably vacuum-packed
50 g (2 oz) fresh breadcrumbs
1.25 ml (¼ tsp) each ground nutmeg, ground cloves, ground
cinnamon and ground coriander
FOR THE ROAST
150 g (5 oz) butter
15 ml (1 tbsp) oil
900 g (2 lb) small onions or shallots, peeled
MADEIRA GRAVY
30 ml (2 tbsp) plain flour
600 ml (1 pint) turkey stock
60 ml (4 tsp) Madeira
TO GARNISH
fresh herbs

1 First prepare the stuffing. Place the dried pears and prunes in a small bowl, cover with cold water and leave to soak overnight. The following day, drain the fruit thoroughly and set aside.

2 Place the sausages in a saucepan and cover with cold water. Bring to the boil and cook gently in the SIMMERING OVEN for 15 minutes or until cooked through. Allow to cool a little in the liquid, then drain, skin and cut into large cubes.

3 Heat the butter in a pan, add the chopped onion, cover and cook in the SIMMERING OVEN for 10 minutes, or until soft; let cool. Mix all the stuffing ingredients together and season well with salt and pepper.

4 Spoon some stuffing into the neck end of the turkey only. Shape into a neat, rounded end then tuck the neck skin under and truss or secure with a wooden skewer or cocktail stick. Weigh the turkey and calculate the cooking time, allowing approximately 20 minutes per lb (450 g).

5 Spoon any remaining stuffing into foil and seal. Refrigerate until required.

6 Place the turkey on a rack in the large roasting tin and spread with 125 g (4 oz) softened butter. Season with a little salt and plenty of pepper. Cover loosely with a large sheet of foil to make a 'tent'.

7 Heat the oil and remaining butter in a frying pan on the BOILING PLATE. Add the onions or shallots, and fry, turning, until browned. Remove from the heat; set aside.

8 Cook the turkey on the grid shelf on the floor of the ROASTING OVEN for the calculated cooking time: 3¼-3½ hours, basting occasionally; see cook's tips. About 1 hour before the end of the cooking time, remove the foil and add the onions to the tin with the turkey, basting them well with the cooking juices. If there isn't room to cook the onions around the turkey, cook in the small roasting tin in the middle of the SIMMERING OVEN for 1¼ hours (or in the BAKING OVEN of a 4-oven cooker for 45 minutes).

9 When the turkey is cooked remove it and the onions from the roasting tin, tipping the bird slightly to let any juices run out. Place on a warmed serving platter, cover with foil and leave to rest in the SIMMERING OVEN for 30 minutes.

10 Meanwhile, prepare the Madeira gravy. Tilt the roasting tin and spoon off all but 30 ml (2 tbsp) fat, leaving the turkey juices. Place the tin on the SIMMERING PLATE. Whisk in the flour and cook for 1-2 minutes. Slowly whisk in the turkey stock. Bring to the boil, and simmer for 3-4 minutes until smooth. Add the Madeira and season with salt and pepper to taste. Transfer to a sauceboat.

11 Garnish the turkey with herbs and serve with the Madeira gravy, and traditional accompaniments.

COOK'S TIPS

▶ Thawing: Leave frozen turkeys in their bags and thaw at cool room temperature, not in the refrigerator. Remove giblets as soon as they are loose. Once there are no ice crystals in the body cavity and the legs are flexible, cover and store in the refrigerator. Cook within 24 hours.

▶ Cooking: Weigh the bird after stuffing and calculate the complete cooking time to be ready 30 minutes before carving; this allows time for the flesh to firm up, making carving easier. Cooking the turkey on a rack makes it easier to transfer to a serving plate.

▶ Testing: Insert a skewer into the thickest part of a thigh. If the juices run clear, it is cooked; if not return to the oven.

▶ Carving: Removing the wishbone from the turkey before cooking will make carving easier.

TURKEY AND HAM POT PIE

■ SERVES 6-8 ■ PREPARATION 40 MINUTES ■ COOKING 40 MINUTES
■ FREEZING SUITABLE: STAGE 6 ■ 735-550 CALS PER SERVING

This tempting supper dish is loosely based on an American recipe in which the 'pie' is topped with 'biscuits' or cobblers to make a homely crust. It is an excellent way of using up turkey and ham leftovers – combining them in a delicious creamy sauce. You will need a chunky piece of ham.

700 g (1¹/₂ lb) cooked boneless turkey
225 g (8 oz) cooked ham
900 ml (1¹/₂ pints) chicken stock
150 ml (¹/₄ pint) dry white wine
1 bay leaf
2 fresh rosemary sprigs
2 carrots, peeled and sliced
1 large leek, peeled and thickly sliced
125 g (4 oz) baby corn cobs, halved
75 g (3 oz) butter
225 g (8 oz) chestnut or button mushrooms, quartered
60 ml (4 tbsp) plain flour
300 ml (¹/₂ pint) single cream
salt and freshly ground black pepper
HERB COBBLERS
350 g (12 oz) self-raising flour
30 ml (2 tbsp) chopped fresh parsley
30 ml (2 tbsp) chopped fresh chives
75 g (3 oz) butter
about 200 ml (7 fl oz) milk
TO GARNISH
coarse sea salt
rosemary leaves

1 Cut the turkey into bite-sized pieces. Cut the ham into large cubes. Place in a 1.7 litre (3 pint) ovenproof dish.

2 Pour the stock into a saucepan and add the wine, bay leaf and rosemary. Bring to the boil on the BOILING PLATE, then add the carrots and cook in the SIMMERING OVEN for 10 minutes. Add the leek and baby corn and cook for about 5 minutes until all of the vegetables are barely tender. Strain the stock into a jug; set the vegetables aside.

3 Melt the butter in a saucepan on the BOILING PLATE. Add the mushrooms and cook until beginning to colour. Sprinkle in the flour. Take off the heat and mix well. Stir in the stock and cream. Return to the heat and bring to the boil, stirring all the time. Simmer for 3-5 minutes; check the seasoning. Cover the surface closely with dampened greaseproof paper, to prevent a skin forming; allow to cool.

4 To make the herb cobblers, sift the flour with 2.5 ml (¹/₂ tsp) salt into a bowl and stir in the chopped herbs. Rub in the butter until the mixture resembles fine breadcrumbs. Stir in enough milk to make a soft scone dough. (Alternatively, you can prepare the dough in a food processor.) Turn out onto a floured surface and knead lightly.

5 Roll out the dough to a 1 cm (¹/₂ inch) thickness and cut out at least nine 7.5 cm (3 inch) squares with a sharp knife. Halve these diagonally to make triangles.

6 Add the vegetables and sauce to the meat and mix well. Arrange the herb cobblers, overlapping, around the edge of the dish. Brush with milk and sprinkle with coarse sea salt.

7 Bake in the ROASTING OVEN with the grid shelf on the third set of runners for 10 minutes until the cobblers are risen and browning, then set the grid shelf on the floor of the oven and bake for a further 20 minutes. Serve garnished with rosemary and accompanied by a green vegetable of your choice.

TRADITIONAL ROAST PHEASANT

■ SERVES 4 ■ PREPARATION 10 MINUTES ■ COOKING ABOUT 1 HOUR
■ FREEZING NOT SUITABLE ■ 800 CALS PER SERVING

2 oven-ready pheasants
salt and freshly ground black pepper
few fresh rosemary or thyme sprigs,
or 12 juniper berries, lightly crushed
100 g (4 oz) butter, softened
175 g (6 oz) streaky bacon rashers
1 small onion, peeled and halved
75 g (3 oz) fresh fine brown or white breadcrumbs
450 ml (3/4 pint) chicken stock
watercress sprigs, to garnish

1 Season the inside of the pheasants with salt and pepper and put the rosemary or thyme sprigs or juniper berries into the cavities. Smear 50 g (2 oz) of the butter all over the pheasants.

2 Place the pheasants, breast-side down, in the small roasting tin. Slide onto the third set of runners in the ROASTING OVEN and cook for 1 hour or until the juices run clear when the thickest part of the thigh is pierced with a sharp knife. Baste the pheasants every 10 minutes during roasting, and lay the streaky bacon rashers over the birds after the first 30 minutes cooking. Turn the pheasants onto their backs for the last 5 minutes cooking to brown the breasts.

3 Meanwhile, place the onion halves, cut-side down, on the floor of the ROASTING OVEN for 5-10 minutes or until charred; take out and put to one side.

4 Melt the remaining butter in a small flameproof pan or dish on the floor of the ROASTING OVEN, add the bread-crumbs and cook, on the floor of the oven, for 10 minutes. Stir and cook for a further 5-10 minutes until lightly browned and crisp. Place in a serving bowl and keep warm at the back of the cooker.

5 Lift the cooked pheasants onto a warmed serving dish. Cut the crisp bacon rashers in half and place around the pheasant. Keep warm in the SIMMERING OVEN.

6 Skim the fat off the juices in the roasting tin, add the onion halves and pour on the stock. Bring to the boil on the BOILING PLATE and boil until reduced by one quarter, and the resulting gravy has a good flavour. Check the seasoning and strain into a sauceboat.

7 Garnish the pheasant with sprigs of watercress. Serve with the fried breadcrumbs, gravy, crisp potatoes and seasonal vegetables.

COOK'S TIPS
▶ *Always carefully check game birds for shot, removing any and rinsing the birds inside and out.*
▶ *Carving is easier if the wish bone is removed with a small, sharp knife before the pheasant is cooked.*

PAN-FRIED GUINEA FOWL WITH RED WINE SAUCE

■ SERVES 6 ■ PREPARATION 15 MINUTES ■ COOKING 30-35 MINUTES
■ FREEZING SUITABLE ■ 425 CALS PER SERVING

Guinea fowl most closely resembles chicken in taste
but it has a superior delicate gamey flavour.
Creamy mashed potato and a steamed green vegetable
perfectly offset this wonderfully rich dish.

25 g (1 oz) butter
15 ml (1 tbsp) oil
6 guinea fowl or corn-fed chicken breast fillets, each
about 150 g (5 oz)
175 g (6 oz) rindless streaky bacon, chopped
225 g (8 oz) button mushrooms
225 g (8 oz) button onions, peeled
30 ml (2tbsp) plain flour
90 ml (6 tbsp) brandy
350 ml (12 fl oz) red wine, such as Cabernet Sauvignon
600 ml (1 pint) chicken stock
15 ml (1 tbsp) redcurrant jelly
salt and freshly ground black pepper

1 Melt the butter and oil in a sauté pan or wide casserole on the BOILING PLATE. Add the guinea fowl, skin-side down, and cook for 3-4 minutes until a deep golden brown. Turn and seal the other side. Transfer the guinea fowl to an ovenproof dish and place in the SIMMERING OVEN, while you make the sauce.

2 Add the bacon, mushrooms and onions to the sauté pan. Cook on the BOILING PLATE for 4-5 minutes or until golden. Add the flour, stirring until smooth. Stir in the brandy and wine, bring to the boil and let bubble furiously until reduced by half, either on the BOILING PLATE or on the floor of the ROASTING OVEN for 5 minutes.

3 Add the stock and redcurrant jelly. Bring to the boil, season and return the guinea fowl to the pan. Cover and cook in the SIMMERING OVEN for 15-20 minutes.

4 Serve at once, accompanied by creamy mashed potatoes and a green vegetable.

Duck Breasts with Rösti and Apple

■ SERVES 4 ■ PREPARATION 30 MINUTES ■ COOKING 20-25 MINUTES
■ FREEZING NOT SUITABLE ■ 430 CALS PER SERVING

Rosy pink, tender slices of 'roasted' duck breast are served on golden apple and potato cakes and accompanied by sautéed caramelised apple slices. The method used to cook the duck breasts encourages most of the fat to run out and the skin becomes deliciously crisp and brown. If possible buy the large French magrets – one of these easily serves 2. Otherwise you will need 4 standard duck breasts.

2 large duck breast fillets, each about 350 g (12 oz),
or 4 medium duck breast fillets (at room temperature)
salt and freshly ground black pepper
15 ml (1 tbsp) red wine vinegar
60 ml (4 tbsp) apple juice
RÖSTI
2 large old potatoes, about 450 g (1 lb) total weight
1 dessert apple
2 fresh sage leaves, finely chopped
oil, for frying
CARAMELISED APPLE
15 ml (1 tbsp) oil
1 dessert apple, cored and sliced
TO GARNISH
sage sprigs

1 Use a sharp knife to lightly score through the skin side of the duck. Rub with salt and pepper. Leave at room temperature for 15 minutes.

2 To make the rösti, peel and finely grate the potatoes and apple. Squeeze out as much moisture as possible and place in a bowl. Add the sage and mix well. Season generously with salt and pepper.

3 Heat 30 ml (2 tbsp) oil in a large heavy-based frying pan on the BOILING PLATE. Place 4 large tablespoonfuls of the potato mixture in the pan, spacing well apart and pressing down hard with a fish slice. Cook for 2 minutes or until golden brown on the underside; turn over and cook the rösti until crisp and golden. Remove and drain on kitchen paper. Repeat with the remaining mixture, adding more oil to the pan as necessary, until you have at least 8 rösti. Keep warm

in the SIMMERING OVEN while cooking the duck breasts and apple slices.

4 For the caramelised apple, heat 15 ml (1 tbsp) oil in a large frying pan on the SIMMERING PLATE, add the apple slices and sauté until golden on both sides. Transfer to a heatproof plate and keep warm in the SIMMERING OVEN with the rösti.

5 Return the frying pan to the SIMMERING PLATE to heat. Add the duck breasts, skin-side down, and cook for 7-10 minutes depending on size and thickness, without moving them; the fat that runs out will prevent them sticking. Turn the breasts over and cook for 3-4 minutes, depending on thickness.

6 Using a slotted spoon, transfer the duck breasts to a warmed serving dish. Cover and leave to rest in the SIMMERING OVEN for 10 minutes. Meanwhile pour off all of the fat from the pan. Add the wine vinegar and apple juice, bring to the boil and reduce slightly.

7 To serve, place 2 rösti on each warmed serving plate. Carve the duck breasts into slices and arrange on top. Spoon on the sauce and garnish with the apple slices and sage. Serve immediately.

Roast Duck with Cherry Sauce

■ SERVES 4 ■ PREPARATION 20 MINUTES ■ COOKING 1¼-1½ HOURS
■ FREEZING NOT SUITABLE ■ 510 CALS PER SERVING

1.8-2 kg (4-4½ lb) oven-ready duck
fine sea salt and freshly ground black pepper
a little oil, for basting
50 g (2 oz) dried cherries
45 ml (3 tbsp) golden syrup
135 ml (9 tbsp) white wine vinegar
120 ml (8 tbsp) brandy
750 ml (1¼ pints) jellied chicken stock (see cook's tips)
125 g (4 oz) pitted fresh or frozen cherries

1 Season the inside of the duck with salt and pepper. Rub the skin of the duck with oil, prick lightly and sprinkle generously with sea salt. Put the dried cherries in a small bowl, pour on 150 ml (¼ pint) boiling water and leave to soak.

2 Place the duck on a rack in the small roasting tin and slide onto the third set of runners in the ROASTING OVEN. Roast for 1¼-1½ hours, or until the juices run clear when the thickest part of the thigh is pierced with a knife. Baste the duck every 20 minutes during roasting and turn it onto its breast after 30-40 minutes. Turn the duck onto its back for the last 10 minutes of cooking.

3 In the meantime, heat the syrup in a wide flameproof pan on the SIMMERING PLATE and cook to a deep brown caramel. Immediately pour on the wine vinegar and reduced by half. Add 60 ml (4 tbsp) of the brandy and bubble to reduce by half. Pour on the stock, bring to the boil and cook on the floor of the ROASTING OVEN for 25-30 minutes or until reduce by one third. Add the fresh and dried cherries together with their soaking liquid and return to the oven for 5 minutes.

4 Lift the duck off the rack onto a serving platter and keep warm in the SIMMERING OVEN. Skim the fat off the cooking juices, add the remaining brandy and bring to the boil on the SIMMERING PLATE. Add to the cherry sauce.

5 Carve the duck into portions and serve with the cherry sauce and vegetables of your choice.

COOK'S TIPS

▶ *If the chicken stock is not jellied, it may be necessary to thicken the sauce with 10 ml (2 tsp) arrowroot mixed to a paste with 30 ml (2 tbsp) cold water at the end of cooking. Cook for 1 minute until slightly thickened.*

▶ *Reserve the duck fat to use for roasting potatoes.*

RABBIT WITH GRAINY MUSTARD

■ SERVES 4 ■ PREPARATION 10 MINUTES ■ COOKING ABOUT 1¾ HOURS
■ FREEZING SUITABLE: STAGE 3 ■ 405 CALS PER SERVING

**4-6 rabbit or chicken joints, about 700-900 g
(1½-2 lb) total weight
salt and freshly ground black pepper
25 g (1 oz) plain flour
30 ml (2 tbsp) oil
15 g (½ oz) butter
2 garlic cloves, peeled and crushed
275 g (10 oz) shallots or button onions, peeled,
and halved if large
225 g (8 oz) carrots, peeled and thickly sliced
150 ml (¼ pint) white wine
300 ml (½ pint) chicken stock
45-60 ml (3-4 tbsp) wholegrain mustard
60 ml (4 tbsp) crème fraîche (optional)
chopped herbs, to garnish**

1 Season the rabbit joints with salt and pepper and toss in half of the flour. Heat the oil and butter in a 2.3 litre (4 pint) flameproof casserole on the BOILING PLATE. Add the rabbit joints and brown on all sides, then transfer the rabbit to an ovenproof dish using a slotted spoon, and place in the SIMMERING OVEN to keep warm.

2 Place the casserole on the SIMMERING PLATE and add the garlic, onions and carrots. Cook for 3-4 minutes, then stir in the remaining flour. Add the wine and bubble for 1 minute. Add the chicken stock and mustard, stir well and bring to the boil. Let bubble for 2-3 minutes.

3 Return the browned rabbit joints to the casserole, then cover and cook in the SIMMERING OVEN for 1½-1¾ hours or until the rabbit is very tender.

4 Transfer the rabbit and vegetables to a warmed serving dish, using a slotted spoon. Place the casserole on the BOILING PLATE and let the sauce bubble for 2-3 minutes to reduce if necessary. Correct the seasoning and stir in the crème fraîche, if using. Pour the sauce over the rabbit and garnish with herbs. Serve with shredded cabbage.

MEAT DISHES

MUSTARD ROAST RIB OF BEEF WITH YORKSHIRE PUDDING

■ SERVES 8-10 ■ PREPARATION 20 MINUTES
■ COOKING ABOUT 2½ HOURS, PLUS 30 MINUTES FOR PUDDING
■ FREEZING NOT SUITABLE ■ 420-335 CALS PER SERVING

Only good quality, tender joints of beef are suitable for roasting. When purchasing a joint, allow about 225 g (8 oz) per person for a boned, rolled joint; 300-350 g (10-12 oz) per person for meat on the bone. Weigh the joint and bring it to room temperature before cooking.

2-bone rib of beef, weighing about 2.7-3.2 kg (6-7 lb)
15 ml (1 tbsp) plain flour
15 ml (1 tbsp) mustard powder
salt and freshly ground black pepper
YORKSHIRE PUDDING
125 g (4 oz) plain flour
2.5 ml (½ tsp) salt
300 ml (½ pint) milk
2 eggs
45 ml (3 tbsp) hot fat from beef
GRAVY
150 ml (¼ pint) red wine, such as Cabernet Sauvignon
600 ml (1 pint) beef stock

1 Place the rib of beef, fat-side up, in the small roasting tin.

2 In a small bowl, mix the flour with the mustard and season with salt and pepper. Rub the mixture over the joint.

3 Slide the roasting tin onto the third set of runners down in the ROASTING OVEN and cook for 20-30 minutes or until the fat is beginning to brown.

4 Baste the beef and lower the roasting tin to the fourth set of runners down. Cook for a further 1½ hours approximately, basting every 20-30 minutes; allow 12 minutes per 450 g (1 lb) for rare beef, 15 minutes per 450 g (1 lb) for medium.

5 Meanwhile, make the Yorkshire pudding batter. Sift the flour and salt into a bowl. Make a well in the centre and whisk in half the milk, then add the eggs and season with pepper. Beat together until smooth, add the rest of the milk and whisk again. Cover and leave the batter to 'rest' in the refrigerator for at least 1 hour.

6 Place the beef on a carving dish, cover loosely with foil and leave to rest in the SIMMERING OVEN while cooking the Yorkshire pudding and making the gravy.

7 Pour 45 ml (3 tbsp) fat from the joint into a 23 x 18 cm (9 x 7 inch) base measurement roasting tin. Place in the ROASTING OVEN on the second set of runners. Heat for 5 minutes or until the fat is so hot that it is almost smoking. Give the pudding batter a stir and pour into the tin. Cook for 25 minutes or until the Yorkshire pudding is well risen, golden and crisp.

8 Meanwhile, make the gravy. Skim any fat off the sediment in the roasting tin. Pour in the wine and boil vigorously on the BOILING PLATE until very syrupy. Pour in the stock and boil until syrupy; there should be about 450 ml (¾ pint) gravy. Check the seasoning.

9 Remove the rib bone and carve the beef. Serve with the gravy, Yorkshire pudding, Golden Roast Vegetables (see page 97), and a green vegetable.

COOK'S TIPS
▶ *Leaving the joint to rest allows the juices that have risen to the surface of the meat during cooking to seep back into the flesh and 'set'.*
▶ *To check the joint is cooked, insert a skewer into the thickest part, press the surface hard and watch the colour of the juices: for rare meat they will be slightly red; for medium they'll be pink; for well done they should run clear.*
▶ *If short of oven space, or concerned about the temperature of the oven dropping, cook the Yorkshire Pudding before the beef and reheat before serving.*

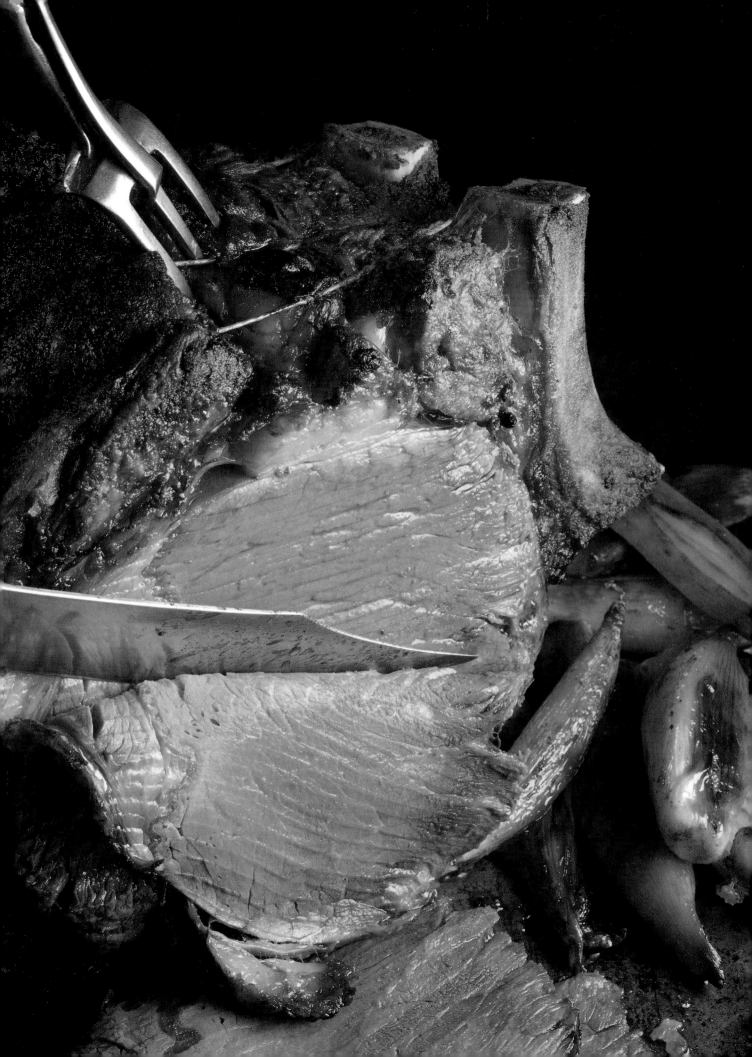

CHILLI WITH POTATO WEDGES

■ SERVES 6 ■ PREPARATION 20 MINUTES
■ COOKING ABOUT 1¹⁄₂ HOURS ■ FREEZING SUITABLE: CHILLI ONLY
■ 700 CALS PER SERVING

This warming family supper dish is perfect for chilly evenings. Crisp roast potato wedges and thick creamy yogurt are the ideal accompaniments.

75 ml (5 tbsp) olive oil
225 g (8 oz) onions, peeled and finely chopped
3 celery sticks, finely chopped
2 red chillies, seeded and finely chopped
900 g (2 lb) good quality lean minced beef
5-10 ml (1-2 tsp) hot chilli powder, to taste
5 ml (1 tsp) ground cumin
15 ml (1 tbsp) tomato purée
10 ml (2 tsp) soft dark brown sugar
30 ml (2 tbsp) Worcestershire sauce
15 ml (1 tbsp) dried oregano
300 ml (¹⁄₂ pint) beef stock
two 400 g (14 oz) cans chopped tomatoes
400 g (14 oz) can red kidney beans, drained and rinsed
1.1 kg (2¹⁄₂ lb) potatoes, scrubbed
salt and freshly ground black pepper
TO SERVE
Greek-style yogurt

1 Heat 30 ml (2 tbsp) olive oil in a large flameproof casserole on the BOILING PLATE, then add the onion, celery and chillies. Stir, then cook on the floor of the ROASTING OVEN for about 10 minutes until the onion is beginning to soften.

2 Place the casserole on the BOILING PLATE, add the minced beef and fry for 1-2 minutes. Return to the floor of the ROASTING OVEN for a further 10-15 minutes, or until the meat is beginning to brown, stirring from time to time.

3 Stir in the chilli powder, ground cumin and tomato purée and fry on the BOILING PLATE for 30 seconds. Add the sugar, Worcestershire sauce, oregano, beef stock, chopped tomatoes and drained kidney beans. Bring to the boil.

4 Cover the casserole with a tight-fitting lid, place on the grid shelf on the floor of the ROASTING OVEN and cook for about 50 minutes.

5 Meanwhile, cut the potatoes into wedges and toss in the remaining olive oil. Place in the large roasting tin and season with plenty of salt and pepper. Hang the tin from the top set of runners in the ROASTING OVEN for 35 minutes before the chilli will be ready. Cook until the potatoes are golden brown.

6 Skim off the fat from the surface of the chilli. Check the seasoning. Serve in bowls topped with a dollop of yogurt, and accompanied by the potato wedges.

COOK'S TIP *If necessary take the chilli out of the oven, keep warm in the* SIMMERING OVEN *and give the potatoes a further 10 minutes cooking.*

ITALIAN MEATBALLS IN TOMATO SAUCE

■ SERVES 4 ■ PREPARATION 20 MINUTES ■ COOKING ABOUT 1¹⁄₄ HOURS
■ FREEZING SUITABLE: STAGE 4 (SAUCE AND MEATBALLS SEPARATELY)
■ 650 CALS PER SERVING

30 ml (2 tbsp) olive oil
350 g (12 oz) onions, peeled and chopped
3 garlic cloves, peeled and crushed
two 400 g (14 oz) cans chopped tomatoes
5 ml (1 tsp) salt
15 ml (1 tbsp) cider vinegar
2.5 ml (¹⁄₂ tsp) ground cinnamon
450 g (1 lb) good quality lean minced beef or pork
75 g (3 oz) fresh breadcrumbs
30 ml (2 tbsp) chopped fresh basil
5 ml (1 tsp) dried oregano, or mixed herbs
1 egg, plus 1 egg yolk, beaten
45 ml (3 tbsp) chopped fresh parsley
45 ml (3 tbsp) freshly grated Parmesan cheese
salt and freshly ground black pepper
12 thin rashers smoked streaky bacon, about 200 g (7 oz)

1 Heat the oil in a shallow flameproof casserole on the SIMMERING PLATE. Add the onions with 2 crushed garlic cloves and fry until beginning to soften, about 5-7 minutes. Add the tomatoes, salt, vinegar and cinnamon. Bring to the boil.

2 ■■ Cover and cook on the grid shelf on the floor of the ROASTING OVEN for 20 minutes.

■■■■ Cook in the BAKING OVEN with the grid shelf on the fourth set of runners for 20 minutes.

3 Place the minced beef or pork in a bowl and, with your hands, work in the breadcrumbs, basil, oregano, remaining crushed garlic, egg and extra yolk, 30 ml (2 tbsp) of the parsley, 15 ml (1 tbsp) Parmesan and seasoning. Shape the mixture into 12 balls with moistened hands, then wrap a bacon rasher round each one.

4 Place the meatballs on top of the tomato sauce and cover the casserole with the lid.
■■ Cook on the grid shelf on the floor of the ROASTING OVEN with the cold plain shelf just above for about 45 minutes or until piping hot and cooked through.
■■■■ Cook in the BAKING OVEN with the grid shelf on the fourth set of runners for 45 minutes to 1 hour.

5 Sprinkle over the remaining Parmesan and parsley. Serve immediately, with steamed couscous, spaghetti or rice.

MEAT PIE WITH CHEESY VEGETABLE TOPPING

■ SERVES 6 ■ PREPARATION 20 MINUTES ■ COOKING ABOUT 1¼ HOURS
■ FREEZING SUITABLE: STAGE 6 ■ 570 CALS PER SERVING

The root vegetable topping for this tasty mince is enriched with Cheddar cheese and mayonnaise.

30 ml (2 tbsp) oil
900 g (2 lb) good quality lean minced beef or lamb
1 large onion, peeled and chopped
1 large carrot, peeled and chopped
30 ml (2 tbsp) plain flour
2.5 ml (½ tsp) ground cinnamon
30 ml (2 tbsp) tomato purée
5 ml (1 tsp) dried thyme
600 ml (1 pint) beef or lamb stock
salt and freshly ground black pepper
30 ml (2 tbsp) chopped fresh parsley
TOPPING
1.1 kg (2½ lb) mixed root vegetables, such as parsnips, turnips and potatoes
45-60 ml (3-4 tbsp) mayonnaise
75 g (3 oz) mature Cheddar cheese, grated
melted butter, for brushing

1 Heat 15 ml (1 tbsp) of the oil in a large flameproof casserole on the BOILING PLATE. Add the minced meat and fry, stirring occasionally, until the meat is browned. Lift out with a slotted spoon onto a plate and set aside.

2 Heat the remaining oil in the casserole on the BOILING PLATE. Add the onion and carrot and fry for 3-5 minutes or until starting to soften and brown lightly.

3 Return the minced meat to the casserole. Add the flour, cinnamon and tomato purée; cook for 1 minute. Stir in the thyme, stock, salt and pepper. Bring to the boil. Cook, uncovered, on the floor of the ROASTING OVEN for 30-35 minutes. Skim off the fat from the surface, then stir in the parsley and adjust the seasoning (see cook's tip).

4 Meanwhile, for the topping, peel the root vegetables and cut into chunks. Place in a saucepan, cover with cold salted water and bring to the boil on the BOILING PLATE. Transfer to the SIMMERING PLATE and simmer, covered, for 5 minutes. Drain off most of the water, then cover and cook in the SIMMERING OVEN for 20-30 minutes until very soft. Drain and dry off completely on the SIMMERING PLATE.

5 Mash the vegetables, leaving some chunks for texture. Stir in the mayonnaise and grated cheese. Season with salt and pepper to taste.

6 Spoon the meat mixture into a 2 litre (3½ pint) ovenproof baking dish, which is about 4 cm (1¾ inch) deep. Pile the mashed vegetables on top and brush with melted butter.

7 Stand the dish on a baking tray. Place on the grid shelf on the highest runners possible in the ROASTING OVEN, positioning the dish towards the back of the oven, and cook for 20-25 minutes or until the topping is golden brown. Serve with Savoy cabbage.

COOK'S TIP *The mince may be cooked the day before to the end of step 3. Cool, cover and chill. It will then be easier to apply the topping. Allow 10 minutes longer in the oven to heat through.*

AROMATIC BRAISED STEAK

■ SERVES 4 ■ PREPARATION 15 MINUTES ■ COOKING 4-5 HOURS
■ FREEZING SUITABLE ■ 520 CALS PER SERVING

This is based on an original French recipe – the anchovies melt into the cooking juices during the long, slow cooking process, resulting in a delicious and full-flavoured dish. If possible, prepare the recipe a day ahead to allow the flavours time to develop.

1 kg (2¼ lb) braising steak
50 g (2 oz) can anchovies, in olive oil
450 g (1 lb) onions, peeled and thinly sliced
6 large garlic cloves, peeled and crushed
30 ml (2 tbsp) capers, drained and chopped
60 ml (4 tbsp) chopped fresh parsley
30 ml (2 tbsp) olive oil
freshly ground black pepper

1 Cut the braising steak into large bite-size pieces.

2 Drain the anchovies, reserving 30 ml (2 tbsp) of the oil, then chop. Place the anchovies and reserved oil in a bowl with the onions, garlic, capers and parsley.

3 Heat the olive oil in a 3.4 litre (6 pint) flameproof casserole on the BOILING PLATE and brown the braising steak, in 2 or 3 batches, evenly on all sides. Remove with a slotted spoon and set aside.

4 Off the heat, add about 45 ml (3 tbsp) water to the hot casserole and scrape with a spoon to loosen the brown sediment.

5 Scatter half of the browned meat pieces over the bottom of the casserole. Layer the remaining meat alternately with the onion mixture, seasoning with pepper as you go.

6 Dampen a large piece of greaseproof paper and place on top of the casserole. Cover with the lid to ensure a tight seal. Place on the SIMMERING PLATE for 5-10 minutes, then transfer to the middle of the SIMMERING OVEN, position the casserole towards the back. Cook for 4-5 hours or until the meat is very, very tender. (See cook's tips.)

7 Remove any fat from the surface, then serve the braised steak with vegetables of your choice.

COOK'S TIPS

▶ The meat should create its own liquid as it cooks, but check the level of liquid after the first hour of cooking. If the lid does not seal completely, you may have to add a little water.

▶ If your SIMMERING OVEN is a little too cool, it may be necessary to place the casserole in the ROASTING OVEN for 15-20 minutes every hour to speed up cooking.

RICH BEEF DAUBE

■ SERVES 6 ■ PREPARATION 25 MINUTES, PLUS SOAKING
■ COOKING ABOUT 2½ HOURS ■ FREEZING SUITABLE: STAGE 4
■ 520 CALS PER SERVING

This tasty, warming stew is quick and easy to prepare. For optimum results, cook it a day ahead and leave at cool room temperature overnight to allow the flavours to mature.

20 g (¾ oz) dried ceps or porcini mushrooms, rinsed
900 g (2 lb) stewing steak
salt and freshly ground black pepper
75 ml (5 tbsp) sunflower oil
225 g (8 oz) shallots or button onions, peeled (see cook's tip)
2 garlic cloves, peeled and crushed
2.5 cm (1 inch) piece fresh root ginger,
peeled and finely chopped
45 ml (3 tbsp) plain flour
125 g (4 oz) sun-dried tomatoes, halved
10 ml (2 tsp) dried mixed herbs
300 ml (½ pint) red wine
300 ml (½ pint) beef stock
10 ml (2 tsp) caster sugar
finely pared rind and juice of 1 large orange
225 g (8 oz) brown-cap mushrooms
125 g (4 oz) black olives
thyme sprigs, to garnish

1 Put the dried mushrooms in a small bowl, pour on 150 ml (¼ pint) water and leave to soak for 1 hour.

2 Cut the meat into 4 cm (1½ inch) cubes. Season with salt and pepper. Heat 30 ml (2 tbsp) oil in a large flameproof casserole on the BOILING PLATE and brown the meat in batches; remove with a slotted spoon and set aside in the SIMMERING OVEN.

3 Add another 15 ml (1 tbsp) oil to the pan and fry the

shallots or onions on the SIMMERING PLATE for 3-5 minutes until golden. Return all of the meat to the casserole and stir in the garlic, ginger, flour, sun-dried tomatoes and herbs. Cook, stirring, for 1 minute.

4 Add the soaked mushrooms, together with their liquid, the wine, stock, sugar, pared orange rind and juice. Bring to a simmer.

■■ Place the casserole on the grid shelf on the floor of the ROASTING OVEN for 30 minutes, then transfer to the SIMMERING OVEN and cook for a further 1½-2 hours until the meat is tender. (Alternatively cook in the SIMMERING OVEN only for 3-4 hours.)

■■■■ Cook the casserole on the grid shelf on the floor of the BAKING OVEN for 2 hours or until the meat is tender.

5 Heat the remaining oil in a frying pan on the BOILING PLATE, add the brown-cap mushrooms and fry briskly for 2-3 minutes, stirring. Add them to the casserole with the olives; discard the orange rind. Return the casserole to the SIMMERING OVEN for a further 15-20 minutes. Check the seasoning and serve garnished with thyme.

COOK'S TIPS

▶ *Dried mushrooms are obtainable from larger supermarkets and good delicatessens. Always use the water the mushrooms are soaked in, as it's full of flavour.*

▶ *To make it easier to peel the shallots, first immerse them in a bowl of boiling water for about 5 minutes to loosen the skins, then drain and peel. To prevent them falling apart, leave the root end intact.*

PAN-FRIED STEAKS WITH ROQUEFORT AND RED PEPPER BUTTER

■ SERVES 4 ■ PREPARATION 15 MINUTES, PLUS CHILLING
■ COOKING ABOUT 3-8 MINUTES ■ FREEZING SUITABLE: FLAVOURED BUTTER ONLY
■ 565 CALS PER SERVING

4 sirloin or fillet steaks, each about 175 g (6 oz) and
1 cm (½ inch) thick
olive oil, for brushing
FLAVOURED BUTTER
75 g (3 oz) unsalted butter, softened
90 g (3½ oz) Roquefort or dolcelatte cheese
1 small red pepper, about 90 g (3½ oz), cored,
seeded and diced
salt and freshly ground black pepper
few drops of Tabasco, to taste

1 To prepare the flavoured butter, cream the butter and cheese together in a bowl, then beat in the red pepper and season lightly with salt and pepper. Add 1 or 2 drops of Tabasco, or to taste.

2 Shape the flavoured butter into a cylinder on a piece of greaseproof paper and roll up tightly. Chill in the refrigerator for 10-15 minutes.

3 Meanwhile, trim off any excess fat from the steaks, season well and brush lightly with olive oil.

4 Heat a ridged skillet or ovenproof frying pan on the floor of the ROASTING OVEN for 10 minutes, then place on the BOILING PLATE. Add the steaks and cook over a high heat, turning just once. Allow about 1½ minutes per side for rare, 2-2½ minutes per side for medium-rare, and 4 minutes per side for well-done steaks.

5 Transfer the steaks to warmed serving plates and top each one with several slices of the flavoured butter. Serve with roast new potatoes and a rocket or watercress salad.

COOK'S TIP *To test how well steak is cooked, press it gently. If rare, the steaks will seem soft and give readily. If medium, the meat will be firm on the outside but with plenty of give in the centre. If well done, it will be completely firm with no give at all.*

RAGÙ ALLA BOLOGNESE

■ SERVES 6 ■ PREPARATION 20 MINUTES ■ COOKING ABOUT 1 HOUR
■ FREEZING SUITABLE: STAGE 5 ■ 980 CALS PER SERVING

There are many variations of this famous sauce, but we think this is the most delicious. If possible, make the ragù the day beforehand in order to remove the solidified fat from the cooled mixture, before reheating.

50 g (2 oz) dried porcini mushrooms
75 g (3 oz) butter
30 ml (2 tbsp) olive oil
275 g (10 oz) onion, peeled and finely chopped
175 g (6 oz) carrot, peeled and finely chopped
175 g (6 oz) celery, finely chopped
350 g (12 oz) lean minced beef
350 g (12 oz) lean minced pork
300 ml (½ pint) dry white wine
pinch of freshly grated nutmeg
60 ml (4 tbsp) sun-dried tomato paste
45 ml (3 tbsp) tomato purée
600 ml (1 pint) beef stock
salt and freshly ground black pepper
700 g (1½ lb) dried tagliatelle
175 g (6 oz) Parma ham, finely chopped
200 ml (7 fl oz) milk
freshly grated Parmesan cheese, to serve

1 Soak the porcini in 75 ml (3 fl oz) warm water for 10 minutes or until most of the water has been absorbed. Drain the mushrooms, reserving the soaking liquor; chop them finely.

2 Melt 50 g (2 oz) butter with the olive oil in a heavy-based ovenproof pan on the SIMMERING PLATE. Add the onion, carrot and celery. Cook, stirring, occasionally, for 10 minutes or until the vegetables have softened.

3 Add the beef and pork, stirring to break up any lumps. Cook for a further 10 minutes or until the meat begins to turn golden brown.

4 Add the wine and bring to the boil. Transfer to the floor of the ROASTING OVEN and cook, uncovered, for about 10 minutes until all the wine has evaporated.

5 Add the nutmeg, sun-dried tomato paste, tomato purée and beef stock. Season generously with salt and pepper.

Cook, uncovered, on the floor of the ROASTING OVEN for 25-30 minutes, then transfer to the SIMMERING OVEN and cook for a further 15-20 minutes.

6 Add the pasta to a large pan of boiling salted water, bring to the boil on the BOILING PLATE, then transfer to the SIMMERING OVEN and cook for 12-15 minutes, or until *al dente*, tender but firm to the bite.

7 In the meantime, add the Parma ham, mushrooms and reserved liquor to the sauce, with the milk and remaining butter. Bring to the boil on the SIMMERING PLATE.

8 Drain the cooked pasta and toss with the sauce. Serve immediately, sprinkled with Parmesan cheese.

TRADITIONAL STEAK AND KIDNEY PIE

■ SERVES 8 ■ PREPARATION 30 MINUTES ■ COOKING 2½-3½ HOURS
■ FREEZING SUITABLE: FILLING ONLY STAGE 2 ■ 695 CALS PER SERVING

This old-fashioned deep-crust pie has a deliciously rich filling encased in a buttery shortcrust pastry.
For best results, make sure you buy good-quality meat, by the piece rather than ready-chopped.

FILLING
1 kg (2¼ lb) piece chuck steak or other stewing beef
350 g (12 oz) ox kidney
45 ml (3 tbsp) plain flour
salt and freshly ground black pepper
90 ml (6 tbsp) oil (approximately)
225 g (8 oz) onion, peeled and chopped
600 ml (1 pint) beef stock, preferably homemade
150 ml (¼ pint) red wine
15 ml (1 tbsp) prepared English mustard
60 ml (4 tbsp) chopped fresh parsley
125 g (4 oz) button mushrooms
SHORTCRUST PASTRY
350 g (12 oz) plain white flour
pinch of salt
225 g (8 oz) butter, diced
2 egg yolks
45 ml (3tbsp) water
beaten egg, to glaze

1 Cut the beef and kidney into 2.5 cm (1 inch) pieces. Season the flour with salt and pepper. Toss the beef in the flour to coat. Heat 45 ml (3 tbsp) of the oil in a flameproof casserole on the BOILING PLATE and quickly brown the meat in batches on all sides, adding more oil to the pan as necessary. Return all the beef with any remaining flour to the casserole. Add the onion, kidney, stock, wine and mustard. Bring to simmering point and cover the casserole.

2 ■■ Cook on the grid shelf on the floor of the ROASTING OVEN for 1 hour, then transfer to the middle of the SIMMERING OVEN and cook for a further 1½ hours.
■■■■ Cook on the grid shelf on the floor of the BAKING OVEN for 1½-2 hours.

3 Meanwhile make the pastry. Sift the flour and salt into a large mixing bowl. Rub in the butter until the mixture resembles breadcrumbs. Beat the egg yolks with 45 ml (3 tbsp) water. Add to the dry ingredients, mixing with a round-bladed knife. Knead lightly until smooth, then wrap the pastry in cling film and chill in the refrigerator for 30 minutes to 1 hour.

4 When the meat is tender, stir in the chopped parsley and check the seasoning, then allow to cool.

5 Thickly roll out three-quarters of the pastry to a round, 38 cm (15 inches) in diameter. Lift into a 20 cm (8 inch) spring-release cake tin and press down onto the base of the tin and up the sides, allowing excess pastry to overhang.

6 Strain the juices from the cooked meat and reserve. Layer the meat and the uncooked mushrooms in the pastry case and pour over 150 ml (¼ pint) meat juice. Roll out the rest of the pastry to make a lid. Carefully position the lid and trim off excess pastry. Pinch the pastry edges together to seal well.

7 Lightly knead the pastry trimmings and re-roll to a thickness of about 5 mm (¼ inch). Cut into leaf shapes, using the back of the knife to mark veins. Arrange the leaves on top of the pie. Make a small hole in the centre of the pie to allow steam to escape. Add a pinch of salt to the beaten egg and brush over pie. Chill in the refrigerator for 30 minutes.

8 Re-glaze the pie; stand it in the large roasting tin and bake on the grid shelf on the floor of the ROASTING OVEN for about 1 hour, positioning the cold plain shelf on the second set of runners for the last 20-30 minutes to avoid over-browning. Leave for 10 minutes, then carefully remove the tin side. Leave the pie on the tin base and place in an edged dish. Serve with the hot meat juices.

ROAST PORK WITH MINTED APPLE AND HORSERADISH SAUCE

■ SERVES 6 ■ PREPARATION 20 MINUTES ■ COOKING ABOUT 1½ HOURS
■ FREEZING NOT SUITABLE ■ 345 CALS PER SERVING

When buying pork for roasting, look for a joint where the eye of the meat is fairly small, ie from a younger animal, as this produces the best crackling.

1.4 kg (3 lb) loin of pork, on the bone, chined (see cook's tips)
salt and freshly ground black pepper
oil, for basting
APPLE AND HORSERADISH SAUCE
450 g (1 lb) cooking apples
25 g (1 oz) butter
30 ml (2 tbsp) creamed horseradish
30 ml (2 tbsp) chopped fresh mint
15 ml (1 tbsp) caster sugar (approximately)

1 To prepare the rind for crackling, thoroughly score the rind with a sharp knife (see cook's tip), rub with salt and leave for 5-10 minutes, then pat dry with kitchen paper. Smear liberally with oil and sprinkle with a little more salt. Put the joint into the small roasting tin.

2 Hang the tin on the highest runners possible in the ROASTING OVEN, positioning it towards the back of the oven. Roast for 15-20 minutes, then lower the tin to the fourth set of runners and cook for a further 1¼ hours or until the pork is cooked through.

3 Meanwhile, make the apple and horseradish sauce. Peel, core and chop the apples. Place them in a pan with 60 ml (4 tbsp) water and bring to the boil on the SIMMERING PLATE. Transfer to the SIMMERING OVEN and cook until the apples are soft. Crush with a potato masher, then stir in the remaining ingredients. Add a little more sugar if the apples are tart and season with pepper to taste.

4 When the pork is cooked, transfer to a warmed serving platter and leave to rest in the SIMMERING OVEN for 15-20 minutes.

5 To serve, remove the crackling with a sharp knife and cut into pieces with kitchen scissors. Carve the pork into thin slices and arrange on the warm platter with the crackling. Serve at once, with the warm apple and horseradish sauce, gravy and vegetables of your choice.

COOK'S TIPS

▶ *If possible, ask the butcher to score the rind for the crackling and to chine the loin (ie remove the backbone); this makes carving much easier.*
▶ *Make a tasty gravy from the skimmed meat juices to serve with the pork.*

ROAST LOIN OF PORK WITH SWEET-SOUR VINAIGRETTE

■ SERVES 6 ■ PREPARATION 10 MINUTES
■ COOKING ABOUT 2¼ HOURS ■ FREEZING NOT SUITABLE
■ 600 CALS PER SERVING

A sweet-sour vinaigrette works well with pork, and makes an interesting change from gravy and apple sauce. To ensure a crisp crackling, make sure the pork rind is well scored.

20 g (¾ oz) dried porcini mushrooms
1.4 kg (3 lb) boned loin of pork (see cook's tip)
15 ml (1 tbsp) oil
5 ml (1 tsp) salt
275 g (10 oz) rindless streaky bacon, roughly chopped
125 g (4 oz) fresh brown-cap mushrooms, thinly sliced
2 garlic cloves, peeled and crushed
45 ml (3 tbsp) balsamic vinegar
30 ml (2 tbsp) soft dark brown sugar
45 ml (3 tbsp) chopped fresh parsley

1 Place the dried porcini mushrooms in a bowl and pour on 425 ml (15 fl oz) boiling hot water; cover and leave to soak.

2 Brush the meat with the oil and rub in the salt. Place in the roasting tin and hang on the lowest set of runners in the ROASTING OVEN. Roast for 2 hours or until the pork is cooked through.

3 Remove the meat from the roasting tin, place on a warmed platter and leave to rest in the SIMMERING OVEN. Pour all the juices and dark sediment from the roasting tin into a jug or gravy separator. Allow the fat and the dark

cooking juices to separate, then pour into separate bowls; reserve the juices for later use.

4 Pour 30 ml (2 tbsp) of the pork fat back into the roasting tin. Add the bacon and fry on the SIMMERING PLATE for 5-7 minutes or until golden brown. Add the fresh mushrooms and garlic; fry for a further 2 minutes or until the mushrooms are beginning to soften.

5 Stir in the porcini mushrooms and their soaking liquor, the balsamic vinegar and sugar. Bring to the boil and simmer gently for about 2 minutes. Remove from the heat and stir in the reserved pork juices. Add the chopped parsley.

6 To serve, carefully remove the crackling with a sharp knife and cut into pieces, using kitchen scissors. Carve the pork into thin slices and arrange on the platter. Spoon the warm vinaigrette over the meat. Serve at once, with the crackling, crispy roast potatoes and seasonal vegetables.

COOK'S TIP *If possible, get your butcher to score the pork rind for the crackling.*

GLAZED SPARE RIBS OF PORK

■ SERVES 4 ■ PREPARATION 10 MINUTES, PLUS MARINATING
■ COOKING 2-2¼ HOURS ■ FREEZING ■ 275 CALS PER SERVING

Sticky and very more-ish, these tasty sweet-sour ribs will be a favourite with all the family. For best results, marinate them overnight before cooking.

300 ml (½ pint) dry cider
120 ml (8 tbsp) marmalade
30 ml (2 tbsp) thin honey
120 ml (8 tbsp) soy sauce
45 ml (3 tbsp) lemon juice
2 garlic cloves, peeled and crushed
freshly ground black pepper
1.8 kg (4 lb) pork spare ribs (see cook's tip)

1 Put the cider, marmalade, honey, soy sauce, lemon juice, crushed garlic and pepper in a small pan and heat on the SIMMERING PLATE, stirring occasionally, until evenly blended; allow to cool.

2 Divide the pork into individual ribs if necessary and trim off excess fat. Place in a large, non-metallic dish and pour on the cooled cider mixture. Turn the ribs to coat with the marinade. Cover and leave to marinate in the refrigerator overnight, turning once.

3 Transfer the ribs and marinade to the large roasting tin. Cover with foil and cook on the grid shelf on the floor of the ROASTING OVEN for 1 hour. Uncover and cook for a further 1 hour on the floor of the oven, or until the ribs are very tender, turning and basting them halfway through cooking.

4 Place the roasting tin on the BOILING PLATE and cook, stirring, for 3-5 minutes until the juices have reduced to a syrupy glaze on the ribs. Serve with rice or Chinese egg noodles, and a crisp salad.

COOK'S TIP *Spare ribs of pork may be sold as barbecue ribs, Chinese-style ribs or American cut ribs. If they come as a whole rack they'll need to be divided.*

PEPPERED GARLIC PORK WITH CRÈME FRAÎCHE

■ SERVES 6 ■ PREPARATION 30 MINUTES ■ COOKING 40-45 MINUTES
■ FREEZING NOT SUITABLE ■ 350 CALS PER SERVING

2 pork tenderloins, each about 350 g (12 oz)
salt
60 ml (4 tbsp) olive oil
8 shallots, peeled and chopped
6 garlic cloves, peeled and chopped
15 ml (1 tbsp) coarsely crushed green peppercorns
15 ml (1 tbsp) chopped fresh chives
15 ml (1 tbsp) chopped fresh parsley
25 g (1 oz) fresh white breadcrumbs
30 ml (2 tbsp) beaten egg
450 ml (¾ pint) chicken stock
150 ml (¼ pint) medium dry white wine
60 ml (4 tbsp) crème fraîche

1 Trim the pork tenderloins and slit each one lengthwise, cutting about halfway into the meat, then open out flat like a book. Cover with a piece of greaseproof paper or cling film and beat with a meat mallet or rolling pin until the pork is rectangular in shape and about 1 cm (½ inch) thick. Season with salt.

2 Heat half the oil in a saucepan on the SIMMERING PLATE. Add the shallots and garlic and fry gently for 5 minutes. Remove from the heat and add the peppercorns, herbs and breadcrumbs. Mix well, then stir in the egg (see cook's tip).

3 Press the mixture along the middle of each tenderloin. Close the pork and tie at regular intervals with string.

4 Heat the remaining oil in a frying pan on the BOILING PLATE. Add the pork tenderloins and fry quickly, turning until brown all over. Transfer to the small roasting tin and drizzle over any juices from the frying pan. Add 200 ml (7 fl oz) stock to the roasting tin.

5 ■■ Cook on the grid shelf on the floor of the ROASTING OVEN with the cold plain shelf on the runners just above for 30-35 minutes or until cooked through, basting frequently with the juices.
■■■■ Hang the roasting tin from the second set of runners in the BAKING OVEN and cook for 25-35 minutes

until cooked through, basting frequently.

6 Lift the pork tenderloins onto a warmed serving platter and keep warm in the SIMMERING OVEN. Add the remaining stock and the wine to the roasting tin and boil rapidly on the BOILING PLATE until reduced by about half. Add the crème fraîche and boil until smooth and creamy.

7 Remove the string from the pork and carve the pork into neat slices. Serve hot with the sauce.

COOK'S TIP *For convenience, the meat can be prepared and stuffed several hours in advance. Allow the mixture to cool completely before adding the egg and stuffing the meat. Set aside in a cool place until ready to cook.*

ROSEMARY AND GARLIC-SCENTED ROAST LEG OF LAMB

■ SERVES 8 ■ PREPARATION 30 MINUTES ■ COOKING ABOUT 1¾ HOURS
■ FREEZING NOT SUITABLE ■ 630 CALS PER SERVING

A leg of lamb studded with garlic and rosemary always makes an excellent roast. This one is cooked on a rack over potatoes, shallots and garlic cloves which are therefore basted with the meat juices – to delicious effect. Roasted whole baby beetroot are the perfect complement.

90 ml (6 tbsp) olive oil
275 g (10 oz) carrots, peeled and roughly chopped
275 g (10 oz) onions, peeled and roughly chopped
275 g (10 oz) celery, roughly chopped
1 bottle red wine
900 ml (1½ pints) lamb stock
45 ml (3 tbsp) redcurrant jelly
2-3 fresh bay leaves
small bunch of fresh rosemary sprigs
small bunch of fresh thyme sprigs
salt and freshly ground black pepper
2.4 kg (5 lb) leg of lamb
2 garlic bulbs, divided into cloves and peeled
8 small, raw beetroot, peeled and trimmed
8 even-sized potatoes, peeled and halved
450 g (1 lb) shallots, or small onions, peeled

1 Prepare the sauce well ahead if possible (see cook's tips). Heat 30 ml (2 tbsp) oil in a large ovenproof saucepan on the SIMMERING PLATE. Add the chopped vegetables and cook, stirring, for 4-5 minutes or until soft and slightly browned.

2 Transfer to the BOILING PLATE, add the wine and boil steadily until reduced by half, then add the stock, redcurrant jelly, bay leaves and 1 or 2 sprigs of rosemary and thyme. Bring to the boil, then transfer the pan to the floor of the ROASTING OVEN and cook, uncovered, until reduced by half. Strain the liquid: there should be about 600 ml (1 pint). Skim off the fat, check the seasoning and set aside.

3 Thinly slice 2 garlic cloves. Make shallow slits in the skin of the lamb and insert a sprig of herbs and a garlic slice into each incision. Rub the lamb with 30 ml (2 tbsp) oil and season with plenty of black pepper. Wrap each beetroot in a piece of foil.

4 Place the lamb on a grid over the large roasting tin and hang from the fourth set of runners in the ROASTING OVEN, with the beetroot parcels alongside. Roast, allowing 30 minutes per kg (2 lb), plus an extra 30 minutes for large joints. After 30 minutes, place the potatoes, shallots and remaining garlic cloves in the roasting tin under the meat and drizzle the remaining oil over them. Add 150 ml (¼ pint) water to the tin. Return to the oven and cook for a further 1 hour or until the lamb and vegetables are tender.

5 When the lamb is cooked, all the liquid should have evaporated and the shallots and garlic should be cooked and glazed with the juices. Transfer the lamb and vegetables to a warmed serving platter and leave to rest in the SIMMERING OVEN for 5-10 minutes.

6 Add the wine sauce to the sediment in the roasting tin. Bring to the boil on the BOILING PLATE, then place in the ROASTING OVEN for 5 minutes, until piping hot.

7 Carve the lamb, slice the beetroot and pour any lamb juices over the meat. Serve the sauce separately.

COOK'S TIPS

▶ *Reducing stocks and sauces lowers the heat of the aga considerably, so it makes sense to do this well in advance of cooking the meat if possible.*
▶ *Ensure the joint is at room temperature before cooking.*

ITALIAN BRAISED LAMB SHANKS

■ SERVES 6-8 ■ PREPARATION 20 MINUTES ■ COOKING 3½-6½ HOURS
■ FREEZING SUITABLE: STAGE 5 ■ 660 CALS PER SERVING

Half-leg knuckles of lamb are part-roasted, then braised with vegetables, sun-dried tomatoes and spicy Italian sausage in a rich red wine stock until meltingly soft.

2 half-leg knuckles of lamb, each 1.2-1.4 kg (2½-3 lb)
30 ml (2 tbsp) olive oil
30 ml (2 tbsp) dried porcini mushrooms,
or 125 g (4 oz) fresh mushrooms
75 g (3 oz) butter
275 g (10 oz) onions, peeled and finely chopped
175 g (6 oz) carrots, peeled and finely chopped
175 g (6 oz) celery sticks, finely chopped
9 sun-dried tomatoes, finely chopped
150 g (5 oz) Italian-style spicy sausage, thickly sliced
600 ml (1 pint) red wine
400 g (14 oz) passata or creamed tomatoes
600 ml (1 pint) vegetable stock
125 g (4 oz) dried pasta shapes
30-45 ml (2-3 tbsp) freshly grated Parmesan cheese

1 Place the lamb knuckles in the small roasting tin and drizzle over 15 ml (1 tbsp) oil. Hang the tin from the highest set of runners possible in the ROASTING OVEN and cook for 35 minutes.

2 If using dried porcini, soak in about 90 ml (3 fl oz) hot water to cover for 30 minutes, then drain, reserving the soaking liquor. Finely chop the soaked porcini, or fresh mushrooms if using.

3 Meanwhile, melt the butter with the remaining oil in a large flameproof casserole on the SIMMERING PLATE, then stir in the vegetables. Cook, stirring, for 10-15 minutes or until soft and golden. (Or cook in the SIMMERING OVEN for 20-25 minutes. Stir in the mushrooms (with the soaking liquid if relevant) and cook for a further 2-3 minutes on the BOILING PLATE.

4 Add the sun-dried tomatoes and sausage to the casserole with the wine, passata and stock. Bring to the boil, then transfer to the SIMMERING PLATE or SIMMERING OVEN and cook for 10 minutes.

5 Lift the lamb from the roasting tin, place in the casserole and cover with a tight-fitting lid.

6 ■■ Cook in the SIMMERING OVEN, towards the back for 5-6 hours or until the lamb is very tender – almost falling off the bone.
■■■■ Cook on the grid shelf on the floor of the BAKING OVEN for 3 hours or until the lamb is very tender.

7 Lift the lamb from the casserole to a deep, heatproof platter. Cover loosely with foil and keep warm in the bottom of the SIMMERING OVEN.

8 Skim off the fat from the surface of the sauce, then stir in the pasta. Bring to the boil on the BOILING PLATE, then transfer to the SIMMERING OVEN for 10-15 minutes, or until the pasta is tender. Off the heat, stir in the grated Parmesan cheese and spoon around the lamb to serve.

COOK'S TIP *To speed up cooking if necessary, at stage 6 place the casserole in the ROASTING OVEN for 15-20 minutes of each hour.*

LAMB STEAKS WITH AUBERGINE RELISH

■ SERVES 4 ■ PREPARATION 10 MINUTES ■ COOKING 30-35 MINUTES
■ FREEZING NOT SUITABLE ■ 455 CALS PER SERVING

3 garlic cloves, peeled and crushed
60 ml (4 tbsp) chopped fresh mint
75 ml (5 tbsp) olive oil
salt and freshly ground black pepper
4 lamb leg steaks or chump chops,
about 450 g (1 lb) total weight
450 g (1 lb) aubergine, diced
125 g (4 oz) onion, peeled and roughly chopped
125 g (4 oz) feta cheese
30 ml (2 tbsp) chopped fresh flat-leaf parsley
30 ml (2 tbsp) lemon juice
lemon wedges and mint leaves, to garnish

1 For the marinade, mix 2 crushed garlic cloves with 30 ml (2 tbsp) mint, 45 ml (3 tbsp) olive oil and seasoning. Score the fat on the meat, then place the lamb in a shallow dish and spoon over the marinade. Cover and leave to marinate in the refrigerator for about 30 minutes.

2 Halve the aubergine lengthwise, score the flesh deeply and drizzle 15 ml (1 tbsp) oil over the cut surfaces. Place, cut-side down, in the small roasting tin on the floor of the ROASTING OVEN and bake for 20-25 minutes until well browned underneath and soft. Leave until cool enough to handle, then dice the flesh.

3 Preheat a grill pan (cast-iron ridged skillet) on the floor of the ROASTING OVEN for 7-10 minutes.

4 Meanwhile, heat the remaining oil in a frying pan on the SIMMERING PLATE. Add the onion and remaining garlic clove and cook, stirring, for 10 minutes.

5 Move the hot grill pan to the BOILING PLATE. Place the lamb steaks in the pan and cook for 5 minutes (see cook's tip). Turn the lamb steaks over, place the grill pan on the floor of the ROASTING OVEN and cook for 5 minutes, until well browned on the outside but still pink in the middle.

6 Add the aubergine to the onion and garlic, together with the remaining mint, crumbled feta cheese, parsley and lemon juice. Season with salt and pepper to taste.

7 Transfer the lamb to warmed serving plates and spoon over any pan juices. Garnish with lemon wedges and mint leaves, and serve with the aubergine relish.

MOUSSAKA

■ SERVES 6 ■ PREPARATION 30 MINUTES ■ COOKING ABOUT 1¾ HOURS
■ FREEZING SUITABLE: STAGE 4 ■ 440 CALS PER SERVING

Serve this classic Greek dish with a crisp, leafy salad, warm crusty bread and a glass of robust red wine. Use small to medium aubergines, rather than large plump ones which require degorging to remove the bitter juices.

60 ml (4 tbsp) sunflower oil
1 large onion, peeled and chopped
450 g (1 lb) lean minced lamb or beef
400 g (14 oz) can chopped tomatoes
1.25 ml (¼ tsp) ground cinnamon
5 ml (1 tsp) dried oregano
salt and freshly ground black pepper
900 g (2 lb) aubergines, sliced
50 g (2 oz) butter
50 g (2 oz) plain flour
600 ml (1 pint) warm milk
25 g (1 oz) Parmesan cheese, freshly grated
1 egg yolk
30 ml (2 tbsp) fresh breadcrumbs

1 Heat the oil in a large ovenproof pan on the SIMMERING PLATE, add the onion and fry gently for about 10 minutes until softened but not coloured. Stir in the meat and cook on the floor of the ROASTING OVEN for 20 minutes until evenly browned, stirring from time to time. Move to the BOILING PLATE and add the tomatoes, cinnamon, oregano and seasoning. Bring to the boil, then cook, uncovered, in the middle of the ROASTING OVEN for 20 minutes.

2 Meanwhile, brush the aubergines with oil and lay in the large roasting tin. Cook on the floor of the ROASTING OVEN for 20 minutes until softened and golden brown, turning the slices from time to time.

3 In the meantime, melt the butter in a pan on the SIMMERING PLATE. Stir in the flour and cook, stirring, for 1 minute. Remove from the heat and gradually whisk in the milk. Bring to the boil, stirring, and cook, stirring, for 3-4

minutes, until thickened and smooth. Allow to cool slightly, then beat in half of the cheese and the egg yolk. Season with salt and pepper to taste.

4 Arrange half of the aubergines in a 2.8 litre (5 pint) shallow ovenproof dish. Cover with the meat mixture, then the remaining aubergines. Spoon the sauce over the top and sprinkle with the breadcrumbs and remaining cheese.

5 ■ ■ Stand the dish on the grid shelf on the floor of the ROASTING OVEN and cook for 20 minutes, or until golden. Position the cold plain shelf on the runners above and bake for a further 30-40 minutes.

■ ■ ■ ■ Cook in the BAKING OVEN with the grid shelf on the fourth set of runners for 45 minutes to 1 hour.

6 Serve piping hot, accompanied by a salad.

TOMATO-CRUSTED LAMB WITH SUMMER VEGETABLES

■ SERVES 6 ■ PREPARATION 20 MINUTES ■ COOKING ABOUT 50 MINUTES
■ FREEZING NOT SUITABLE ■ 550 CALS PER SERVING

2 garlic cloves, peeled
100 ml (3½ fl oz) olive oil
125 g (4 oz) sun-dried tomatoes
5 ml (1 tsp) chopped fresh thyme or 2.5 ml (½ tsp) dried
salt and freshly ground black pepper
2-3 fully trimmed racks of lamb (see cook's tip)
450 g (1 lb) new potatoes, roughly chopped
450 g (1 lb) young carrots, peeled and roughly chopped
450 g (1 lb) summer squash, peeled and roughly chopped
about 18 pitted black olives
1.25 ml (¼ tsp) fennel seeds
juice of 1 lemon
5 ml (1 tsp) caster sugar
chopped parsley, to garnish

1 Put the garlic, 30 ml (2 tbsp) of the olive oil, the sun-dried tomatoes and thyme in a blender or food processor and process to a smooth paste. Season with salt and pepper.

2 Trim the lamb of most of the fat, then lightly score the thin fat layer at regular intervals. Press the tomato mixture firmly over the lamb to coat.

3 Add the potatoes to a pan of boiling salted water and cook on the SIMMERING PLATE for 1-2 minutes; drain well. Put the potatoes, carrots and squash in the large roasting tin with the olives, fennel seeds, lemon juice, sugar and remaining oil. Toss well to coat the vegetables with the oil.

4 Hang the roasting tin from the fourth set of runners in the ROASTING OVEN and cook for about 20 minutes.

5 Place the racks of lamb on a rack over the vegetables (or on the grid shelf directly over the roasting tin). Roast, allowing 20-25 minutes for medium-rare; 30-35 minutes for well done meat; cover the lamb loosely with foil if the crust starts to burn.

6 Transfer the vegetables to a serving dish; keep warm in the SIMMERING OVEN. Transfer the lamb to the roasting tin and leave to rest in the SIMMERING OVEN for 5 minutes before carving.

7 Carve the lamb into cutlets and arrange on warmed plates with the vegetables. Pour any pan juices over the lamb. Garnish with parsley and serve immediately.

COOK'S TIP *New season's racks of lamb are smaller than those obtained later in the season, so you may need 3 racks to serve 6. Allow approximately 10 minutes extra cooking for larger racks.*

JAMAICAN JERK LAMB

■ SERVES 6 ■ PREPARATION 15 MINUTES, PLUS OVERNIGHT MARINATING
■ COOKING ABOUT 45 MINUTES ■ FREEZING NOT SUITABLE
■ 200 CALS PER SERVING

15 ml (1 tbsp) oil
1 large onion, peeled and finely diced
2 red chillies, seeded and finely chopped
2 large garlic cloves, peeled and crushed
5 ml (1 tsp) dried thyme
2.5 ml (½ tsp) ground allspice
finely grated zest and juice of 1 lime
30 ml (2 tbsp) dark rum or Bacardi
salt and freshly ground black pepper
3 fully trimmed racks of lamb, about 700 g (1½ lb) total weight
(see cook's tip)

1 Heat the oil in a saucepan on the SIMMERING PLATE. Add the onion and fry for about 10 minutes or until soft and golden brown. Add the chillies, garlic, thyme and allspice. Fry for a further 2-3 minutes. Stir in the lime zest and juice, the rum and 30 ml (2 tbsp) water. Simmer gently, uncovered, for about 4 minutes or until all the liquid has evaporated and the mixture is a dry, dark paste. Season well, then leave to cool.

2 Make about six 1 cm (½ inch) deep cuts at regular intervals along the back of the lamb. Rub the cooled jerk paste into the cuts and over the lamb, pressing firmly to coat. Cover and refrigerate overnight.

3 Place the lamb in the large roasting tin and with the grid shelf on the fourth set of runners, cook in the ROASTING OVEN, allowing 20-25 minutes for medium-rare lamb; 30-35 minutes for well done; see cook's tips. Leave to rest in the SIMMERING OVEN for 10-15 minutes.

4 Carve the lamb into individual cutlets and serve at once on a bed of rice, accompanied by fine green beans.

COOK'S TIPS

▶ *Mid and late season racks of lamb will be larger – about 350 g (12 oz) each, so 2 racks will be sufficient to serve 6, allowing 2-3 cutlets per person. For these larger racks, allow 30-35 minutes for medium; 35-40 for well done lamb.*

▶ *To ensure even cooking, turn the roasting tin around halfway through cooking.*

KOFTAS ON GREEN HERBS WITH TOMATO RICE

■ SERVES 4 ■ PREPARATION 20 MINUTES ■ COOKING ABOUT 25 MINUTES
■ FREEZING NOT SUITABLE ■ 590 CALS PER SERVING

For this African dish, spiced minced lamb is packed cylindrically around skewers, then cooked in the grill pan. The koftas are served on a bed of herbs and spring onions, accompanied by tasty tomato-flavoured rice.

575 g (1¼ lb) finely minced lamb
1 onion, peeled and grated
6 fresh mint leaves, shredded, or 5 ml (1 tsp) dried mint
5 ml (1 tsp) ground allspice
salt and freshly ground black pepper
olive oil, for brushing
TOMATO RICE
30 ml (2 tbsp) olive oil
2 garlic cloves, peeled and finely chopped
225 g (8 oz) long-grain rice
200 g (7 oz) can peeled plum tomatoes
TO SERVE
3 spring onions, trimmed and chopped
45 ml (3 tbsp) chopped fresh parsley
lemon wedges
parsley sprigs

1 Put the minced lamb into a bowl with the onion. Add the mint, allspice, salt and pepper, and use your hands to mix together thoroughly to a paste. Divide into 8 portions and mould each into a sausage around a skewer. Brush them all over with olive oil.

2 Preheat the grill pan (cast-iron ridged skillet) on the floor of the ROASTING OVEN for 7-10 minutes.

3 Meanwhile, prepare the tomato rice. Heat the oil in a heavy-based saucepan (which has a close-fitting lid) on the SIMMERING PLATE. Add the garlic and fry gently for 30 seconds. Add the rice and stir over the heat for 1 minute until glossy.

4 Tip the can of tomatoes into a sieve over the saucepan and press through, then fill the can with cold water and pour that in too. Bring to the boil and season with salt and pepper. Cover with a tight-fitting lid and cook in the SIMMERING OVEN for 15-20 minutes.

5 Meanwhile, transfer the preheated grill pan to the BOILING PLATE and arrange the meat skewers in the pan. Cook, turning regularly, for about 10-12 minutes until well browned all over and cooked through.

6 Meanwhile, mix the spring onions and parsley together and spoon onto serving plates. Lay the koftas on top. Fork up the rice gently, correct the seasoning and serve with the koftas. Garnish with lemon wedges and parsley.

VARIATION Use good quality finely minced beef instead of lamb, or a mixture of both.

CALVES LIVER WITH BLACK PUDDING AND BACON

■ SERVES 4-6 ■ PREPARATION 15 MINUTES ■ COOKING 7 MINUTES
■ FREEZING NOT SUITABLE ■ 695-465 CALS PER SERVING

Tender calves liver is flash-fried with black pudding and bacon, and served with a quick sauce – made by enriching the pan juices with cream and cider. Tangy dessert apples are wrapped in the bacon to add a refreshing contrast.

4 rashers smoked streaky bacon, derinded
1 dessert apple
700 g (1½ lb) calves liver, trimmed
15 ml (1 tbsp) oil
25 g (1 oz) butter
125 g (4 oz) black pudding, sliced
150 ml (¼ pint) double cream
125 ml (4 fl oz) medium cider
20 ml (4 tsp) chopped fresh sage
salt and freshly ground black pepper
sage sprigs, to garnish

1 Stretch each bacon rasher with the back of a knife, then cut in half to give 8 strips. Cut the apple into 8 wedges, cutting away the core.

2 Cut the liver into slightly smaller pieces. Heat the oil with the butter in a large frying pan on the SIMMERING PLATE. Add the apple slices and fry for 1 minute each side, until golden; remove with a slotted spoon.

3 Wrap an apple wedge in each bacon strip and secure with a wooden cocktail stick. Return to the pan and fry on the SIMMERING PLATE for 2 minutes, turning once. Add the black pudding to the pan and cook for 1 minute on each side. Transfer the bacon rolls and black pudding to an ovenproof serving dish using a slotted spoon; keep warm.

4 Move the frying pan to the BOILING PLATE. Add the calves liver to the pan and sear quickly for 30 seconds on each side until golden brown. Place in the dish with the black pudding and bacon.

5 Add the cream, cider and sage to the frying pan. Bring to the boil on the BOILING PLATE and let bubble for 1-2 minutes. Season with salt and pepper to taste.

6 Arrange the liver and black pudding on warmed serving plates and pour over the sauce. Garnish with the bacon apple rolls and sage. Serve immediately.

ITALIAN SAUSAGE RAGÙ WITH SOFT POLENTA

■ SERVES 4 ■ PREPARATION 30 MINUTES ■ COOKING 30 MINUTES
■ FREEZING SUITABLE ■ 785 CALS PER SERVING

Soft, golden polenta is the perfect foil for this thick, rich, spicy sausage and tomato sauce. If you haven't time to make your own sausagemeat, buy fresh Italian sausages from a delicatessen or good butcher.

SAUSAGEMEAT
225 g (8 oz) shoulder of pork
125 g (4 oz) piece unsmoked gammon
125 g (4 oz) belly of pork
1 large garlic clove, peeled and crushed
5 ml (1 tsp) coarse sea salt
5 ml (1 tsp) granulated sugar
15 ml (1 tbsp) coarsely crushed black pepper
5 ml (1 tsp) fennel seeds
RAGÙ
30 ml (2 tbsp) olive oil
1 onion, peeled and chopped
2 red peppers, cored, seeded and diced
2.5 ml (½ tsp) mild chilli powder
500 g (1 lb 2 oz) passata or creamed tomatoes
150 ml (¼ pint) dry red wine
6 sun-dried tomatoes in oil, drained and sliced
salt and freshly ground black pepper
TO SERVE
300 g (10 oz) quick-cook (instant) polenta
freshly grated Parmesan cheese

1 To prepare the sausagemeat, trim the shoulder of pork, gammon and belly pork of any skin or connective tissue, then cut into rough chunks. Pass through the coarse blade of a mincer or chop with a large sharp knife or cleaver. (Do not use a food processor as this gives a poor texture.) Place the meat in a large bowl with the garlic, sea salt, sugar, pepper and fennel seeds. Mix thoroughly.

2 To prepare the ragù, heat the oil in a saucepan on the

SIMMERING PLATE. Add the onion and red peppers, and cook for 5 minutes until soft and golden.

3 Add the sausagemeat and chilli powder. Transfer to the BOILING PLATE and fry until evenly browned, stirring with a wooden spoon to break up the lumps. Pour in the passata and wine. Bring to the boil and add the sun-dried tomatoes.

4 Cook, uncovered, on the grid shelf on the floor of the ROASTING OVEN for 30 minutes or until well reduced, stirring occasionally. Season with salt and pepper to taste.

5 Meanwhile, pour 1.4 litres (2½ pints) boiling water into a large saucepan. Add 5 ml (1 tsp) salt and bring to the boil on the BOILING PLATE. Sprinkle in the polenta, stirring to prevent lumps forming. Simmer, stirring constantly, for 30 seconds, then cover and cook in the SIMMERING OVEN for 10 minutes until thickened to the consistency of soft mashed potato. Season generously with salt and pepper.

6 Spoon the polenta into 4 warmed large soup plates and make a shallow dip in the centre of each. Top with the sausage ragù and serve with grated Parmesan cheese.

VEGETABLE COUSCOUS WITH HARISSA

■ SERVES 4-6 ■ PREPARATION 30 MINUTES ■ COOKING 25-45 MINUTES
■ FREEZING NOT SUITABLE ■ 345-235 CALS PER SERVING

This tasty vegetable stew originates from North Africa. Harissa, the traditional accompaniment, is a fiery hot red chilli paste flavoured with garlic, coriander, cumin and mint. It is used widely in North African cookery and is available from ethnic shops in tubes or small cans. If you can't find it, make your own substitute (see cook's tip).

350 g (12 oz) quick-cook couscous
40 g (1½ oz) butter
2 small onions, peeled and quartered
2 garlic cloves, crushed
1 bunch of baby fennel, trimmed, or 1 large fennel bulb, cored and cut into wedges
225 g (8 oz) pumpkin, peeled and chopped
225 g (8 oz) small whole baby carrots, trimmed and scrubbed
good pinch of saffron strands
2 cinnamon sticks
30 ml (2 tbsp) coriander seeds, crushed, or ground coriander
5 ml (1 tsp) paprika
300 ml (½ pint) vegetable stock
salt and freshly ground black pepper
225 g (8 oz) courgettes, thickly sliced
1 red chilli, finely sliced
225 g (8 oz) tomatoes, skinned and chopped
50 g (2 oz) raisins
175 g (6 oz) shelled sliced frozen broad beans, skinned
15 ml (1 tbsp) harissa paste (see right)
chopped coriander, to garnish

1 Put the couscous in a bowl and add sufficient cold water to cover by 2.5 cm (1 inch). Leave to stand for 2-3 minutes (or according to packet instructions) then drain and place in a steamer or metal colander lined with damp muslin over boiling water; cover tightly.

2 ■■ Steam on the grid shelf on the floor of the ROASTING OVEN for 20-25 minutes, forking it through occasionally.
■■■■ Steam on the grid shelf on the floor of the BAKING OVEN for 40-45 minutes, forking it through occasionally, until tender and fluffed up.

3 Meanwhile, cook the vegetables. Melt the butter in a large casserole on the SIMMERING PLATE. Add the onions, cover and cook for 3-4 minutes, then add the garlic, fennel, pumpkin and carrots. Cover and cook in the SIMMERING OVEN for 10 minutes. Crumble in the saffron and stir in the cinnamon, coriander, paprika, stock and seasoning. Cover and cook in the SIMMERING OVEN for 8-10 minutes or until the vegetables are almost tender.

4 Add the courgettes to the casserole and stir-fry on the BOILING PLATE for 2-3 minutes. Add the chilli, tomatoes, raisins, and broad beans. Cover and place in the SIMMERING OVEN for 5 minutes.

5 Just before serving, pour about 200 ml (7 fl oz) of the cooking liquor into a small bowl and stir in the harissa paste.

6 Pile the couscous onto a warmed platter or individual plates and top with the vegetables. Sprinkle with chopped coriander and serve with the harissa sauce.

COOK'S TIP *If harissa paste is unobtainable, flavour 30 ml (2 tbsp) tomato purée with a little crushed garlic, and paprika and cayenne to taste. Use as a substitute.*

VARIATION Use 125 g (4oz) frozen peas in place of the broad beans.

VEGETABLE CHILLI

■ SERVES 8 ■ PREPARATION 20 MINUTES ■ COOKING ABOUT 1 HOUR
■ FREEZING SUITABLE ■ 225 CALS PER SERVING

Serve this tasty chilli accompanied by plain boiled rice
and topped with soured cream or thick Greek yogurt,
grated cheese and a little extra chopped fresh coriander.
Alternatively, use it to top baked potatoes,
or to fill shop-bought tacos.

30 ml (2 tbsp) oil
2 onions, peeled and chopped
2 large garlic cloves, peeled and crushed
1-2 green chillies, seeded and chopped
1 bay leaf
1 cinnamon stick
4 cloves
15 ml (1 tbsp) mild paprika
10 ml (2 tsp) cumin powder
2.5 ml (½ tsp) chilli powder, or to taste
5 ml (1 tsp) dried marjoram
30 ml (2 tbsp) tomato purée
225 g (8 oz) button mushrooms, sliced
1 large green pepper, cored, seeded and chopped
900 g (2 lb) mixed vegetables, including carrots, aubergines,
parsnips, potato and celery, prepared as necessary
and cut into chunks
two 400 g (14 oz) cans chopped tomatoes
two 425 g (15 oz) cans red kidney beans, drained and rinsed
pinch of sugar
5 ml (1 tsp) malt vinegar
45 ml (3 tbsp) chopped fresh coriander
salt and freshly ground black pepper

1 Heat the oil in a large saucepan or flameproof casserole
on the SIMMERING PLATE. Add the onions, garlic and
chillies and fry for 3-4 minutes, stirring continuously. Add the
bay leaf, spices, marjoram and tomato purée, and fry for a
further 2 minutes, stirring.

2 Add all the fresh vegetables and stir to coat in the spice
mixture. Fry for 1-2 minutes, then add the tomatoes. Move to
the BOILING PLATE and bring to the boil, stirring
occasionally. Add enough water just to cover the vegetables
and cook, uncovered, on the grid shelf on the floor of the
ROASTING OVEN for 35-45 minutes.

3 Add the kidney beans with the sugar, vinegar and half
the coriander. Season with salt and pepper. Bring back to
the boil on the BOILING PLATE, cover and return to the
ROASTING OVEN for 15 minutes, stirring occasionally. If the
chilli looks dry, add a little extra water. If it is wet, leave the
lid off during this time.

4 Stir in the remaining coriander, then leave to stand for
5 minutes. Taste and adjust the seasoning, if necessary.
Serve with plain boiled rice.

COOK'S TIP *If preferred, use cooked dried kidney beans.
You will need 225 g (8 oz) dried weight. Soak overnight in
cold water to cover before cooking.*

VEGETABLE PASANDA

■ SERVES 6 ■ PREPARATION 30 MINUTES ■ COOKING ABOUT 50 MINUTES
■ FREEZING NOT SUITABLE ■ 450 CALS PER SERVING

Dry-frying whole spices, such as cumin, fennel and
coriander releases maximum aroma and lends a subtle
smoky flavour. The technique is used here to enhance
the pasanda's rich, creamy flavour.

75 g (3 oz) blanched almonds
10 ml (2 tsp) cumin seeds
5 ml (1 tsp) fennel seeds
10 ml (2 tsp) coriander seeds
5 cm (1 inch) piece fresh root ginger, peeled
and roughly chopped
2 garlic cloves, peeled
6 cloves
8 black peppercorns
oil, for frying
2 onions, peeled and thinly sliced
300 ml (½ pint) double cream
350 g (12 oz) waxy potatoes, peeled and cut into chunks
3 courgettes, cut into chunks
1 medium aubergine, cut into chunks
125 g (4 oz) green beans, halved
225 g (8 oz) small cauliflower florets
450 g (1 lb) spinach leaves, stalks removed
salt
TO GARNISH
crisp-fried onions (optional)
toasted shredded almonds

1 Put the almonds in a heavy-based frying pan and dry-fry on the SIMMERING PLATE until just golden brown. Remove from the pan and leave to cool. Add the cumin, fennel and coriander seeds to the pan and dry-fry in the same way, shaking the pan all the time until the spices release their aroma. Leave to cool.

2 Tip the almonds into a food processor or blender and process until finely chopped. Add the ginger, garlic and 15 ml (1 tbsp) water. Work to a purée.

3 Crush the dry-fried spices with the cloves and black peppercorns, using a pestle and mortar or spice grinder.

4 Heat 30 ml (2 tbsp) oil in a large saucepan on the BOILING PLATE. Add the onions and cook until tinged with brown. Transfer to the SIMMERING PLATE, add the almond mixture and cook for 2 minutes.

5 Add the crushed spices and cook for 2 minutes. Add the cream and 175 ml (6 fl oz) water. Cover and cook in the SIMMERING OVEN for 10-15 minutes.

6 Meanwhile, heat a little oil in a frying pan on the BOILING PLATE and fry the potatoes until thoroughly browned on all sides. Repeat with the courgettes and aubergine. Drain on crumpled kitchen paper.

7 Add the fried vegetables to the sauce with the beans and cauliflower. Bring to the boil and simmer for 2-3 minutes, then cover and cook in the SIMMERING OVEN for 20-30 minutes or until the vegetables are tender. If the mixture becomes too dry, add a little extra water.

8 Meanwhile, roughly tear the spinach leaves. Add to the pan and simmer for 1-2 minutes until just wilted. Add salt to taste. Serve garnished with crisp-fried onions if desired, and toasted almonds.

COOK'S TIPS

▶ To toast the spices and almonds in the ROASTING OVEN, place in a shallow baking tin, with the grid shelf on the top set of runners. Toast the spices for 1 minute; almonds for 3-4 minutes.

▶ It isn't absolutely essential to fry the potatoes, courgettes and aubergines. You can stir them straight into the sauce once it has simmered for 10-15 minutes, but they will take longer to cook.

STIR-FRIED VEGETABLES

■ SERVES 4-6 ■ PREPARATION 15 MINUTES ■ COOKING 5 MINUTES
■ FREEZING NOT SUITABLE ■ 440-290 CALS PER SERVING

60 ml (4 tbsp) oil
2 garlic cloves, peeled and crushed
2.5 cm (1 inch) piece fresh root ginger, peeled and sliced
1-2 fresh chillies, seeded and chopped (optional)
125 g (4 oz) cashew nuts, peanuts or almonds
900 g (2 lb) mixed vegetables, prepared as necessary and cut into thin strips or slices (see cook's tip)
15 ml (1 tbsp) light soy sauce
15 ml (1 tbsp) dry sherry
5 ml (1 tsp) sugar
5 ml (1 tsp) five-spice powder (optional)
TO SERVE
Chinese egg noodles, or plain boiled rice

1 Heat the oil in a large deep frying pan (see cook's tip) on the SIMMERING PLATE. Add the garlic, ginger and chillies if using, and stir-fry for about 30 seconds until softened. Add the nuts and cook, stirring, for 1 minute, until golden; remove the nuts with a slotted spoon and set aside.

2 Move the pan to the BOILING PLATE. Add the slower-cooking vegetables (see cook's tip) and cook for 1-1½ minutes, stirring frequently. Add the remaining vegetables and cook for a further 1-2 minutes or until heated through but still very crisp.

3 Add the soy sauce, sherry, sugar and five-spice powder, if using. Cook for a further 15-20 seconds, then transfer to a warmed serving dish, sprinkle with the nuts and serve immediately, with noodles or rice.

COOK'S TIPS

▶ Vegetable stir-fries are delicious made with whatever vegetables you have to hand, though it's important to cut them into pieces of a similar size. First add tougher, slower-cooking vegetables, such as baby corn, carrots, spring onions, celery, fennel and radish. Delicate fast-cooking vegetables, such as bean sprouts, Chinese leaves, mangetout, courgettes and mushrooms, need only 1-2 minutes. When cooked, the vegetables should be served right away, so make sure accompanying noodles or rice are almost cooked when you begin stir-frying.

▶ Use a frying pan rather than a narrow-based wok for stir-frying on an aga, as it will conduct heat more efficiently.

POTATO GNOCCHI WITH RED PESTO

■ SERVES 6 ■ PREPARATION 30 MINUTES ■ COOKING ABOUT 40 MINUTES
■ FREEZING NOT SUITABLE ■ 625 CALS PER SERVING

Classic potato gnocchi originate from Northern Italy, where they are a staple food. Here they're tossed with a red pesto made from basil, toasted pine nuts, sun-dried tomatoes, fresh tomatoes, chilli and roasted red peppers. It takes a little practice to make gnocchi really light – overworking makes them tough.

PESTO
1 large red pepper
50 g (2 oz) fresh basil leaves
1 garlic clove, crushed
30 ml (2 tbsp) toasted pine nuts
6 sun-dried tomatoes in oil, drained
2 ripe tomatoes, skinned
45 ml (3 tbsp) tomato purée
2.5 ml (½ tsp) chilli powder
50 g (2 oz) freshly grated Parmesan cheese
150 ml (¼ pint) olive oil
GNOCCHI
900 g (2 lb) floury potatoes
salt
50 g (2 oz) butter
1 egg, beaten
225-275 g (8-10 oz) plain white flour
TO GARNISH
basil leaves

1 Place the pepper in the small roasting tin and hang from the highest set of runners possible at the back of the ROASTING OVEN. Cook, turning occasionally, for 10-15 minutes until beginning to blacken all over. Place in a covered bowl until cool enough to handle, then peel off the skin. Halve the pepper and remove the core and seeds. Place in a blender or food processor with the remaining pesto ingredients except the oil. Blend until smooth, then with the machine running, slowly add the oil.

2 To make the gnocchi, add the unpeeled potatoes to a pan of boiling water and cook in the SIMMERING OVEN for 20-30 minutes until very tender; drain well. Halve and press through a potato ricer, or peel and press through a sieve into a bowl.

3 While still warm, add 5 ml (1 tsp) salt, the butter, beaten egg and half the flour. Lightly mix together, then turn out onto a floured board. Gradually knead in enough of the remaining flour to yield a smooth, soft, slightly sticky dough.

4 Roll the dough into thick sausages, 2.5 cm (1 inch) in diameter, then cut into 2 cm (¾ inch) pieces. Roll each piece over the back of a fork with your floured thumb to form ridges on one side and an indentation on the other. Lay on a floured tea-towel.

5 Bring a large pan of well salted water to the boil on the BOILING PLATE, then move to the SIMMERING PLATE. Cook the gnocchi in batches. Drop them into the boiling water and cook for 2-3 minutes, until they float to the surface. Remove with a slotted spoon and transfer to a warmed serving dish. Keep hot in the SIMMERING OVEN while cooking the remainder. Toss with the red pesto and serve immediately, garnished with basil.

COOK'S TIP *The red pesto can be stored in a jar, covered with a layer of oil, for up to 2 weeks in the refrigerator.*

VARIATION Serve the gnocchi with a classic pesto. Use 50 g (2 oz) fresh basil leaves; 1 garlic clove, crushed; 45 ml (3 tbsp) freshly grated Parmesan cheese; 25 g (1 oz) pine nuts; 90 ml (6 tbsp) olive oil; pepper to taste. Process all the ingredients, except the oil, then add the oil as above.

CRUSTY MEDITERRANEAN PARCELS

■ SERVES 8 ■ PREPARATION 30 MINUTES ■ COOKING ABOUT 1 HOUR
■ FREEZING SUITABLE: STAGE 7 ■ 480 CALS PER SERVING

700 g (1½ lb) mixed vegetables, such as carrots, leeks,
courgettes, red peppers, aubergines, sweet potatoes,
prepared as necessary
30 ml (2 tbsp) olive oil
coarse sea salt and freshly ground black pepper
225 g (8 oz) onions, peeled and roughly chopped
2 garlic cloves, peeled and crushed
400 g (14 oz) can chopped tomatoes
15 ml (1 tbsp) sun-dried tomato paste
125 g (4 oz) Gruyère cheese, grated
200 g (7 oz) mascarpone cheese
60 ml (2 fl oz) single cream
30 ml (2 tbsp) finely chopped fresh chives
50 g (2 oz) pine nuts
450 g (1 lb) ready-made puff pastry
1 egg
chopped chives, to garnish

1 Cut the mixed vegetables into 2.5 cm (1 inch) chunks.
Place in the small roasting tin with 15 ml (1 tbsp) olive oil.
Turn to coat with the oil and season with salt and pepper to
taste. Cook on the grid shelf on the floor of the ROASTING
OVEN for 40-45 minutes or until just tender, stirring
occasionally. Remove from the oven and allow to cool.

2 Meanwhile, heat the remaining olive oil in a frying pan on
the SIMMERING PLATE. Add the onions and garlic and fry
for 5 minutes or until lightly coloured. Add the chopped
tomatoes and sun-dried tomato paste and cook,
uncovered, on the floor of the SIMMERING OVEN for
10-15 minutes or until thick and pulpy. Set aside.

3 Mix 75 g (3 oz) of the Gruyère cheese with the
mascarpone cheese, single cream and chopped chives.

4 Spread 25 g (1 oz) of the pine nuts in the small roasting
tin and toast in the middle of the ROASTING OVEN for
about 3 minutes until pale golden. Mix the vegetables with
the tomato sauce, toasted pine nuts and seasoning.

5 Roll out the pastry quite thinly to 2 oblongs, each about
35 x 30 cm (14 x 12 inches).

6 Beat the egg with a pinch of salt. Place half of the
vegetables along the middle of each pastry oblong, in a
10 cm (4 inch) wide band. Top the vegetables with the
cheese mixture. Brush the pastry with the egg glaze.

7 With a sharp knife, make diagonal slits in the pastry, at
2.5 cm (1 inch) intervals, along each side to within 2.5 cm
(1 inch) of the filling. Plait from the top by overlapping
alternate strips from either side across the filling. Make sure
that the strips cross or the pastry may burst open during
cooking. Tuck any loose pastry under the base. Brush
liberally with the egg glaze and sprinkle with pepper, salt,
the remaining grated cheese and pine nuts.

8 Carefully transfer the plaits to a baking sheet. Cook on
the floor of the ROASTING OVEN for 15-20 minutes, covering with foil halfway through cooking if the pastry appears to
be browning too quickly. Serve, cut into slices, and
sprinkled with chopped chives.

PASTA AND AUBERGINE GRATIN

■ SERVES 4 ■ PREPARATION 15 MINUTES ■ COOKING 40 MINUTES
■ FREEZING NOT SUITABLE ■ 565 CALS PER SERVING

30 ml (2 tbsp) olive oil
1 onion, peeled and chopped
1 garlic clove, peeled and crushed
10 ml (2 tsp) mild paprika
10 ml (2 tsp) tomato purée
350 g (12 oz) aubergine, roughly chopped
400 g (14 oz) can chopped tomatoes
5 ml (1 tsp) sugar
2 small courgettes, thinly sliced
salt and freshly ground black pepper
275 g (10 oz) dried rigatoni or other pasta shapes
15 ml (1 tbsp) pesto
150 g (5 oz) Gruyère or mature Cheddar cheese, grated
25 g (1 oz) Parmesan cheese, freshly grated

1 Heat the oil in a heavy-based ovenproof saucepan on the
SIMMERING PLATE. Add the onion and crushed garlic and
fry until softened. Add the paprika and tomato purée and
cook, stirring, for 30 seconds. Add the aubergine and cook
for a further 2 minutes, stirring to coat in the tomato and
onion mixture.

2 Add the tomatoes, sugar and 75 ml (5 tbsp) water. Bring to the boil, then cover.
■■ Place on the grid shelf on floor of ROASTING OVEN.
■■■ Place on the grid shelf on the fourth set of runners in the BAKING OVEN.
Cook for about 15 minutes or until the aubergine is just tender. Add the courgettes, recover and cook for a further 5 minutes. Season with salt and pepper to taste.

3 Meanwhile, add the pasta to a large pan of boiling salted water and bring to the boil on the BOILING PLATE. Cover and cook in the SIMMERING OVEN for approximately 12 minutes until *al dente*, tender but firm to the bite. Drain well, then return to the pan and toss with the pesto.

4 Toss the pasta with the aubergine sauce and check the seasoning. Transfer to an ovenproof dish and top with the grated cheeses. Bake in the ROASTING OVEN with the grid shelf on the highest set of runners possible for about 20 minutes until golden brown and bubbling. Serve with warm crusty bread and a crisp leafy salad.

AUBERGINE, RED ONION AND MUSHROOM PIZZA

■ SERVES 8-10 ■ PREPARATION 40 MINUTES, PLUS RISING

■ COOKING ABOUT 45 MINUTES ■ FREEZING NOT SUITABLE

■ 485-385 CALS PER SERVING

PIZZA DOUGH
15 g (½ oz) fresh yeast, or 15 ml (1 tbsp) dried yeast
pinch of sugar
250 ml (8 fl oz) warm water
350 g (12 oz) strong plain white flour
30 ml (2 tbsp) olive oil
5 ml (1 tsp) salt
TOPPING
2 aubergines, about 700 g (1½ lb) total weight
105 ml (9 tbsp) olive oil (approximately)
salt and freshly ground black pepper
700 g (1½ lb) red onions, peeled and thinly sliced
4 large garlic cloves, peeled and crushed
700 g (1½ lb) brown cap or firm flat mushrooms, thickly sliced
15 ml (1 tbsp) chopped fresh thyme
30 ml (2 tbsp) balsamic vinegar
45 ml (3 tbsp) sun-dried tomato paste
3 packets mozzarella cheese, 375 g (13 oz)

1 To make the pizza dough, in a bowl, cream the fresh yeast with the sugar, then whisk in the warm water. Leave for 10 minutes until frothy. If using dried yeast, follow the packet instructions.

2 Sift the flour into a large bowl and make a well in the centre. Pour in the yeast mixture, olive oil and salt. Mix together with a round-bladed knife, then using your hands until the dough comes together.

3 Tip out onto a floured surface. With clean, dry hands, knead the dough for 10 minutes until smooth, elastic and quite soft. If too soft to handle, knead in a little more flour.

4 Place in a clean oiled bowl, cover with a damp tea-towel and set on a folded towel on the lid of the SIMMERING PLATE. Leave to rise for about 1 hour until doubled in size.

5 Thinly slice the aubergines lengthwise. Lay the aubergine slices in a single layer on lightly oiled baking sheets. Season with salt and pepper and brush with a little oil. Bake in batches on the top shelf of the ROASTING OVEN for 10 minutes, turning halfway through cooking.

6 Heat 30 ml (2 tbsp) olive oil in a large ovenproof frying pan on the SIMMERING PLATE. Add the onions and cook for 5 minutes. Season with salt and pepper, then transfer to the floor of the ROASTING OVEN for 20-25 minutes or until soft, stirring from time to time.

7 Meanwhile, heat 45 ml (3 tbsp) olive oil in a large frying pan on the BOILING PLATE. Add half of the mushrooms and fry briskly; season and drain off excess liquid. Repeat with the remaining mushrooms, then add the chopped thyme.

8 Add the balsamic vinegar to the onions.

9 Oil the cold plain Aga shelf. Knock back the risen pizza dough and roll out to cover the cool shelf.

10 Spread the sun-dried tomato paste over the dough. Spoon over the onions, then cover with the mushrooms. Arrange the aubergine slices on top and finally cover with the sliced mozzarella. Drizzle over 45 ml (3 tbsp) olive oil.

11 Slide the shelf onto the top set of runners in the ROASTING OVEN and bake for 10-15 minutes, then lower to the floor of the oven and cook for a further 5-10 minutes or until the pizza is golden brown and cooked through to the centre. Serve at once.

CRESPOLINE

■ SERVES 4 ■ PREPARATION 30 MINUTES, PLUS STANDING

■ COOKING ABOUT 1-1¼ HOURS

■ FREEZING NOT SUITABLE ■ 345 CALS PER SERVING

Cannelloni tubes are filled with a tasty spinach and ricotta stuffing, then baked in a tomato sauce, topped with a Parmesan sauce.

8 dried pasta cannelloni tubes, about 75 g (3 oz) total weight

salt and freshly ground black pepper

TOMATO SAUCE

15 ml (1 tbsp) oil

50 g (2 oz) onion, peeled and chopped

50 g (2 oz) carrot, peeled and chopped

50 g (2 oz) celery, peeled and chopped

1 garlic clove, peeled and crushed

50 ml (2 fl oz) dry white wine

50 g (2 oz) sun-dried tomatoes in oil, drained and finely chopped

400 g (14 oz) can chopped tomatoes

100 ml (3½ fl oz) vegetable stock

FILLING

225 g (8 oz) spinach leaves

175 g (6 oz) ricotta cheese

pinch of freshly grated nutmeg

1 garlic clove, peeled and crushed

PARMESAN SAUCE

40 g (1½ oz) butter

25 g (1 oz) plain white flour

450 ml (¾ pint) milk

50 g (2 oz) Parmesan cheese, freshly grated

1 To make the tomato sauce, heat the oil in a saucepan on the SIMMERING PLATE. Add the onion, carrot, celery and garlic and cook for 1-2 minutes. Transfer to the SIMMERING OVEN and cook for 15 minutes or until beginning to soften. Add the wine, bring to the boil and let bubble to reduce by half on the BOILING PLATE. Add the sun-dried tomatoes, tomatoes, stock and seasoning. Bring to the boil, cover and cook in the SIMMERING OVEN for 30-40 minutes or until pulpy.

2 Cook the spinach in a large saucepan on the SIMMERING PLATE with just the water clinging to the leaves after washing for 3-4 minutes or until wilted. Drain well, allow to cool, then chop roughly.

3 To prepare the filling, mix the spinach with the ricotta, nutmeg and garlic, and season with salt and pepper to taste. Fill the cannelloni tubes with the mixture.

4 To make the Parmesan sauce, melt the butter in a small saucepan on the SIMMERING PLATE. Stir in the flour and cook for 1-2 minutes, stirring. Remove from the heat and gradually whisk in the milk. Slowly bring to the boil, stirring. Simmer gently for 1-2 minutes, whisking again if necessary. Stir in two thirds of the Parmesan cheese and season with salt and pepper.

5 Pour the tomato sauce into an ovenproof dish and place the stuffed cannelloni on top in a single layer. Pour the Parmesan sauce over the top and sprinkle over the remaining cheese. Leave to stand for 30 minutes.

6 ■■ Cook on the grid shelf on the floor of the ROASTING OVEN for 15-20 minutes.

■■■■ Cook in the BAKING OVEN with the grid shelf on the third set of runners for 30-40 minutes or until piping hot and golden brown.

COOK'S TIPS

▶ Most cannelloni does not need any pre-cooking, but do check the packet instructions first.

▶ If the cheese sauce gets too hot it may separate a little around the edges, but this won't impair the flavour.

WHITE ONION PIZZA

■ SERVES 4-6 ■ PREPARATION 30 MINUTES, PLUS RISING
■ COOKING ABOUT 1 HOUR ■ FREEZING NOT SUITABLE
■ 705-470 CALS PER SERVING

This succulent golden pizza is the forerunner of the French pissaladière. The onions are cooked in olive oil to a creamy softness, then spread onto the pizza base before baking. Add more herbs if you like – dried herbs work well in this pizza. If you hate anchovies, leave them out, but they do add a delicious savoury saltiness to the sweet onions!

PIZZA DOUGH
15 g (1/2 oz) fresh yeast, or 15 ml (1 tbsp) dried yeast
pinch of sugar
250 ml (8 fl oz) warm water
350 g (12 oz) strong plain white flour
30 ml (2 tbsp) olive oil
5 ml (1 tsp) salt
TOPPING
100 ml (3½ fl oz) olive oil
900 g (2 lb) onions, peeled and finely sliced
15 ml (1 tbsp) chopped fresh oregano
15 ml (1 tbsp) chopped fresh rosemary
12 anchovy fillets in oil, drained
16 black olives, stoned
TO GARNISH
rosemary sprigs
oregano leaves

1 To make the pizza dough, in a bowl, cream the fresh yeast with the sugar, then whisk in the warm water. Leave for 10 minutes until frothy. If using dried yeast, follow the packet instructions.

2 Sift the flour into a large bowl and make a well in the centre. Pour in the yeast mixture, olive oil and salt. Mix together with a round-bladed knife, then using your hands until the dough comes together.

3 Tip out onto a floured surface. With clean, dry hands, knead the dough for 10 minutes until smooth, elastic and quite soft. If too soft to handle, knead in a little more flour.

4 Place in a clean oiled bowl, cover with a damp tea-towel and set on a folded towel on the lid of the SIMMERING PLATE. Leave to rise for about 1 hour until doubled in size.

5 Meanwhile, heat the oil in a heavy-based saucepan on the SIMMERING PLATE. Add the onions, cover and cook for 10-15 minutes, stirring occasionally. Transfer to the SIMMERING OVEN and cook for a further 40 minutes until the onions are very soft and golden, but not brown. Stir in the chopped herbs.

6 Knock back the dough and roll out, or stretch with your fingers, to a 30 cm (12 inch) circle on the large floured baking sheet.

7 Spoon the onions on top of the pizza and spread evenly. Scatter over the anchovy fillets and olives. Slide the baking sheet onto the top set of runners in the ROASTING OVEN and bake for 10 minutes, then transfer to the floor of the oven and cook for a further 5 minutes to crisp the base. Scatter over the rosemary sprigs and oregano leaves. Serve immediately.

COOK'S TIP *To make two smaller pizzas, halve the dough and roll out two 20 cm (8 inch) circles.*

VARIATION
Tomato, Artichoke and Proscuitto Pizza: Prepare the base as above, then spread with 45 ml (3 tbsp) sun-dried tomato paste. Slice 150 g (5 oz) mozzarella and arrange half over the base. Scatter over 4 sliced plum tomatoes, 8 sliced artichoke hearts in oil, and 4 finely sliced garlic cloves. Scrunch up 6 slices of prosciutto and drape over the pizza. Scatter over the remaining mozzarella and drizzle with olive oil. Sprinkle with Parmesan and bake as above. Omit the rosemary garnish, scattering with oregano only.

MELTING CHEESE AND HAM PARCEL

■ SERVES 4 ■ PREPARATION 15 MINUTES, PLUS CHILLING
■ COOKING ABOUT 20 MINUTES ■ FREEZING NOT SUITABLE
■ 685 CALS PER SERVING

A crunchy cucumber and watercress salad, tossed in a dill-flavoured vinaigrette, is the ideal accompaniment for this sustaining supper.

45 ml (3 tbsp) crème fraîche
15 ml (1 tbsp) Dijon mustard
350 g (12 oz) ready-made puff pastry
350 g (12 oz) good-quality cooked ham, sliced
175 g (6 oz) Gruyère cheese, thinly sliced
1 egg yolk, beaten
coarse sea salt

1 Mix together the crème fraîche and mustard in a small bowl.

2 Roll out one third of the puff pastry to a 30 x 25 cm (12 x 10 inch) rectangle and place on a baking sheet.

3 Spread a third of the mustard mixture evenly over the pastry, leaving a 1 cm (½ inch) border. Cover with a layer of ham. Spread with half the remaining mustard mixture, then top with all the cheese and finally the remaining ham.

4 Spread the remaining mustard mixture over the ham and brush the pastry border with beaten egg.

5 Roll out the remaining pastry to a rectangle about 2.5 cm (1 inch) larger all round than the parcel base. Position over the filling and press the pastry edges firmly together. Trim if necessary. Knock up the edges with a knife. Brush with beaten egg and chill in the refrigerator for 15 minutes.

6 Cook the parcel on the grid shelf on the top set of runners in the ROASTING OVEN for 10-15 minutes until golden, then transfer to the floor of the oven and cook for a further 5-10 minutes until crisp underneath. If the pastry edges show signs of over-browning, cover with a rim of foil during baking. Season with salt and serve with a mixed salad.

CALABRIAN PASTA

■ SERVES 4-6 ■ PREPARATION 10 MINUTES ■ COOKING 12-18 MINUTES
■ FREEZING NOT SUITABLE ■ 695-465 CALS PER SERVING

The finest broccoli is grown right down in the toe of Italy, in Calabria – and called calabrese after the region. Fried with pine nuts, sultanas, garlic and breadcrumbs, it makes a delicious sauce to serve with the local pasta, ziti – which resembles spaghetti-length macaroni. You can, of course, use spaghetti or long fusilli instead.

150 g (5 oz) broccoli
50 g (2 oz) sultanas
300-350 g (10-12 oz) dried ziti, long fusilli or spaghetti
salt and freshly ground black pepper
125 ml (4 fl oz) olive oil
75 g (3 oz) white breadcrumbs
2 garlic cloves, peeled and finely chopped
25 g (1 oz) pine nuts
10 ml (2 tsp) anchovy essence
45 ml (3 tbsp) chopped fresh parsley
cayenne pepper, to taste

1 Break the broccoli into small florets; peel thicker stems and cut into pieces about the same size. Place in a saucepan of boiling water on the SIMMERING PLATE, bring to the boil and simmer for 30 seconds; drain and refresh in a bowl of iced water.

2 Put the sultanas in a bowl, pour on a little boiling water and leave to soak.

3 Meanwhile, add the pasta to a large pan of boiling salted water. Bring to the boil on the BOILING PLATE, then cover and cook in the SIMMERING OVEN for 12-18 minutes until *al dente*, tender but firm to the bite.

4 In the meantime, heat the oil in a frying pan and add the breadcrumbs. Fry, stirring until they begin to crisp, then add the garlic and pine nuts. Continue to fry, stirring, until the pine nuts begin to colour. Drain the broccoli thoroughly, add to the frying pan and stir until heated through.

5 Drain the pasta in a colander, setting it back on top of the saucepan to catch the last 15 ml (1 tbsp) cooking water. Stir the anchovy essence into this liquid, then return the pasta to the saucepan.

6 Drain the sultanas and add them to the pasta with a generous grinding of pepper and half of the chopped parsley. Toss to mix and transfer to a heated serving bowl. Mix the remaining parsley into the crumb mixture and sprinkle over the pasta. Sprinkle with a little cayenne pepper and serve at once.

COOK'S TIP *It's an Italian trick to toss the pasta with a little of its cooking water. This helps to keep the pasta hot, as well as preventing it from drying out.*

TOMATO, AUBERGINE AND PEPPER PARMIGIANA

Serve this tasty gratin with plenty of crusty bread and a crisp, leafy salad.

■ SERVES 6 ■ PREPARATION 15 MINUTES ■ COOKING ABOUT 1½ HOURS
■ FREEZING SUITABLE: STAGE 5 ■ 360 CALS PER SERVING

two 400 g (14 oz) cans chopped tomatoes
45 ml (3 tbsp) olive oil
2 garlic cloves, peeled and crushed
30 ml (2 tbsp) chopped fresh basil
5 ml (1 tsp) grated lemon rind
pinch of sugar
salt and freshly ground black pepper
4 large red peppers
3 aubergines
225 g (8 oz) Cheddar cheese, grated
50 g (2 oz) Parmesan cheese, freshly grated

1 Place the chopped tomatoes in a saucepan and add 15 ml (1 tbsp) oil, the garlic, basil, lemon rind, sugar and seasoning. Bring to the boil on the BOILING PLATE. Let bubble for 2-3 minutes, then cover and transfer to the SIMMERING OVEN for 30-40 minutes. Remove the lid and return to the oven for a further 15 minutes. Allow to cool.

2 Meanwhile, place the whole red peppers in the small roasting tin and hang from the top set of runners in the ROASTING OVEN for 20-25 minutes, turning occasionally until the skins are charred all over. Transfer to a bowl, cover tightly and leave to cool.

3 In the meantime, cut the aubergines lengthways into thick slices and place in the large roasting tin. Brush with

the remaining oil. Cook on the floor of the ROASTING OVEN for 20 minutes until the undersides are charred. Leave to cool.

4 Peel away the skins from the cooked peppers, then cut into quarters, discarding the cores and seeds.

5 Spoon a little of the tomato sauce over the base of a large greased ovenproof dish and top with a layer of aubergines and peppers. Sprinkle over a little of the Cheddar cheese. Continue layering in this way, finishing with a layer of Cheddar cheese. Sprinkle over the Parmesan.

6 Bake on the grid shelf on the floor of the ROASTING OVEN for 30-40 minutes until bubbling and golden. Serve immediately.

VARIATIONS
▶ Replace the Cheddar cheese with diced mozzarella.
▶ Use a mixture of red, yellow and orange peppers.
▶ Replace the basil with chopped fresh coriander.

BACON, POTATO AND MUSHROOM GRATIN

■ SERVES 2 ■ PREPARATION 10 MINUTES ■ COOKING ABOUT 25 MINUTES
■ FREEZING NOT SUITABLE ■ 595 CALS PER SERVING

A quick and easy supper for two. Accompany with a crisp salad and a glass of wine.

250 g (9 oz) small new potatoes
salt and freshly ground black pepper
30 ml (2 tbsp) olive oil
1 small onion, peeled and chopped
125 g (4 oz) bacon, derinded and diced
125 g (4 oz) mushrooms, sliced if large
125 g (4 oz) Cheddar cheese, grated

1 Wash the potatoes and halve them (unless very small). Add to a pan of boiling salted water, bring to the boil, then cook in the SIMMERING OVEN for 15-20 minutes until tender. Drain thoroughly.

2 In the meantime, heat the olive oil in a frying pan on the SIMMERING PLATE. Add the onion and bacon and cook gently, stirring frequently, until the onion is softened.

3 Add the mushrooms and transfer the frying pan to the BOILING PLATE. Stir-fry for 2-3 minutes until the mushrooms are cooked.

4 Transfer the bacon, onion and mushroom mixture to a flameproof gratin dish and stir in the potatoes. Season with pepper to taste and top with the grated cheese. Place in the ROASTING OVEN with the grid shelf on the second set of runners, positioning the dish towards the back of the oven. Cook for 7-10 minutes until the cheese is bubbling. Serve immediately.

VARIATION

For a vegetarian version, replace the bacon with sliced leeks, increasing the olive oil by 15 ml (1 tbsp) and adding a sprinkling of chopped thyme.

ASPARAGUS AND BROAD BEAN FRITTATA

■ SERVES 3-4 ■ PREPARATION 20 MINUTES ■ COOKING 15-20 MINUTES
■ FREEZING NOT SUITABLE ■ 480-360 CALS PER SERVING

175 g (6 oz) small new potatoes
225 g (8 oz) asparagus
225 g (8 oz) frozen broad beans, thawed
6 eggs
salt and freshly ground black pepper
50 g (2 oz) Parmesan cheese, freshly grated
45 ml (3 tbsp) chopped mixed fresh herbs, such as parsley, oregano and thyme
50 g (2 oz) unsalted butter

1 Add the potatoes to a pan of boiling salted water, bring to the boil on the BOILING PLATE, then transfer to the SIMMERING OVEN for 15-20 minutes until tender. Allow to cool, then slice thickly.

2 Meanwhile, trim the asparagus, removing any woody parts of the stems. Add to a pan of boiling salted water and cook briskly on the BOILING PLATE until just tender. Drain, then immerse in a bowl of cold water to cool.

3 Slip the broad beans out of their waxy skins. Drain the asparagus, pat dry, then cut into short lengths.

4 Put the eggs in a bowl with a good pinch of salt, plenty of pepper and half of the Parmesan cheese. Beat thoroughly until evenly blended, then stir in the asparagus, broad beans and chopped herbs.

5 Put 40 g (1½ oz) butter in a large ovenproof cast-iron frying pan, about 25 cm (10 inch) in diameter. Place on the floor of the ROASTING OVEN until the butter is melted and the pan is very hot; about 4-5 minutes. Transfer to the SIMMERING PLATE. When the butter is foaming, pour in the egg mixture. Cook for about 8-10 minutes, until the frittata is beginning to set and the top is still a little runny.

6 Scatter the cooked potato over the frittata and sprinkle with the remaining Parmesan. Dot with the rest of the butter. Transfer the pan to the ROASTING OVEN, positioning it at the back of the grid shelf on the second set of runners. Cook for about 2-3 minutes, or until the frittata is just set; don't overcook or it will dry out. Cut into wedges to serve.

WARM CHICKEN, CASHEW AND NOODLE SALAD

■ SERVES 4 ■ PREPARATION 25 MINUTES, PLUS MARINATING

■ COOKING 4-5 MINUTES ■ FREEZING NOT SUITABLE ■ 470 CALS PER SERVING

350 g (12 oz) skinless chicken breast fillet

30 ml (2 tbsp) sunflower oil

5 ml (1 tsp) sesame oil

5 ml (1 tsp) ground coriander

1.25 ml (¼ tsp) chilli powder

pinch of Chinese five-spice powder

125 g (4 oz) dried egg noodles (½ packet)

50 g (2 oz) mangetout

50 g (2 oz) fine green beans, halved

15 ml (1 tbsp) chopped fresh mint

15 ml (1 tbsp) chopped fresh coriander

25 g (1 oz) cashew nuts, toasted (see cook's tip)

DRESSING

45 ml (3 tbsp) peanut or sunflower oil

10 ml (2 tsp) sesame oil

1 garlic clove, peeled and crushed

5 ml (1 tsp) grated fresh root ginger

2.5 ml (½ tsp) dried red chilli flakes, crushed

15 ml (1 tbsp) dark soy sauce

15 ml (1 tbsp) lemon juice

TO GARNISH

coriander sprigs

1 Very thinly slice the chicken breast, across the grain, then place in a shallow dish. Combine 15 ml (1 tbsp) of the sunflower oil with the sesame oil, coriander, chilli powder and Chinese five-spice powder. Add to the chicken and stir until evenly coated. Cover and leave to marinate for at least 30 minutes.

2 Add the noodles to a large pan of boiling salted water, cover and place in the SIMMERING OVEN for about 3-4 minutes until *al dente*, tender but firm to the bite.

3 Meanwhile, heat the remaining sunflower oil in a large non-stick frying pan on the BOILING PLATE. When hot, add the marinated chicken pieces and stir-fry for 2 minutes until golden and crispy. Drain on kitchen paper. Place in an ovenproof dish, cover and keep warm in the SIMMERING OVEN.

4 Add the vegetables and herbs to the pan and stir-fry for 1 minute until tender. Add to the chicken pieces.

5 To make the dressing, heat both oils in a small pan on the SIMMERING PLATE. Add the garlic, ginger and chilli flakes and fry gently until softened but not coloured. Whisk in the soy sauce, lemon juice and 30 ml (2 tbsp) water. Bring to the boil and remove from the heat.

6 Drain the cooked noodles and immediately toss with the hot soy dressing and chicken and vegetable mixture. Sprinkle over the toasted cashews. Serve warm or cool, garnished with coriander.

COOK'S TIP *To toast pine nuts, spread on a baking sheet and with the grid shelf on the top set of runners, cook in the* ROASTING OVEN *for 2 minutes. Use a timer to remind you – they will quickly burn!*

VARIATION Replace the chicken with the same weight of peeled, raw tiger prawns and add 10 ml (2 tsp) grated lime to the marinade. Stir-fry for 3-4 minutes until the prawns have turned pink. Use basil instead of mint and replace the lemon juice in the dressing with lime juice.

ACCOMPANIMENTS

OVEN-BAKED TOMATOES

■ SERVES 4-6 ■ PREPARATION 10 MINUTES ■ COOKING 10-12 MINUTES
■ FREEZING NOT SUITABLE ■ 210-140 CALS PER SERVING

Large tomato halves are baked with a mozzarella and garlic-flavoured breadcrumb topping to make this appetizing accompaniment, which goes well with most meat and poultry dishes.

3 large beef tomatoes
salt and freshly ground black pepper
150 g (5 oz) mozzarella cheese, finely diced
25 g (1 oz) fresh white breadcrumbs
1 garlic clove, peeled and crushed
30 ml (2 tbsp) olive oil

1 Cut the beef tomatoes in half horizontally and season with salt and pepper.

2 Mix the diced mozzarella with the breadcrumbs, garlic and seasoning.

3 Place the tomato halves, cut-side up, in the small roasting tin. Spoon the crumb mixture on top of the tomatoes and drizzle with the olive oil. Hang the tin from the top set of runners in the ROASTING OVEN and bake for 10-12 minutes or until golden brown.

BAKED AUBERGINES

Use baby or small aubergines for this recipe if obtainable, as they do not require degorging. Serve as an accompaniment to grilled meat or fish.

■ SERVES 8 ■ PREPARATION 10 MINUTES ■ COOKING ABOUT 25 MINUTES
■ FREEZING NOT SUITABLE ■ 80 CALS PER SERVING

9 baby or 4 small aubergines
olive oil, for brushing
salt and freshly ground black pepper
1 green or red chilli, seeded and finely diced
finely grated rind and juice of 1 lemon
45 ml (3 tbsp) chopped fresh parsley

1 Halve the aubergines lengthways, then score the flesh deeply in a criss-cross pattern. Brush generously with olive oil. Season with salt and pepper and place, cut-side down, in the large roasting tin.

2 Bake on the floor of the ROASTING OVEN for 12-18 minutes until browned underneath and almost cooked through. Transfer the aubergines to a shallow ovenproof dish, placing them cut-side up.

3 Mix the chilli with the grated lemon rind and parsley. Sprinkle the mixture over the aubergines. Drizzle with a little more olive oil and cook on the grid shelf on the floor of the ROASTING OVEN for a further 10 minutes, or until the aubergines are tender.

4 Sprinkle with lemon juice to serve.

BAKED VEGETABLE PURSES

■ SERVES 6 ■ PREPARATION 20 MINUTES ■ COOKING 30-40 MINUTES
■ FREEZING NOT SUITABLE ■ 110 CALS PER SERVING

This recipe is simple to prepare and baby vegetables look lovely in the little purses. If baby vegetables are unobtainable, use ordinary-sized ones and shape into batons or cut into bite-sized pieces.

900 g (2 lb) mixed baby vegetables, such as carrots, turnips, fennel, parsnips and button onions
50 g (2 oz) unsalted butter
4 garlic cloves, peeled and crushed
90 ml (3 fl oz) vegetable stock
90 ml (3 fl oz) orange juice
15 ml (1 tbsp) thin honey
5 ml (1 tsp) dried thyme
salt and freshly ground black pepper

1 Cut six 30 cm (12 inch) squares of foil. Trim the carrots, turnips, fennel and parsnips. Peel the onions and halve if necessary.

2 Melt the butter in a frying pan on the BOILING PLATE. Add slower-cooking vegetables, such as onion and parsnip, and stir-fry for about 2 minutes. Add the rest of the vegetables and stir-fry for a further 1 minute or until beginning to brown.

3 Divide the vegetables evenly between the squares of foil, pulling the edges up to make open purses.

4 Add the crushed garlic, stock, orange juice, honey and thyme to the frying pan. Bring to the boil and let bubble for 1-2 minutes. Season with salt and pepper to taste. Pour over the vegetables and seal the foil over the purses tightly.

5 Stand the purses on a baking sheet and bake on the grid shelf on the floor of the ROASTING OVEN for 30-40 minutes until just tender. Serve the vegetables wrapped in the foil so that each guest can open their own purse at the table.

GRILLED PEPPER SALAD

■ SERVES 6 ■ PREPARATION 20 MINUTES ■ COOKING 20-25 MINUTES
■ FREEZING NOT SUITABLE ■ 200 CALS PER SERVING

A colourful salad full of flavours evocative of the Mediterranean – smoky grilled peppers, aromatic fennel and garlic, and a sweet balsamic vinegar dressing. Serve it accompanied by some firm, country bread.

3 small onions
3 red peppers
3 yellow peppers
3 garlic cloves, peeled
45 ml (3 tbsp) capers
25 ml (1½ tbsp) fennel seeds
90 ml (6 tbsp) olive oil
30 ml (2 tbsp) balsamic vinegar
45 ml (3 tbsp) roughly torn fresh flat-leaf parsley
coarse sea salt and freshly ground black pepper

1 Peel the onions, leaving the root end intact, and cut into quarters. Drop them into a pan of boiling water and cook for 1 minute; drain well.

2 Halve the peppers lengthwise cutting through the stems, then core and deseed. Arrange in the large roasting tin, skin-side up, in a single layer. Place the onion quarters and garlic cloves in the tin too. Slide the tin onto the highest set of runners possible in the ROASTING OVEN and bake, turning occasionally, for 20-25 minutes until the pepper skins are blistered and charred all over. Turn the onions and garlic as necessary, but let them char slightly too.

3 Place the peppers in a bowl, cover with a plate and allow to cool slightly, then peel away their skins. Arrange the peppers on a serving platter. Fill the cavities with the grilled onions and capers.

4 Put the fennel seeds in a dry frying pan and toast on the SIMMERING PLATE for a few minutes until they begin to pop and release their aroma. Transfer to a mortar and coarsely grind with the pestle. Add the grilled garlic and grind to a paste. Transfer the garlic paste to a small bowl and whisk in the oil and vinegar.

5 Sprinkle the parsley, sea salt and pepper over the salad and spoon on the dressing. Serve at room temperature.

POTATO PARSNIP GALETTE

■ SERVES 6 ■ PREPARATION 25 MINUTES ■ COOKING 35-40 MINUTES
■ FREEZING NOT SUITABLE ■ 340 CALS PER SERVING

This golden cake of butter-basted potatoes and sweet parsnips with a hint of honey and lemon is a perfect partner to roasts and game dishes. It is really important to clarify the butter – as it lends a wonderful colour to the potatoes and intensifies the flavour.

900 g (2 lb) firm potatoes, such as Desirée, Romano, Estima or Wilja
225 g (8 oz) young parsnips
75 g (3 oz) unsalted butter, diced
45 ml (3 tbsp) thin honey
30 ml (2 tbsp) lemon juice
freshly grated nutmeg
salt and freshly ground black pepper

1 Peel the potatoes and parsnips. Slice them very thinly either by hand, with a mandoline, or in a food processor. Divide the potatoes into three equal portions and cover with a tea-towel. Don't worry if they discolour (see cook's tips).

2 To clarify the butter, melt in a heatproof bowl on the back of the Aga or in the SIMMERING OVEN, then skim off any white residue; keep warm. Melt the honey and lemon juice together in a small pan; keep warm.

3 Pour 30 ml (2 tbsp) butter into a heavy 20 cm (8 inch) non-stick frying pan, suitable for oven use (see cook's tips). Layer one third of the potatoes over the bottom of the pan in neat overlapping circles, seasoning well.

4 Lay half the sliced parsnips over the potato layer. Drizzle over half of the honey and lemon juice and season with nutmeg, salt and pepper.

5 Cover with another third of the potato slices and season well. Layer the remaining parsnips on top. Drizzle with the remaining honey and lemon juice, and season with nutmeg, salt and pepper. Finish with the remaining potato slices, butter and seasoning. Cover with buttered foil.

6 Place the pan on the SIMMERING PLATE and cook carefully for about 5 minutes or until the underside is just beginning to turn golden brown. Test by carefully lifting up the edge of the galette with a palette knife. Press the potatoes down firmly.

7 Transfer the frying pan to the floor of the ROASTING OVEN for 10-15 minutes until the underside is deep golden brown. Move to the grid shelf on the fourth set of runners and bake for 20 minutes, or until the potatoes and parsnips in the centre are tender when pierced with a sharp knife and the underside is a deep golden brown colour. Allow to stand for 5 minutes.

8 Loosen the galette with a palette knife. Place a warmed serving plate over the pan and quickly invert the galette onto the dish. Serve immediately.

COOK'S TIPS
▶ *Don't rinse the potato slices – the starch is needed to help them stick together.*
▶ *Ideally you need a non-stick frying pan with an integral metal handle which can therefore be placed in the oven. Alternatively, use a shallow flameproof dish or cake tin (lined with foil if not non-stick).*

DESSERTS

COCONUT CRÈME BRULÉE

■ SERVES 8 ■ PREPARATION 25 MINUTES, PLUS CHILLING
■ COOKING 40 MINUTES-1¼ HOURS ■ FREEZING NOT SUITABLE
■ 260 CALS PER SERVING

A tempting variation of this classic rich baked custard,
flavoured with coconut and served with a
medley of tropical fruits.

600 ml (1 pint) milk
75 g (3 oz) creamed coconut, grated,
or 25 g (1 oz) coconut powder
3 eggs
3 egg yolks
150 ml (¼ pint) double cream
150 g (5 oz) caster sugar
45 ml (3 tbsp) water
pinch of cream of tartar
TO SERVE
1 banana, peeled and sliced
15 ml (1 tbsp) lemon juice
1 small mango, peeled, stoned and roughly chopped
2 or 3 slices fresh or canned pineapple, cut into chunks

1 Put the milk and grated or powdered coconut in a saucepan on the SIMMERING PLATE and warm through gently until dissolved.

2 Whisk the whole eggs and egg yolks together in a bowl until evenly blended. Gradually whisk in the coconut milk, cream and 25 g (1 oz) of the sugar.

3 Strain the mixture into a shallow 1.1-1.4 litre (2-2½ pint) ovenproof dish, which is about 4 cm (1½ inches) deep. Stand the dish in the small roasting tin and pour in enough warm water to come halfway up the sides of the dish.

4 ■■ Slide the tin onto the fourth set of runners in the ROASTING OVEN and bake for 10-15 minutes, or until a skin begins to form on the surface. Carefully transfer to the middle of the SIMMERING OVEN and cook for a further 45-50 minutes or until just set.
■■■■ Slide the tin onto the fourth set of runners in the BAKING OVEN and cook for 25-30 minutes or until just set.

5 Cool, cover and chill thoroughly for several hours until firm.

6 Meanwhile, put the remaining sugar in a shallow heavy-based saucepan with the 45 ml (3 tbsp) water and the cream of tartar. Place on the SIMMERING PLATE until the sugar is dissolved, then transfer to the BOILING PLATE and boil steadily to a rich brown caramel. Immediately remove from the heat and pour onto a lightly oiled or non-stick baking tray. Leave the caramel to cool and harden, then break into pieces and grind to a powder in a food processor or blender.

7 Sprinkle a thin, even layer on top of the well chilled custard; reserve the remaining crushed caramel. Stand the dish in the small roasting tin and surround with ice and cold water. Slide the tin onto the top or second set of runners in the ROASTING OVEN and cook for 5-10 minutes until the caramel has melted. Take the dish out of the roasting tin and allow to cool completely.

8 To serve, toss the banana in the lemon juice, then mix with the mango and pineapple. Place in a serving bowl and sprinkle with the remaining crushed caramel. Serve with the crème brulée.

CARAMELISED RICE PUDDINGS

■ SERVES 8 ■ PREPARATION 20 MINUTES ■ COOKING ABOUT 1-1¼ HOURS
■ FREEZING NOT SUITABLE ■ 425 CALS PER SERVING

125 g (4 oz) short-grain pudding rice
600 ml (1 pint) milk
1 vanilla pod, split, or 2.5 ml (½ tsp) vanilla essence
225 g (8 oz) caster sugar
45 ml (3 tbsp) water
300 ml (½ pint) double cream
5 egg yolks

1 Place the rice, milk, split vanilla pod and 125 g (4 oz) sugar in a saucepan on the SIMMERING PLATE and bring slowly to the boil. Simmer for 1-2 minutes, then cover and transfer to the floor of the SIMMERING OVEN. Cook, stirring occasionally, for 35 minutes, or until all the liquid is absorbed and the rice is tender. Allow to cool.

2 Meanwhile, put 75 g (3 oz) sugar in a heavy-based saucepan with the 45 ml (3 tbsp) water; place on the SIMMERING PLATE. Once the sugar has dissolved, transfer to the BOILING PLATE and cook for a further 2-3 minutes or until the syrup turns a dark caramel. Immediately pour into 8 warmed dariole moulds or ramekins and set aside.

3 Pour the cream into a heavy-based saucepan and slowly bring to the boil on the SIMMERING PLATE. Meanwhile, whisk the egg yolks with the remaining 25 g (1 oz) sugar in a bowl until pale and thick. Pour on the cream, then stir in the rice. Fill the moulds with the rice mixture.

4 Stand the moulds in the small roasting tin and pour in enough hot water to come halfway up the sides of the moulds. Loosely cover with foil.
■■ Slide the roasting tin onto the fourth set of runners in the ROASTING OVEN and cook for 15 minutes, then transfer to the middle of the SIMMERING OVEN and cook for a further 30 minutes or until just set.
■■■ Slide the roasting tin onto the fourth set of runners in the BAKING OVEN and cook for 20-30 minutes or until just set.

5 Serve warm or cold, with Vanilla Custard (see page 104).

APPLE AND BLACKBERRY PUDDING

■ SERVES 6 ■ PREPARATION 25 MINUTES ■ COOKING ABOUT 1 HOUR
■ FREEZING NOT SUITABLE ■ 435 CALS PER SERVING

450 g (1 lb) Bramley apples
125 g (4 oz) caster sugar (approximately)
125 g (4 oz) butter
50 g (2 oz) soft light brown sugar
3 eggs, beaten
175 g (6 oz) self-raising flour
5 ml (1 tsp) baking powder
5 ml (1 tsp) ground cinnamon
175 g (6 oz) blackberries, loganberries or blackcurrants

1 Peel, core and roughly chop the apples. Place in a saucepan with 45 ml (3 tbsp) water, cover and bring to the boil on the SIMMERING PLATE. Transfer to the SIMMERING OVEN and cook for about 15 minutes or until just softened, but still in chunks. Sweeten with about 50 g (2 oz) caster sugar, to taste. Allow to cool.

2 Cream the butter, brown sugar and 50 g (2 oz) caster sugar together in a bowl. Gradually beat in the eggs. Sift in the flour, baking powder and cinnamon; fold in, using a metal spoon. Add the berries or blackcurrants and cooled apple. Fold in lightly.

3 Spoon the mixture into a buttered shallow 2 litre (3½ pint) ovenproof dish.
■■ Bake on the grid shelf on the floor of the ROASTING OVEN with the cold plain shelf on the second set of runners for 30 minutes or until golden brown, then move the plain shelf to the middle of the SIMMERING OVEN. Transfer the pudding to this shelf and cook for about 15 minutes until just firm in the centre.
■■■■ Bake on the grid shelf on the floor of the BAKING OVEN for 40-50 minutes until just firm in the centre.

4 Serve hot, with Vanilla Custard (see page 104) or cream.

COOK'S TIP *When fresh berries or blackcurrants are unavailable use frozen fruit, draining off all excess juice once the fruit is thawed.*

GOLDEN CROISSANT PUDDING

■ SERVES 6 ■ PREPARATION 15 MINUTES ■ COOKING 35 MINUTES-1 HOUR
■ FREEZING SUITABLE: BEFORE BAKING ■ 565 CALS PER SERVING

For this updated version of traditional bread and butter pudding light, flaky croissants replace the usual bread and the baking dish is set in a bain-marie – so the custard cooks to a softly set, wonderfully creamy consistency. Soak the sultanas in a little brandy to plump them up, if you like. Serve the pudding just warm, with cream.

3 large croissants (see cook's tip)
75 g (3 oz) unsalted butter (at room temperature)
40 g (1½ oz) sultanas
40 g (1½ oz) raisins
CUSTARD
300 ml (½ pint) milk
300 ml (½ pint) double cream
1 vanilla pod, split
2 eggs
40 g (1½ oz) caster sugar
TO FINISH
icing sugar, for dusting

1 Slice the croissants thickly, then spread with the butter. Arrange the croissant slices, butter-side up and overlapping, in a buttered 1.7 litre (3 pint) shallow baking dish, scattering in the sultanas and raisins as you do so.

2 To make the custard, pour the milk and cream into a saucepan. Add the vanilla pod and slowly bring to just below boiling point on the SIMMERING PLATE. Cover and place in the SIMMERING OVEN for 10-15 minutes until well-flavoured with vanilla.

3 Meanwhile, in a large bowl, whisk together the eggs and 25 g (1 oz) caster sugar until light and foamy. Strain the flavoured milk on to the egg mixture, whisking all the time.

4 Pour the egg mixture evenly over the croissants and leave to stand for 15 minutes. Sprinkle over the remaining sugar and stand the dish in a bain-marie or large roasting tin. Pour in enough boiling water to come halfway up the sides of the dish.

5 ■ ■ Cook on the grid shelf on the floor of the ROASTING OVEN for 10 minutes, then transfer to the middle of the SIMMERING OVEN and cook for 50 minutes or until just set in the middle.
■ ■ ■ Slide the roasting tin onto the fourth set of runners in the BAKING OVEN and cook for 35-40 minutes or until just set in the centre.

6 Remove from the oven and leave the pudding to stand in the bain-marie until just warm. Sprinkle with icing sugar and serve with cream.

COOK'S TIP *The croissants are better used when slightly stale. Leave them in a cool place for a day or two, to dry and firm up before slicing.*

VARIATION Replace the croissants with 3-4 individual brioche (depending on size) and substitute roughly chopped, ready-to-eat dried apricots for the sultanas. Flavour the custard with the pared rind of 1 orange instead of the vanilla pod.

CHOCOLATE, WALNUT AND MAPLE PUDDINGS

■ SERVES 8 ■ PREPARATION 25 MINUTES ■ COOKING 25-30 MINUTES
■ FREEZING SUITABLE: STAGE 4 (SEE COOK'S TIP) ■ 525 CALS PER SERVING

Unlike most steamed puds, these pretty individual ones are made from a whisked mixture – of eggs, cocoa, walnuts and ground almonds – resulting in an exceptionally light, soufflé-like texture. Serve with a generous spoonful of crème fraîche.

150 g (5 oz) unsalted butter, softened
175 g (6 oz) light muscovado sugar
1.25 ml (¼ tsp) ground nutmeg
25 g (1 oz) plain white flour
60 ml (4 tbsp) cocoa powder
5 eggs, separated
125 g (4 oz) ground almonds
50 g (2 oz) breadcrumbs
50 g (2 oz) shelled walnuts, chopped
TO SERVE
maple syrup
extra chopped walnuts, for sprinkling

1 Grease eight 150 ml (¼ pint) individual pudding basins and line the bases with greaseproof paper.

2 In a bowl, cream the butter with 50 g (2 oz) of the sugar and the nutmeg until fluffy. Sift the flour and cocoa into the bowl. Add the egg yolks, ground almonds, breadcrumbs and walnuts; stir until just combined.

3 Whisk the egg whites until stiff. Gradually whisk in the remaining sugar. Fold a quarter into the chocolate mixture, to lighten it, using a metal spoon. Carefully fold in the remaining mixture.

4 Spoon the mixture into the prepared basins, filling them no more than two-thirds full.

5 Stand the pudding basins in the large roasting tin and pour in sufficient boiling water to give a 1 cm (½ inch) depth. Cover the tin with a sheet of foil tucking the edges into the water around the puddings. Hang the tin from the fourth set of runners in the ROASTING OVEN and bake for 25-30 minutes or until the puddings feel firm.

6 Loosen the edges of the puddings with a knife and turn out onto warmed serving plates. Drizzle with maple syrup and sprinkle with chopped walnuts. Serve with crème fraîche or Vanilla Custard (see below).

COOK'S TIP These puddings can be baked from frozen, allowing an extra 5 minutes.

VANILLA CUSTARD

■ SERVES 6 ■ PREPARATION 15 MINUTES ■ COOKING ABOUT 15-20 MINUTES
■ FREEZING NOT SUITABLE ■ 130 CALS PER SERVING

600 ml (1 pint) milk
1 vanilla pod, split
4 egg yolks
25-40 g (1-1½ oz) caster sugar
15 ml (1 tbsp) cornflour

1 Pour the milk into a saucepan, add the vanilla pod and bring to just below boiling point on the SIMMERING PLATE. Cover and transfer to the SIMMERING OVEN to infuse for 10-15 minutes or until well flavoured with vanilla.

2 Meanwhile, in a large bowl, whisk together the egg yolks, sugar and cornflour until light and foamy. Strain the flavoured milk onto the egg mixture, whisking all the time.

3 Return to the saucepan and heat, stirring, on the SIMMERING PLATE until thickened enough to coat the back of the spoon; do not boil or the custard will curdle.

4 Immediately remove from the heat and pour into a cold heatproof bowl. Cover the surface with a piece of dampened greaseproof paper to prevent a skin forming and keep warm on the back of the Aga until ready to serve.

GOOD HOUSEKEEPING CHRISTMAS PUDDING

■ SERVES 8 ■ PREPARATION 30 MINUTES ■ COOKING 8½-10½ HOURS
■ FREEZING SUITABLE ■ 445 CALS PER SERVING

125 g (4 oz) butter, softened
finely grated rind of 1 lemon
125 g (4 oz) soft dark brown sugar
2 eggs, beaten
350 g (12 oz) mixed seedless raisins, currants and sultanas
50 g (2 oz) blanched almonds, roughly chopped
50 g (2 oz) walnuts, roughly chopped
50 g (2 oz) brazil nuts, roughly chopped
75 g (3 oz) carrots, coarsely grated
75 g (3 oz) no-soak pitted dried prunes, roughly chopped
25 g (1 oz) chopped mixed peel
50 g (2 oz) fresh brown breadcrumbs
125 g (4 oz) plain wholemeal flour
50 g (2 oz) plain white flour
15 ml (1 tbsp) ground mixed spice
200 ml (7 fl oz) Guinness
30 ml (2 tbsp) brandy
30 ml (2 tbsp) black treacle
TO SERVE
60 ml (4 tbsp) brandy
Sabayon Sauce (see right)

1 In a large mixing bowl, beat together the butter and lemon rind. Gradually beat in the sugar, then the eggs. Mix in all of the remaining ingredients, stirring well. Cover and leave in a cool place (not the refrigerator) overnight.

2 The next day, lightly grease a 1.4-1.6 litre (2½-2¾ pint) heatproof pudding basin and line the base with non-stick baking parchment. Beat the pudding mixture again and spoon into the basin. Cover the surface with a disc of greaseproof paper. Ensure the rim of the bowl is clean, then cover the bowl with a double layer of microwave (non-PVC) film.

3 Stand the pudding basin in a large saucepan containing enough boiling water to come halfway up the sides of the basin. Cover tightly and boil on the SIMMERING PLATE for 30 minutes. Transfer to the SIMMERING OVEN and cook for 8-10 hours; ie all day or overnight. Cool the pudding completely (see cook's tips). Store in the refrigerator for up to 2 months.

4 On the day, place the covered pudding basin in the middle of the SIMMERING OVEN towards the back and leave for 1-1½ hours to heat through (see cook's tips).

5 Turn out the pudding on to a warm serving plate. Warm the brandy in a small saucepan, pour over the pudding and set alight. When the flames have died down, serve cut into wedges, accompanied by the Sabayon Sauce.

COOK'S TIPS

▶ Do not uncover the cooked pudding; the microwave film will form a shrink wrap as it cools.
▶ It isn't necessary to re-steam the pudding (which would cool the Aga) to serve.
▶ Leftover pudding can be reheated in the SIMMERING OVEN.

SABAYON SAUCE

■ SERVES 8 ■ PREPARATION 15 MINUTES ■ COOKING ABOUT 5 MINUTES
■ FREEZING NOT SUITABLE ■ 115 CALS PER SERVING

75 g (3 oz) caster sugar
120 ml (4 fl oz) water
3 egg yolks
120 ml (4 fl oz) double cream
grated rind and juice of 1 lemon

1 Place the sugar and water in a small saucepan on the SIMMERING PLATE until dissolved. Transfer to the BOILING PLATE and boil for about 3 minutes until the syrup registers 105°C (225°F) on a sugar thermometer (and looks very syrupy with large pea-size bubbles).

2 Whisk the egg yolks in a small bowl, then gradually pour on the hot syrup in a thin steady stream, whisking all the time. Continue to whisk until the mixture is thick, mousse-like and cool.

3 In a separate bowl, whisk the cream until it forms stiff peaks, then add the lemon rind and juice and whip again to soft peaks. Fold the cream into the mousse.

4 Cover and chill in the refrigerator until required. Whisk well before serving.

TARTE TATIN

■ SERVES 8 ■ PREPARATION 30 MINUTES ■ COOKING ABOUT 50 MINUTES
■ FREEZING NOT SUITABLE ■ 535 CALS PER SERVING

This classic French dessert is cooked upside down.
The apples are cooked first in a buttery caramel, then
covered with a layer of pâte sucrée and baked in the hot
oven. To serve, the tarte is inverted so the apples
sit atop the rich pastry base.

PASTRY
225 g (8 oz) plain flour
150 g (5 oz) butter
1.25 ml (¼ tsp) salt
50 g (2 oz) icing sugar
1 egg
few drops of vanilla essence
CARAMEL
125 g (4 oz) butter
1-1.2 kg (2-2½ lb) large dessert apples, preferably Cox's,
Russets, Braeburn or Worcester Pearmains
200 g (7 oz) caster sugar
juice of ½ lemon

1 To make the pastry, sift the flour on to a work surface.
Make a hollow in the centre and add the butter with the salt.
Work the butter and salt together using the fingers of one
hand until smooth and pliable. Add the icing sugar to the
well and mix into the butter in the same way. Add the egg
and vanilla essence and combine with the ingredients in the
well, until the mixture resembles scrambled egg. Cut the
flour into the butter mixture, using a palette knife to form a
dough. Knead lightly until smooth. Wrap in cling film and
chill in the refrigerator for 30 minutes or until firm enough to
roll (see cook's tips).

2 For the caramel, melt the butter in a 25 cm (10 inch) tarte
tatin mould or heavy-based shallow cake tin in the
SIMMERING OVEN. Meanwhile, peel, quarter and core the
apples. Sprinkle the sugar evenly over the melted butter,
then tightly pack the apples in the tin.

3 Cook on the floor of the ROASTING OVEN for 12-15 minutes, then turn the apples over, baste with the juices and
cook on the SIMMERING PLATE until the juices cook to a
golden caramel; about 7-15 minutes depending on the
apple variety. Sprinkle with the lemon juice. Allow to cool.

4 Roll out the pastry to a round, 2.5 cm (1 inch) larger all
round than the top of the tarte tatin tin. Lay over the top of
the cooked apples, tucking the edges of the pastry down the
side of the tin. Prick the pastry with the tip of a sharp knife.
Bake on the grid shelf on the floor of the ROASTING OVEN
for 25 minutes or until the pastry is golden brown all over.

5 Leave in the tin to cool slightly for 10 minutes, then turn
out on to a serving plate. Serve warm, with cream, custard
or ice cream.

COOK'S TIPS
▶ *To save time, mix all the pastry ingredients together in a
food processor until the mixture resembles coarse crumbs;
knead lightly to a smooth dough.*
▶ *If the pastry is firm enough to roll, there is no need to
chill it.*
▶ *Do not use a loose-based cake tin.*

BRAMLEY APPLES WITH GINGER

■ SERVES 4 ■ PREPARATION 15 MINUTES, PLUS SOAKING
■ COOKING 1-1½ HOURS ■ FREEZING NOT SUITABLE ■ 275 CALS PER SERVING

175 g (6 oz) pitted no-soak prunes, roughly chopped
150 ml (¼ pint) apple or orange juice
15 g (½ oz) preserved stem ginger in syrup, plus
15 ml (1 tbsp) syrup from the jar
finely grated rind and juice of 1 lemon
125 g (4 oz) soft light brown sugar
4 Bramley apples, each about 225 g (8 oz)

1 Put the prunes into a small bowl, pour on the fruit juice
and leave to soak for 30 minutes.

2 Finely chop the stem ginger and mix with the ginger
syrup, lemon rind and juice, and the sugar. Drain the
prunes, reserving the juice, and add to the ginger mixture.

3 Wash the apples and remove the cores with an apple
corer. Make shallow cuts in the skin around the centre of
each apple to prevent the skins bursting in the oven. Place
in an ovenproof dish.

4 Fill the centre of each apple with the prune mixture,
sprinkling any extra over the top. Pour on the reserved fruit

juice. Cover the prune filling in each apple with a small piece of foil.

5 ■■ Bake on the grid shelf on the floor of the ROASTING OVEN for 20 minutes, then transfer the dish to the SIMMERING OVEN and cook for about 1¼ hours until the apples are soft in the centre.

■■■■ Bake on the grid shelf on the floor of the BAKING OVEN for approximately 1 hour until the apples are soft in the centre.

COOK'S TIP *If you haven't any stem ginger in your store-cupboard, use 2.5 ml (½ tsp) ground ginger and omit the ginger syrup.*

TRADITIONAL MINCE PIES

■ MAKES 12 PIES; 1.8 KG (4 LB) MINCEMEAT: SEE COOK'S TIPS

■ PREPARATION 30 MINUTES, PLUS STANDING ■ COOKING 20-25 MINUTES

■ FREEZING SUITABLE: SEE COOK'S TIPS ■ 260 CALS PER MINCE PIE

To make perfect mince pies, homemade mincemeat must be given time – ideally at least 1 week – to mature and absorb all the brandy before use or it will seep through the pastry edges, causing the pies to stick to the patty tins. For last-minute panics, buy a good-quality mincemeat and add a few chopped nuts and a dash of brandy.

APRICOT MINCEMEAT

225 g (8 oz) no-soak dried apricots, roughly chopped

finely grated rind of 1 orange

45 ml (3 tbsp) orange juice

900 g (2 lb) mixed currants, sultanas and raisins

60 ml (4 tbsp) orange marmalade

450 g (1 lb) demerara sugar

7.5 ml (1½ tsp) ground mixed spice

1.25 ml (¼ tsp) ground nutmeg

300 ml (½ pint) brandy

PASTRY

225 g (8 oz) plain white flour

pinch of salt

150 g (5 oz) butter

30 ml (2 tbsp) caster sugar

1 egg yolk

TO FINISH

1 egg white, lightly beaten

caster sugar, for sprinkling

1 To prepare the mincemeat, mix all of the ingredients together in a large bowl. Cover and leave in a cool place for 48 hours, stirring occasionally. Pot in sterilised jars, cover and store in a cool place for up to 2 months.

2 To make the pastry, sift the flour and salt into a large mixing bowl. Using a round-bladed knife, roughly cut in the butter, then rub in using your fingertips until the mixture resembles coarse breadcrumbs. Stir in the sugar.

3 Mix the egg yolk with about 45 ml (3 tbsp) cold water, then add to the dry ingredients, mixing with a round-bladed knife to form a dough. Knead gently until just smooth. Wrap in cling film and chill in the refrigerator for about 30 minutes.

4 On a lightly floured surface, roll out half of the pastry to a 3 mm (⅛ inch) thickness. Using a 7.5 cm (3 inch) fluted cutter, stamp out 12 circles of pastry. Gently press these into patty tins – the pastry should just protrude above the tins to allow for shrinkage when cooked. Spoon about 10-15 ml (2-3 tsp) mincemeat into each tin.

5 Roll out the remaining pastry and stamp out 12 circles, using a 6 cm (2½ inch) fluted cutter. Dampen the edges of the pastry in the patty tins, then top with the smaller pastry circles. Press the edges together to seal. Brush the tops with egg white, then sprinkle lightly with caster sugar.

6 ■■ Bake on the grid shelf on the floor of the ROASTING OVEN with the cold plain shelf on the second set of runners for 20-25 minutes.
■■■■ Cook in the BAKING OVEN with the grid shelf on the third set of runners for 20-25 minutes, turning the tray of patty tins around halfway through cooking.

7 Leave in the tins for 5 minutes, then transfer to a wire rack. Serve warm, with pouring cream if desired.

COOK'S TIPS

▶ *You will only need to use about 225 g (8 oz) of the mincemeat for this quantity of mince pies.*

▶ *Freeze the uncooked mince pies. Glaze and bake from frozen as above, allowing an extra 10-15 minutes baking.*

VARIATION At stage 5, cut the remaining pastry into holly leaves, using a suitable cutter, and shape small berries too. Arrange, overlapping, over the mincemeat to form the pastry lids. Glaze and bake as above.

APPLE AND CINNAMON PANCAKES WITH MASCARPONE CREAM

■ SERVES 8 ■ PREPARATION 30 MINUTES ■ COOKING ABOUT 40 MINUTES
■ FREEZING SUITABLE: STAGE 6 (PANCAKES AND FILLING SEPARATELY)
■ 340 CALS PER SERVING

Pancakes should be as thin as possible – almost lacy in texture. The following quantity of batter will make 12 pancakes, 16 if you're an expert!

PANCAKES
200 ml (7 fl oz) milk
100 ml (3 fl oz) water
75 g (3 oz) plain white flour
pinch of salt
2.5 ml (½ tsp) ground cinnamon
15 ml (1 tbsp) caster sugar
1 egg
1 egg yolk
15 ml (1 tbsp) oil
a little oil, for cooking
APPLE FILLING
900 g (2 lb) cooking apples
75 g (3 oz) butter
50 g (2 oz) soft light brown sugar
15 ml (1 tbsp) lemon juice
75 g (3 oz) seedless raisins
90 ml (6 tbsp) maple syrup
MASCARPONE CREAM
125 g (4 oz) mascarpone or full-fat soft cheese
150 ml (¼ pint) Greek-style yogurt
15 ml (1 tbsp) icing sugar

1 To make the pancake batter, mix the milk and water together. Sift the flour, salt and cinnamon into a mixing bowl, stir in the sugar and make a well in the centre. Add the egg, egg yolk and half the milk mixture. Beat until smooth, then stir in the remaining milk mixture and oil. Cover and leave to stand for about 1 hour.

2 Mix the ingredients for the mascarpone cream together in a bowl until evenly blended. Cover and chill until required.

3 To prepare the filling, peel, quarter, core and thickly slice the apples. Melt 50 g (2 oz) butter in a saucepan on the SIMMERING PLATE. Add the apples, sugar and lemon juice. Cover tightly and cook for about 10 minutes or until the apples are beginning to soften but retain some shape. Stir in the raisins and 60 ml (4 tbsp) of the maple syrup.

4 Whisk the batter again, then pour into a jug. Heat a little oil in a 15 cm (6 inch) pancake pan on the BOILING PLATE until very hot; pour away excess oil. Wipe the SIMMERING PLATE with oiled kitchen paper and close the lid.

5 Pour a thin layer of batter into the pan, tilting the pan to spread it evenly. Cook for 30 seconds-1 minute or until brown around the edges and beginning to curl away from the pan. Flip onto the SIMMERING PLATE, close the lid and cook for about 30 seconds until the underside is browned. (In the meantime, start cooking the second pancake in the pan on the BOILING PLATE.)

6 Lift the first pancake off the SIMMERING PLATE, using a palette knife. Turn on to a wire rack lined with a tea-towel. Fold the towel over the pancake to keep it moist. Continue to make about 12 pancakes in all, stacking them as they are cooked. If the pancakes start to stick when cooking add a little more oil to the pan.

7 Divide the apple mixture between the pancakes. Roll up and place in a buttered ovenproof dish. Melt remaining 25 g (1 oz) butter and mix with the rest of the maple syrup. Drizzle over the pancakes and cover the dish with foil.

8 Place in the SIMMERING OVEN for about 20 minutes (while eating the main course) until piping hot. Serve with the mascarpone cream.

VARIATION
Traditional Pancakes: Omit cinnamon and sugar from batter. Omit the apple filling and mascarpone cream. Serve warm, sprinkled with lemon juice and caster sugar.

RHUBARB AND CINNAMON COBBLER

■ SERVES 4-6 ■ PREPARATION 15 MINUTES ■ COOKING 40 MINUTES
■ FREEZING SUITABLE ■ 565-375 CALS PER SERVING

PASTRY
175 g (6 oz) plain white flour
125 g (4 oz) butter
25 g (1 oz) caster sugar
45 ml (3 tbsp) chilled water
FILLING
700 g (1½ lb) rhubarb, trimmed and cut into bite-sized chunks
125 g (4 oz) caster sugar
30 ml (2 tbsp) cornflour
2.5 ml (½ tsp) ground cinnamon
a little milk and sugar, for glazing

1 To make the pastry, place the flour, butter and sugar in a food processor and process until the mixture resembles fine breadcrumbs. Add the cold water and process briefly until the pastry comes together to form a ball. If it is slightly sticky, roll in some flour and chill for 20 minutes or until firm enough to handle.

2 Butter a 23 cm (9 inch) flan tin or round ovenproof dish, which is at least 4 cm (1½ inches) deep. Roll out the pastry to a circle, large enough to line the tin or ovenproof dish and to overhang the sides generously. Lift the pastry into the tin or dish keeping the edges ragged and uneven.

3 For the filling, toss the rhubarb in the sugar, cornflour and cinnamon. Spoon into the pastry case. Bring the pastry edges up and over the fruit, leaving a gap in the centre to reveal the filling. Brush the pastry with milk and sprinkle with a little sugar to glaze.

4 Stand the dish in a roasting tin and bake on the floor of the ROASTING OVEN for 20 minutes, then lift the roasting tin onto the fourth set of runners and bake for a further 20 minutes or until the pastry is golden brown. Serve hot, with ice cream or cream.

COOK'S TIP *This pie is cooked in a roasting tin to prevent any juices which might bubble over spilling onto the cooker.*

VARIATIONS Use ripe plums or apricots, quartered and stoned, instead of rhubarb with only 50 g (2 oz) sugar.

LEMON CHEESECAKE

■ SERVES 6 ■ PREPARATION 20 MINUTES ■ COOKING ABOUT 1 HOUR
■ FREEZING NOT SUITABLE ■ 345 CALS PER SERVING

This cheesecake is unusually light in texture – the sharpness of the lemon cuts the richness of the cream cheese to create an irresistible dessert. A simple berry compote is the perfect complement.

BASE
150 g (5 oz) digestive biscuits
25 g (1 oz) butter, melted
3 pieces of stem ginger preserved in syrup, about 50 g (2 oz) total weight
FILLING
two 200 g (7 oz) packs full-fat soft cheese
finely grated rind of 1 large or 2 small lemons
60 ml (4 tbsp) lemon juice
125 g (4 oz) caster sugar
60 ml (4 tbsp) crème fraîche
1 egg
TO FINISH
icing sugar, for dusting

1 Line the base of an 18 cm (7 inch) round spring-release cake tin with non-stick baking parchment.

2 For the base, put the digestive biscuits, butter and stem ginger in a food processor and work until crumbed and evenly blended. Transfer the mixture to the cake tin and spread evenly. Press onto the base of the cake tin, using a potato masher.

3 ■ ■ Bake on the grid shelf on the floor of the ROASTING OVEN with the cold plain shelf set on the runners just above for 15 minutes or until just beginning to change colour. Remove the plain shelf from the oven to cool.

■ ■ ■ ■ Place on the grid shelf on the fourth set of runners in the BAKING OVEN and cook for 15 minutes until beginning to colour.

4 Place the ingredients for the filling in the food processor and blend until smooth. Spoon the cheese mixture onto the warm biscuit base, spreading evenly.

5 ■ ■ Bake on the grid shelf on the floor of the ROASTING OVEN with the cold plain shelf just above for 25 minutes, then transfer the plain shelf to the middle of the SIMMERING

OVEN. Position the cheesecake tin on this shelf towards the back and cook for a further 15 minutes.

■ ■ ■ ■ With the grid shelf on the fourth set of runners in the BAKING OVEN bake the cheesecake for 40-45 minutes or until just set.

6 Leave the cheesecake to cool in the tin on the back of the cooker for 30 minutes. Loosen the edge of the cheesecake with a palette knife, then remove the side of the tin. Carefully transfer the cheesecake to a serving plate (or leave on the tin base if preferred). Serve warm or cold, generously dusted with icing sugar if desired.

VARIATION Omit the stem ginger from the base. Use an extra 25 g (1 oz) digestive biscuits.

BrulÉed Lemon Tartlets

■ SERVES 8 ■ PREPARATION 35 MINUTES, PLUS CHILLING
■ COOKING 25-30 MINUTES ■ FREEZING NOT SUITABLE
■ 325 CALS PER SERVING

These light souffléed lemon tartlets are cooked until just
setting, dusted with icing sugar and cooked again
until lightly browned. Serve with a dollop of crème
fraîche and fresh raspberries.

PÂTE SUCRÉE
200 g (7 oz) plain white flour
2.5 ml (½ tsp) salt
100 g (3½ oz) butter, softened
45 ml (3 tbsp) sugar
1 egg yolk
LEMON FILLING
4 eggs, separated
150 g (5 oz) caster sugar
finely grated rind of 2 lemons
juice of 1 lemon
pinch of salt
TO FINISH
icing sugar, for dusting
raspberries, to decorate

1 To make the pastry, sift the flour and salt onto a sheet of
greaseproof paper. Place the butter, sugar and egg yolk in a
food processor and blend until smooth. Shoot in the flour
and blend until just combined. Turn out onto a lightly floured
surface and knead gently until smooth. Wrap in cling film
and chill in the refrigerator for at least 30 minutes. Allow to
come to room temperature before rolling out.

2 Divide the pastry into 8 equal pieces. Roll out each piece
and use to line individual 10 cm (4 inch) loose-bottomed
flan tins. Prick the bases with a fork and line with greaseproof paper and baking beans. Stand the flan tins in the
large roasting tin and bake blind on the floor of the
ROASTING OVEN for 5 minutes, then remove the paper and
beans. Return to the oven, turning the tins around to ensure
even cooking, for 5 minutes until set and beginning to
brown. Allow to cool.

3 To make the filling, whisk the egg yolks and 75 g (3 oz) of
the sugar together in a bowl until the mixture is pale, thick
and mousse-like. Whisk in the lemon rind and juice. Transfer

the mixture to a small pan and stand in the small roasting
tin, half-filled with boiling water, on the SIMMERING PLATE.
Stir until the mixture thickens slightly – just enough to thinly
coat the back of a wooden spoon; about 4 minutes. Stand
the pan in a roasting tin containing cold water and allow to
cool, stirring occasionally.

4 In a separate bowl, whisk the egg whites with the salt
until stiff but not dry. Gradually whisk in the remaining sugar,
a spoonful at a time. Beat a spoonful into the lemon custard
to loosen it, then carefully fold in the remainder.

5 Spoon the filling into the tartlet cases set in the large
roasting tin.
■■ Place on the grid shelf on the floor of the ROASTING
OVEN, positioning the cold plain shelf on the third set of
runners. Bake for 10-12 minutes until beginning to rise. Take
out the plain shelf.
■■■ Place on the grid shelf on the fourth set of runners
in the BAKING OVEN and bake for 10-15 minutes until
beginning to rise.

6 Sprinkle with icing sugar and return to the oven for
4-5 minutes until just beginning to brown. Serve warm or
cold, decorated with a few raspberries and accompanied
by crème fraîche.

COOK'S TIPS
▶ *The filling rises on baking, but will sink again as it cools.*
▶ *The tartlets can be prepared a few hours ahead and
warmed through in the SIMMERING OVEN while the main
course is served.*

VARIATIONS Use 2 small oranges or 3 limes instead of the
lemons.

PROFITEROLES WITH CHOCOLATE SAUCE

■ SERVES 4 ■ PREPARATION 30 MINUTES, PLUS COOLING
■ COOKING ABOUT 35 MINUTES
■ FREEZING SUITABLE: UNFILLED CHOUX BUNS AND SAUCE SEPARATELY
■ 595 CALS PER SERVING

It is essential to weigh the ingredients for choux pastry accurately and before you begin preparation. During baking, the moisture in the dough turns to steam and puffs up the mixture, leaving the centre hollow. Thorough cooking is important; if insufficiently cooked, the choux may collapse when taken from the oven and there will be uncooked pastry in the centre to scoop out.

CHOUX PASTRY
65 g (2½ oz) plain white flour
50 g (2 oz) butter
150 ml (¼ pint) water
2 eggs, lightly beaten
CHOCOLATE SAUCE
125 g (4 oz) plain chocolate
15 g (½ oz) butter
30 ml (2 tbsp) water
30 ml (2 tbsp) golden syrup
2-3 drops of vanilla essence
TO ASSEMBLE
250 ml (8 fl oz) double cream
icing sugar, for dusting

1 To make the choux pastry, sift the flour on to a sheet of greaseproof paper. Put the butter and 150 ml (¼ pint) water in a saucepan and heat on the SIMMERING PLATE until the butter has melted. Transfer to the BOILING PLATE and bring to a fast boil. Remove the pan from the heat and immediately tip in the flour all at once, beating thoroughly with a wooden spoon. Continue beating until the mixture is smooth and forms a ball in the centre of the pan. (Take care to avoid overbeating or the mixture will become fatty.) Remove from the heat and let cool slightly for 1-2 minutes.

2 Beat in the eggs, a little at a time, adding only just enough to give a piping consistency. It is important to beat the mixture vigorously at this stage to trap in as much air as possible. Continue beating until the mixture develops a sheen.

3 Spoon the choux pastry into a piping bag fitted with a 1 cm (½ inch) plain nozzle. Pipe about 20 small bun shapes onto the dampened plain Aga shelf.

4 Slide the shelf onto the third set of runners in the ROASTING OVEN and bake for 17-20 minutes or until well risen and golden brown.

5 Remove the buns from the oven and make a hole in the side of each with the tip of a knife to release the steam. Return to the ROASTING OVEN, turning the shelf around, for 3-5 minutes to crisp and brown the profiteroles evenly. Transfer to the SIMMERING OVEN for 15 minutes to dry out completely. Leave to cool on a wire rack.

6 To make the chocolate sauce, melt all of the ingredients together in a small heavy-based pan on the SIMMERING PLATE. Stir well until smooth and evenly blended.

7 Meanwhile, whip the cream until it just holds its shape. Spoon into a piping bag fitted with a medium plain nozzle and use to fill the choux buns through the holes in the sides.

8 Dust the profiteroles with icing sugar and serve with the warm chocolate sauce spooned over or served separately.

BAKED BANANAS WITH CARDAMOM AND RUM

■ SERVES 6 ■ PREPARATION 5 MINUTES ■ COOKING 20 MINUTES
■ FREEZING NOT SUITABLE ■ 210 CALS PER SERVING

Baked in an aromatic syrup, these bananas melt in the mouth. They are equally delicious served with ice cream or crème fraîche.

5 cardamom pods
grated rind and juice of 1 orange
grated rind and juice of 1 lemon
30 ml (2 tbsp) soft brown sugar
60 ml (4 tbsp) apricot jam
25 g (1 oz) butter
60 ml (4 tbsp) rum or brandy
6 large bananas

1 Extract the seeds from the cardamom pods and crush with a pestle and mortar.

2 Combine the crushed cardamom seeds, orange and lemon juices, sugar, apricot jam, butter and rum or brandy in a large shallow ovenproof dish and warm in the SIMMERING OVEN until the butter has melted.

3 Peel and quarter the bananas. Add to the juice mixture and turn to coat. Cook on the grid shelf on the floor of the ROASTING OVEN for 20 minutes or until the bananas are soft. Serve immediately, with ice cream or crème fraîche.

VARIATION Instead of cardamom, use ground cinnamon to taste.

HAZELNUT MERINGUE GÂTEAU

■ SERVES 10 ■ PREPARATION 40 MINUTES, PLUS COOLING
■ COOKING ABOUT 3½ HOURS ■ FREEZING SUITABLE: STAGE 4
■ 630 CALS PER SLICE

Tiers of lightly spiced meringue – laced with two-tone chocolate pieces – form a delicious case for lightly whipped cream and a hazelnut praline. For a lighter gâteau, replace half of the cream with thick Greek-style yogurt or fromage frais. You can also increase the amount of spice if you prefer a more intense flavour.

MERINGUE
125 g (4 oz) shelled hazelnuts
5 egg whites
250 g (9 oz) caster sugar
2.5 cm (½ tsp) ground mixed spice
75 g (3 oz) white chocolate, chopped
75 g (3 oz) plain chocolate, chopped
PRALINE
125 g (4 oz) caster sugar
75 g (3 oz) shelled hazelnuts, toasted
TO ASSEMBLE
300 ml (½ pint) double cream
cocoa powder, for dusting

1 Line 2 baking sheets with non-stick baking parchment. Draw a 23 cm (9 inch) circle onto one sheet, using a plate as a guide. On the other sheet, draw an 18 cm (7 inch) circle. Turn the paper over.

2 To make the meringue, spread the hazelnuts in a shallow baking tin and toast on the grid shelf on the floor of the ROASTING OVEN for 8-10 minutes, turning from time to time. Allow to cool, then chop roughly.

3 Whisk the egg whites in a bowl until stiff but not dry. Gradually whisk in half of the sugar, a tablespoon at a time, whisking well between each addition until the meringue is stiff and shiny. Carefully fold in the remaining sugar with the spice, then fold in the chopped hazelnuts and white and plain chocolate.

4 Spoon the meringue onto the drawn circles, then spread neatly into rounds. Bake in the SIMMERING OVEN for

about 3½ hours until dry in the centre and the undersides are firm when tapped.

■ ■ ■ ■ Alternatively cook in the PLATE WARMING OVEN for approximately 7 hours.

5 For the praline, put the sugar in a small heavy-based pan on the SIMMERING PLATE for 5-10 minutes until the sugar is melted. Transfer to the BOILING PLATE and cook to a rich golden brown caramel, tilting the pan from time to time; do not stir. Add the toasted hazelnuts, then pour onto an oiled baking sheet. Leave to cool and harden.

6 Place the praline between 2 sheets of greaseproof paper (or in a strong polythene bag) and beat with a rolling pin until very coarsely crushed.

7 Carefully transfer the largest meringue round to a serving plate. Whip the cream until softly peaking, then spread over the meringue. Scatter with the praline. Top with the smaller meringue round and leave to stand for 1-2 hours. Dust the top of the gâteau with cocoa powder to serve.

COOK'S TIPS

▶ *Remember to switch the baking sheets around halfway through cooking the meringue rounds, to ensure an even result.*

▶ *For convenience, toast all the hazelnuts together, then set aside 75 g (3 oz) for the praline.*

VARIATION Replace the praline with 350 g (12 oz) fresh raspberries or sliced strawberries.

Brown Sugar Meringues with Raspberry Sauce

■ SERVES 6-8 ■ PREPARATION 35 MINUTES, PLUS COOLING

■ COOKING 2½-3 HOURS ■ FREEZING NOT SUITABLE

■ 380-285 CALS PER SERVING

Generous clouds of meringue are filled with whipped cream and sliced peaches and served on a sharp ruby red sauce. Soft brown sugar adds a slight caramel flavour to the meringues and colours them a pretty, pale beige. Use nectarines instead of peaches, or strawberries, if you prefer.

MERINGUE
4 egg whites
25 g (1 oz) caster sugar
225 g (8 oz) soft light brown sugar
RASPBERRY SAUCE
450 g (1 lb) fresh or frozen raspberries, thawed
30 ml (2 tbsp) lemon juice
icing sugar, to taste
30 ml (2 tbsp) kirsch (optional)
TO ASSEMBLE
2-3 ripe peaches
15 ml (1 tbsp) kirsch (optional)
300 ml (½ pint) double cream

1 Put the egg whites in a large bowl and whisk until very stiff but not dry. Whisk in the caster sugar, until stiff and shiny. Whisk in half of the brown sugar, a spoonful at a time, until the meringue is very stiff. Carefully fold in the rest of the brown sugar, using a large metal spoon.

2 Spoon or pipe about 12-16 meringues onto a baking sheet lined with non-stick baking parchment. Bake on the floor of the SIMMERING OVEN for 2½-3 hours until thoroughly dried out, gently pressing the base of the meringues halfway through cooking.

3 Remove the meringues from the oven and leave to cool on the parchment. Carefully lift off when cool and store in an airtight container until required.

4 To make the raspberry sauce, place the raspberries in a blender or food processor with the lemon juice and icing sugar to taste. Work to a purée, then pass through a sieve to remove any seeds. Stir in the kirsch if using. Cover and chill in the refrigerator.

5 Immerse the peaches in a bowl of boiling water for 20 seconds to loosen the skins. Lift out and plunge into cold water to stop further cooking. Peel off the skins. Halve the peaches and remove the stones. Slice neatly and sprinkle with 15 ml (1 tbsp) kirsch if using.

6 To serve, whip the cream until it just holds soft peaks. Spoon the cream onto half of the meringues. Arrange the sliced peaches on top and sandwich together with the remaining meringues. Place on individual serving plates and pour over the raspberry sauce. Serve immediately.

COOK'S TIPS

▶ *The secret to making these meringues is to whisk the egg whites initially until very stiff and to whisk until stiff between each addition of sugar. Do not add the sugar too quickly, or the meringue will become thin.*

▶ *If the meringues are not quite dried out after 3 hours, place them on a cloth on the lid of the SIMMERING PLATE or on the WARMING PLATE (of a 4-oven Aga) until dry.*

RICOTTA STRUDEL

■ SERVES 8 ■ PREPARATION 30 MINUTES, PLUS SOAKING

■ COOKING 30-40 MINUTES ■ FREEZING NOT SUITABLE

■ 350 CALS PER SERVING

For this delicious Austrian strudel, ricotta, fruit and nuts
are spiced with cinnamon and enveloped in
filo pastry. Serve warm, dusted liberally with icing sugar
and accompanied by cinnamon-flavoured
cream, or crème fraîche.

125 g (4 oz) sultanas
90 ml (6 tbsp) rum or brandy
50 g (2 oz) pine nuts
125 g (4 oz) ricotta cheese
45 ml (3 tbsp) double cream
1 egg yolk
finely grated rind of 1 orange
finely grated rind of 1 lemon
50 g (2 oz) chopped mixed peel
30 ml (2 tbsp) icing sugar
2.5 ml (½ tsp) ground cinnamon
50 g (2 oz) butter
450 g (1 lb) Bramley apples
175 g (6 oz) filo pastry (approximately)
25 g (1 oz) ground almonds
30 ml (2 tbsp) caster sugar
TO SERVE
icing sugar, for dusting

1 Put the sultanas in a small heatproof bowl, pour on the
rum or brandy and place at one side of the Aga (where it is
warm). Leave to soak for 1-2 hours.

2 Spread the pine nuts on a baking sheet and toast on the
grid shelf on the floor of the ROASTING OVEN for about
3 minutes until golden brown, taking care to avoid burning.

3 Beat the ricotta cheese, cream and egg yolk together in
a large mixing bowl. Stir in the sultanas and any remaining
soaking liquor, pine nuts, orange and lemon rind, mixed
peel, icing sugar and cinnamon.

4 Melt the butter in a heatproof bowl in the SIMMERING
OVEN. In the meantime, peel, core and slice the apples.

5 Layer 2-3 sheets of filo pastry on a clean tea-towel to
make a 28 x 45 cm (11 x 18 inch) rectangle, with a long
edge towards you. Brush lightly with melted butter. Layer a
few more sheets of filo on top, then brush again with melted
butter. Sprinkle the ground almonds evenly over the surface.

6 Starting 5 cm (2 inches) in from the long edge of the
pastry, arrange the apple slices, overlapping, along its
length. Sprinkle with the caster sugar, then spread the
ricotta filling evenly on top. Fold the short pastry sides over
to seal in the filling. Using the tea-towel to help you lift the
pastry, carefully roll the strudel up as tightly as you can.

7 Carefully transfer the strudel to the Aga plain shelf,
curving it a little to fit if necessary. Brush lightly with butter.
■ ■ Cook on the grid shelf on the floor of the ROASTING
OVEN for 10 minutes. Turn the shelf around (to ensure even
cooking) and re-position on the grid shelf, setting the cold
plain shelf (or roasting tin) about 7-10 cm (3-4 inches)
above. Bake for a further 15 minutes until golden brown.
Transfer to the SIMMERING OVEN and cook for a further
10 minutes or until the apples are tender.
■ ■ ■ ■ Bake on the grid shelf on the third set of runners in
the BAKING OVEN for 30-40 minutes or until golden brown
and the apples are tender, turning the shelf around halfway
through cooking.

8 Leave to stand for 10 minutes, then slide the strudel onto
a warmed serving plate and dust with icing sugar. Serve
with cinnamon cream or crème fraîche.

COOK'S TIP *To make cinnamon cream, lightly whip 300 ml
(½ pint) whipping cream with 15 ml (1 tbsp) icing sugar and
5 ml (1 tsp) ground cinnamon.*

PINEAPPLE AND ALMOND ROULADE

■ SERVES 6-8 ■ PREPARATION 25 MINUTES, PLUS COOLING
■ COOKING 13-20 MINUTES ■ FREEZING SUITABLE: SEE COOK'S TIPS
■ 525 CALS PER SERVING

This irresistible, moist roulade is flecked with
grated marzipan to give a superb almond flavour.
In perfect contrast, chopped fresh pineapple and
whipped cream are encased inside. You will probably
find that the roulade cracks as you roll it – but this
is all part of its charm!

25 g (1 oz) flaked almonds
5 eggs, separated
150 g (5 oz) caster sugar
5 ml (1 tsp) vanilla essence
75 g (3 oz) white marzipan, coarsely grated or finely chopped
45 ml (3 tbsp) plain white flour
TO ASSEMBLE
300 ml (¹/₂ pint) double cream
25 g (1 oz) caster sugar
275 g (10 oz) fresh pineapple, chopped
icing sugar, for dusting

1 Spread the flaked almonds on a baking sheet and toast on the grid shelf on the floor of the ROASTING OVEN for 3-4 minutes or until golden brown.

2 Lightly grease a 33 x 23 cm (13 x 9 inch) Swiss roll tin and line with non-stick baking parchment. Scatter the toasted almonds evenly over the paper.

3 Put the egg yolks and 125 g (4 oz) of the caster sugar into a bowl and whisk, using an electric beater, until pale and thick. Fold in the vanilla essence and grated marzipan. Sift the flour over the mixture, then lightly fold in using a large metal spoon.

4 Whisk the egg whites in another bowl until stiff, but not dry. Whisk in the remaining 25 g (1 oz) caster sugar, a spoonful at a time. Using a large metal spoon, carefully fold a quarter of the egg whites into the almond mixture to lighten it, then gradually fold in the rest.

5 Turn the mixture into the prepared tin and spread evenly, gently easing it into the corners.

6 ■■ Place the tin on the grid shelf on the floor of the ROASTING OVEN with the cold plain shelf on the third set of runners. Bake for 13-15 minutes until well risen and firm to the touch, carefully turning the tin around after 8 minutes to ensure even cooking.
■■■■ Place the tin on the grid shelf on the fourth set of runners in the BAKING OVEN. Cook for 17-20 minutes, until well risen and firm to the touch, carefully turning the tin around after 10 minutes.

7 Leave to stand for 5 minutes, then cover the sponge with a sheet of non-stick baking parchment and a damp tea-towel and leave until cold.

8 Remove the tea-towel and invert the sponge with the covering paper onto the work surface. Peel off the lining paper and trim the long edges to neaten.

9 For the filling, lightly whip the cream in a bowl until soft peaks form, then fold in the caster sugar.

10 Spread the cream over the sponge and scatter the chopped pineapple evenly on top. Carefully roll up the sponge from one of the narrow ends,using the paper to help.

11 Transfer to a serving plate and dust with icing sugar.

COOK'S TIPS

▶ *You will need a 900 g-1 kg (2-2½ lb) pineapple to give this quantity of prepared weight.*

▶ *For a decorative effect, place a long metal skewer directly on the BOILING PLATE, close the lid and leave until it is red hot. Protecting your hand with an oven glove, use the skewer to mark lines diagonally along the length of the roulade.*

▶ Freeze the pineapple roulade at the end of stage 10. To use, thaw overnight in the refrigerator and dust with icing sugar to serve.

VARIATIONS

▶ Replace the chopped fresh pineapple with raspberries or ripe, stoned apricots.

▶ Add 15 ml (1tbsp) amaretto liqueur to the roulade mixture at stage 3.

CAKES, BISCUITS AND BREADS

WHISKED SPONGE WITH CREAM AND STRAWBERRIES

■ 8 SLICES ■ PREPARATION 25 MINUTES, PLUS COOLING

■ COOKING 18-20 MINUTES ■ FREEZING SUITABLE: STAGE 4

■ 240 CALS PER SERVING

This classic whisked fatless sponge is best eaten on the day it is made.

3 eggs
75 g (3 oz) caster sugar
75 g (3 oz) plain white flour, sifted
FILLING
250 ml (8 fl oz) double cream
5 ml (1 tsp) caster sugar
few drops of vanilla essence
45-60 ml (3-4 tbsp) strawberry conserve, or
225 g (8 oz) strawberries, sliced
TO FINISH
icing sugar, for dusting

1 Grease and base-line a 20 cm (8 inch) spring-release cake tin. Grease the paper. Sprinkle a thin layer of caster sugar over the inside, then dust with a little flour.

2 Whisk the eggs and sugar together in a bowl, using an electric beater at high speed, until thick and light in colour. Carefully fold in the flour, using a large metal spoon. Immediately pour into the prepared cake tin.

3 ■■ Bake on the grid shelf on the floor of the ROASTING OVEN with the cold plain shelf on the third set of runners for 18-20 minutes or until just firm in the centre, turning the cake around carefully after 10-12 minutes.
■■■■ Bake on the grid shelf on the fourth set of runners in the BAKING OVEN for 18-20 minutes or until just firm in the centre, turning the cake around carefully after 10-12 minutes.

4 Leave the sponge in the tin for 5 minutes, then carefully turn out onto a wire rack to cool.

5 Lightly whip the cream until soft peaks form, then add the caster sugar and vanilla essence to taste. Chill in the refrigerator until needed.

6 Carefully split the cake in half, using a serrated knife. If using strawberry conserve, spread over the bottom layer, then cover with the cream. If using strawberries, spread half of the whipped cream on the bottom layer, cover with the strawberries, then top with the remaining cream.

7 Position the top cake layer over the filling and press down lightly. Chill until ready to serve.

8 Sprinkle the top of the cake with icing sugar to serve.

APPLE AND WALNUT CAKE

■ 8 SLICES ■ PREPARATION 25 MINUTES, PLUS COOLING

■ COOKING 40 MINUTES ■ FREEZING NOT SUITABLE

■ 375 CALS PER SLICE

175 g (6 oz) soft light brown sugar (see cook's tips)
250 g (9 oz) butter
900 g (2 lb) dessert apples, such as Cox's
grated rind of 1 lemon
2.5 ml (1/2 tsp) ground nutmeg
2.5 ml (1/2 tsp) ground cinnamon
50 g (2 oz) walnut pieces
175 g (6 oz) caster sugar
3 eggs, separated
15 ml (1 tbsp) milk
175 g (6 oz) plain white flour
TO SERVE
crème fraîche
1-2 pieces preserved stem ginger in syrup, drained and
chopped

1 Put the brown sugar and 75 g (3 oz) of the butter in a heavy-based saucepan in the SIMMERING OVEN until melted. Transfer to the SIMMERING PLATE, bring to the boil and cook for 2 minutes, stirring. Spread two-thirds over the base of a 25 cm (10 inch) spring-release cake tin. Carefully add 150 ml (1/4 pint) water to the caramel remaining in the pan and return to the heat. Bring to the boil and simmer until the caramel is dissolved and syrupy.

2 Peel, core and thickly slice the apples. Arrange over the base of the tin. Mix together the grated lemon rind, nutmeg, cinnamon and walnuts. Scatter over the apples.

3 Cream the remaining butter and caster sugar together in a bowl. Gradually beat in the egg yolks with the milk. In a separate bowl, whisk the egg whites until stiff. Fold into the creamed mixture, alternately with the flour. Spoon the mixture over the apples in the tin and smooth evenly.

4 Bake on the grid shelf on the floor of the ROASTING OVEN for 40 minutes. Slide the cold plain shelf onto the runners just above towards the end of cooking if the cake appears to be over-browning.

5 Leave to cool in the tin for 5 minutes, then invert onto a wire rack and brush the apples with the remaining caramel. Serve while still slightly warm, with crème fraîche flavoured with a little chopped stem ginger.

COOK'S TIPS

▶ For optimum colour and flavour, use light muscovado sugar.

▶ This cake will keep well wrapped in foil and stored in an airtight container in a cool place for up to 2 days.

RICH CHOCOLATE CAKE

■ 16 SLICES ■ PREPARATION 25 MINUTES, PLUS COOLING

■ COOKING 50 MINUTES-1½ HOURS ■ FREEZING SUITABLE: STAGE 6

■ 495 CALS PER SLICE

A moist, dark chocolate cake – flavoured with a hint of orange and enriched with almonds – is covered with an indulgent chocolate ganache.

375 g (13 oz) plain chocolate, in pieces
175 g (6 oz) butter, softened
175 g (6 oz) caster sugar
175 g (6 oz) ground almonds
6 eggs, separated
75 g (3 oz) fresh brown breadcrumbs
45 ml (3 tbsp) cocoa powder
grated rind and juice of 1 orange
pinch of salt
125 g (4 oz) white chocolate, roughly chopped
125 g (4 oz) milk chocolate, roughly chopped
150 ml (¼ pint) double cream

1 Grease and line a deep 23 cm (9 inch) round cake tin.

2 Put 225 g (8 oz) of the plain chocolate in a heatproof bowl in the SIMMERING OVEN and leave for approximately 20 minutes (or place at the back of the Aga) until melted; cool slightly.

3 Beat the butter and sugar together in a bowl until light and fluffy. Stir in the melted chocolate, together with the ground almonds, egg yolks, breadcrumbs, cocoa powder, orange rind and juice.

4 Whisk the egg whites in another bowl with the salt until soft peaks form. Stir a quarter into the chocolate mixture to lighten it, then fold in the remainder together with the chopped white and milk chocolate.

5 Pour the mixture into the prepared tin and spread evenly. ■■ Bake on the grid shelf on the floor of the ROASTING OVEN, towards the front of the oven, with the cold plain shelf on the second set of runners, for 30-35 minutes until the top is set and beginning to colour. Transfer the plain shelf to the middle of the SIMMERING OVEN. Carefully transfer the cake to this shelf, positioning it towards the back of the oven and bake for a further 50-60 minutes, until a skewer inserted in the centre comes out clean.
■■■ Place on the grid shelf on the floor of the BAKING OVEN, positioning the cake towards the front right hand side. Bake for 50 minutes or until cooked through to the centre; check after 30-35 minutes and cover loosely with foil if the cake appears to be over-browning.

6 Leave to cool in the tin for 15 minutes before turning out on to a wire rack.

7 For the ganache topping, place the remaining 150 g (5 oz) plain chocolate and cream in a small heavy-based pan on the SIMMERING PLATE and stir occasionally until melted. Allow to cool for about 30 minutes or until slightly thickened. Pour the chocolate ganache over the cake to cover the top and sides. Leave until cool and set.

COOK'S TIP This cake will keep well stored in an airtight container for up to 5 days.

CARROT CAKE WITH MASCARPONE TOPPING

■ 8-10 SLICES ■ PREPARATION 30 MINUTES, PLUS COOLING
■ COOKING 30-40 MINUTES ■ FREEZING SUITABLE: STAGE 4
■ 735-570 CALS PER SLICE

For this carrot cake, Brazil nuts replace the more familiar walnuts and mild, creamy mascarpone provides a delicious smooth frosting. The crowning glory is a rich decoration of fried carrot shavings – crisp, golden and lightly sugared. You could, of course, apply a sprinkling of chopped toasted nuts instead.

125 g (4 oz) Brazil nuts, coarsely chopped
225 g (8 oz) unsalted butter, softened
225 g (8 oz) caster sugar
175 g (6 oz) self-raising white flour
5 ml (1 tsp) baking powder
2.5 ml (½ tsp) ground allspice
4 eggs
grated rind of 1 orange
15 ml (1 tbsp) orange juice
50 g (2 oz) ground almonds
350 g (12 oz) carrots, peeled and finely grated
FROSTING
250 g (9 oz) mascarpone or low-fat cream cheese
5 ml (1 tsp) finely grated orange rind (optional)
30 ml (2 tbsp) orange juice
30 ml (2 tbsp) icing sugar
TO DECORATE
1 large carrot
oil, for frying
icing sugar, for dusting

1 Grease and base-line two 20 cm (8 inch) sandwich tins. Spread the Brazil nuts on a baking sheet and lightly toast on the grid shelf on the floor of the ROASTING OVEN for 5-10 minutes.

2 Cream the butter and sugar together in a bowl until pale and fluffy. Sift the flour, baking powder and allspice over the mixture. Add the eggs, orange rind and juice, and the ground almonds; beat well. Stir in the grated carrots and Brazil nuts.

3 Divide the mixture between the prepared tins and level the surfaces.
■ ■ Bake on the grid shelf on the floor of the ROASTING OVEN with the cold plain shelf on the second set of runners for 30-40 minutes until firm to the touch.
■ ■ ■ ■ Bake on the grid shelf on the fourth set of runners in the BAKING OVEN for 35-40 minutes until firm to the touch.

4 Leave in the tins for a few minutes, then turn out onto a wire rack to cool.

5 For the topping, beat the cheese, orange rind if using, orange juice and icing sugar together in a bowl until smooth. Use half to sandwich the cakes together. Spread the remainder over the top of the cake, swirling it attractively.

6 For the decoration, peel the carrot and pare into long thin ribbons, using a swivel vegetable peeler. Dry the carrot ribbons on kitchen paper. Heat a 1 cm (½ inch) depth of oil in a frying pan on the BOILING PLATE until a piece of carrot added to the hot oil sizzles on the surface. Fry the carrots, in two batches, until they shrink and turn golden. Drain with a slotted spoon and dry on kitchen paper.

7 Scatter the carrot ribbons over the top of the cake and dust with icing sugar. Chill until ready to serve.

COOK'S TIP *It is important to thoroughly dry the carrot ribbons before frying to ensure a crisp result.*

VARIATION For a simple finish, omit the carrot topping and sprinkle with chopped toasted Brazil nuts instead.

CHOCOLATE PECAN FUDGE CAKE

■ 16 SLICES ■ PREPARATION 50 MINUTES, PLUS COOLING
■ COOKING 15-20 MINUTES ■ FREEZING SUITABLE: STAGE 3
■ 465 CALS PER SLICE

Layers of dark, moist chocolate cake are sandwiched together with a filling of chocolate fudge icing, toasted pecan nuts and sweet maple syrup. Piled high with chocolate curls, this cake really is the ultimate taste in chocolate.

175 g (6 oz) butter, softened
175 g (6 oz) caster sugar
175 g (6 oz) self-raising white flour
50 g (2 oz) cocoa powder
10 ml (2 tsp) baking powder
4 eggs
10 ml (2 tsp) vanilla essence
45 ml (3 tbsp) water
ICING
300 g (10 oz) plain dark chocolate
50 g (2 oz) unsalted butter
60 ml (4 tbsp) milk
225 g (8 oz) icing sugar
FILLING
50 g (2 oz) pecan nuts, roughly chopped
60 ml (4 tbsp) maple syrup
TO DECORATE
200 g (7 oz) plain dark chocolate
cocoa powder, for dusting

1 Grease and base-line two 20 cm (8 inch) sandwich tins.

2 Beat the butter and sugar together in a bowl until light and fluffy. Sift the flour, cocoa and baking powder together over the creamed mixture. Add the eggs, vanilla essence and water. Beat, using an electric whisk, for 2 minutes until smooth and paler in colour.

3 Divide the mixture between the prepared tins and level the surfaces.
■ ■ Bake on the grid shelf on the floor of the ROASTING OVEN with the cold plain shelf on the second set of runners for 20-25 minutes until just firm in the centre, transposing the cakes after about 15 minutes to ensure even cooking.
■ ■ ■ Bake on the grid shelf on the fourth set of runners in the BAKING OVEN for 20 minutes or until just firm in the centre, swapping the cakes around after 15 minutes. Turn out onto a wire rack to cool.

4 To make the icing, break up the chocolate and place in a saucepan with the butter and milk. Cover and place in the SIMMERING OVEN for 10-15 minutes until the chocolate and butter are melted. Beat in the icing sugar. Place on the SIMMERING PLATE and stir gently until evenly combined.

5 Set aside three quarters of the icing for the topping. Add the chopped pecans and maple syrup to the remaining quarter and use to sandwich the cakes together. Swirl the rest of the icing over the top and sides of the cake with a palette knife.

6 To make the chocolate curls for the decoration, break up the chocolate and place in a heatproof bowl in the SIMMERING OVEN or at the back of the Aga, until melted, then spread evenly onto a marble slab or work surface. Leave until just set, then draw the blade of a knife, held at a 45° angle, across the chocolate to shave off curls.

7 Scatter the chocolate curls over the top of the cake and dust lightly with cocoa powder to serve.

COOK'S TIP *If the chocolate breaks as you shape the curls, it has set too hard and should be left in a warm place for a few minutes before trying again.*

VARIATION For a simple finish, omit the chocolate curls and decorate the top with pecan halves.

CHRISTMAS CAKE

■ 16 SLICES ■ PREPARATION 1 HOUR, PLUS STANDING

■ COOKING 4-5 HOURS ■ FREEZING UNNECESSARY

■ 660 CALS PER SLICE

This is best made 4-6 weeks ahead to allow time to mature. For convenience, cover with ready-made almond paste and ready-to-roll icing. Finish with a festive ribbon and decorations of your choice.

150 g (5 oz) glacé cherries
150 g (5 oz) dried figs
150 g (5 oz) apricots
150 g (5 oz) dates
150 g (5 oz) raisins
150 g (5 oz) sultanas
50 g (2 oz) mixed peel, chopped
175 ml (6 fl oz) dark rum
175 g (6 oz) skinned, roasted hazelnuts
225 g (8 oz) butter, softened
grated rind of 1 lemon
225 g (8 oz) soft dark brown sugar
4 eggs, beaten
30 ml (2 tbsp) black treacle
225 g (8 oz) plain white flour
10 ml (2 tsp) ground mixed spice
TO FINISH
30-45 ml (2-3 tbsp) apricot jam, warmed and sieved
450 g (1 lb) white almond paste
450 g (1 lb) ready-to-roll fondant icing

1 Grease and line a deep 20 cm (8 inch) round cake tin with a double thickness of greaseproof paper. Rinse the glacé cherries under cold water to remove all the syrup; drain and dry on kitchen paper.

2 Very roughly chop the cherries, figs, apricots and dates. Put all the fruit and the peel in a bowl. Pour on two thirds of the dark rum and leave to soak.

3 Finely grind 50 g (2 oz) of the hazelnuts in a blender or food processor; roughly chop the remainder.

4 In a large mixing bowl, beat the butter with the lemon rind until soft and pale. Gradually beat in the sugar until well mixed. Slowly beat the eggs into the creamed ingredients. Add the treacle, beating again until evenly blended.

5 Sift the flour and spice together and fold half into the creamed mixture with the ground and chopped hazelnuts. Gently fold in all of the fruit, followed by the remaining flour. Spoon into the prepared cake tin, then level off the surface. Tie a band of brown paper around the outside of the tin. Brush a little cold water on top of the cake.

6 ■ ■ Bake on the grid shelf on the floor of the ROASTING OVEN, with the cold plain shelf set on the runners just above, for 1 hour. Move the plain shelf to the middle of the SIMMERING OVEN. Transfer the cake to this shelf, positioning it towards the back and bake for a further 3-4 hours, or until a skewer inserted into the centre comes out clean.
■ ■ ■ Bake on the grid shelf on the fourth set of runners in the BAKING OVEN for 1 hour, until the top is beginning to set and darken. Transfer to the hot plain shelf in the middle of the SIMMERING OVEN, positioning towards the back and bake for a further 3-4 hours or until a skewer inserted into the centre comes out clean.

7 Pierce the surface with a fine skewer and spoon over the remaining rum. Leave the cake in the tin for 1 hour, then turn out and cool on a wire rack. When cold, remove all the lining paper and wrap tightly in fresh greaseproof paper and foil. Store in a cool, dry place for at least 1 week.

8 To finish the cake, brush the top and sides with the warm apricot jam. On a surface lightly dusted with icing sugar, roll out the almond paste to a circle, large enough to cover the top and sides of the cake, ie about 10 cm (4 inches) bigger than the cake top. Place over the cake, press gently around the sides, then trim the edges to neaten. Leave in a cool dry place for 1-2 days before applying the icing.

9 Sprinkle a work surface and rolling pin with cornflour. Roll out the fondant icing to a round, about 10 cm (4 inches) larger than the cake top. With the help of the rolling pin, lift the icing on top of the cake, allowing it to drape over the edges. Dust your hands with cornflour and press the icing onto the sides of the cake; trim off excess at the base. Gently rub the surface in a circular movement to buff the icing and make it smooth. Apply the ribbon, securing with dots of icing and add decorations of your choice.

COOK'S TIPS

▶ *If preferred, bake this cake in the middle of the SIMMERING OVEN only, for about 11 hours until cooked through to the centre. The resulting cake will have a very moist texture.*
▶ *Ideally make the cake up to 6 weeks ahead and feed weekly (as in step 7) with 15-30 ml (1-2 tbsp) rum.*

RIPPLED DATE AND BANANA LOAF

■ 8-10 SLICES ■ PREPARATION 20 MINUTES, PLUS COOLING
■ COOKING 1¼-1¾ HOURS ■ FREEZING SUITABLE
■ 495-395 CALS PER SLICE

**250 g (9 oz) stoned dried dates
grated rind and juice of 1 lemon
2 ripe bananas
175 g (6 oz) unsalted butter, softened
175 g (6 oz) caster sugar
3 eggs
5 ml (1 tsp) vanilla essence
225 g (8 oz) self-raising white flour
2.5 ml (½ tsp) baking powder**

1 Grease and base-line a 1.1 litre (2 pint) loaf tin. Set aside 4 dates. Place the remainder in a small heavy-based pan and add the lemon rind and juice, and 90 ml (3 fl oz) water. Cover and bring to the boil on the SIMMERING PLATE, then cook in the SIMMERING OVEN for 15 minutes until the dates are soft and pulpy. Mash with a fork.

2 Mash the bananas until smooth. Cream the butter and sugar together in a bowl until pale and fluffy. Add the banana purée, eggs and vanilla. Sift the flour and baking powder into the bowl and beat until thoroughly combined.

3 Spoon a third of the banana mixture into the prepared loaf tin and level the surface. Spread half of the date purée over the surface. Repeat these layers, then cover with the remaining banana mixture. Cut the reserved dates into thin lengths and scatter them over the surface.

4 ■■ Bake on the grid shelf on the floor of the ROASTING OVEN with the cold plain shelf on the second set of runners for 20 minutes or until golden brown. Move the plain shelf to the middle of the SIMMERING OVEN. Carefully transfer the cake to this shelf, positioning it towards the back. Bake for a further 1¼-1½ hours, until cooked through to the centre.
■■■■ Bake on the grid shelf on the floor of the BAKING OVEN towards the front right hand side for 1¼-1½ hours, until firm to the touch, covering with foil after 30 minutes if the top appears to be over-browning.

5 Leave in the tin for 15 minutes, then transfer to a wire rack to cool. Store in an airtight container for up to 1 week.

COOK'S TIP The date purée must be similar in consistency to the banana mixture. If too thick, add a little water.

CRUMBLY APPLE AND CHEESE CAKE

■ 10 SLICES ■ PREPARATION 20 MINUTES, PLUS COOLING
■ COOKING 50 MINUTES-1½ HOURS ■ FREEZING SUITABLE
345 CALS PER SLICE

This moist, crumbly fruit cake conceals a layer of tart cheese, which perfectly complements the sweet tang of the apples. Serve still slightly warm – to accentuate the flavours. You will also find that the cake reheats well.

**575 g (1¼ lb) dessert apples
175 g (6 oz) self-raising white flour
5 ml (1 tsp) baking powder
75 g (3 oz) light muscovado sugar
50 g (2 oz) raisins
50 g (2 oz) sultanas
50 g (2 oz) Brazil nuts, roughly chopped
2 eggs
90 ml (3 fl oz) sunflower oil
225 g (8 oz) Caerphilly or Wensleydale cheese
TO FINISH
icing sugar, for sprinkling**

1 Grease and base-line a 5 cm (2 inch) deep, 23 cm (9 inch) round loose-based flan tin. Peel, core and thinly slice the apples.

2 Sift the flour and baking powder into a bowl. Stir in the sugar, raisins, sultanas, nuts and apples, and mix until evenly combined. Beat the eggs with the oil and add to the dry ingredients. Stir until evenly incorporated.

3 Turn half the mixture into the prepared cake tin and level the surface. Crumble the cheese over the surface, then spoon on the remaining cake mixture. Spread the mixture to the edges of the tin, but do not smooth; a rough surface gives a more interesting finish.

4 ■■ Bake on the grid shelf on the floor of the ROASTING OVEN with the cold plain shelf on the second set of runners for 30 minutes or until just firm in the centre, turning the

cake around after 20 minutes. Move the plain shelf to the middle of the SIMMERING OVEN. Carefully transfer the cake to this shelf, positioning it towards the back of the oven and cook for a further 1 hour or until just firm.

▪▪▪▪ Bake on the grid shelf on the fourth set of runners in the BAKING OVEN for 50 minutes or until just firm in the centre, turning the cake around after 20 minutes to ensure even cooking. If the cake appears to be over-browning towards the end of cooking, cover with foil.

5 Leave to cool in the tin for 10 minutes, then transfer to a wire rack. Serve warm, sprinkled with icing sugar.

STICKY ORANGE FLAPJACKS

■ MAKES 18 ■ PREPARATION 15 MINUTES

■ COOKING 20-30 MINUTES ■ FREEZING SUITABLE

■ 300 CALS PER FLAPJACK

2 small oranges
250 g (9 oz) unsalted butter, in pieces
250 g (9 oz) caster sugar
175 g (6 oz) golden syrup
425 g (15 oz) porridge oats
30 ml (2 tbsp) sunflower seeds
45 ml (3 tbsp) fine-shred orange marmalade

1 Grease and base-line the small roasting tin. Using a citrus zester, finely pare the rind from the oranges in strips.

2 Place the orange rind in a heavy-based saucepan with the butter, sugar and syrup. Melt on the SIMMERING PLATE, then remove from the heat and stir in the oats, until evenly coated in syrup.

3 Turn the mixture into the prepared tin and level the surface. Sprinkle with the sunflower seeds.

■ ■ Bake on the grid shelf on the floor of the ROASTING OVEN, with the cold plain shelf on the second set of runners for 20-25 minutes until deep golden brown all over, turning the tin around after 10 minutes to ensure even baking.
■ ■ ■ ■ Hang from the third set of runners in the BAKING OVEN for 25-30 minutes until deep golden brown, turning the tin around after 15 minutes.

4 Leave in the tin until almost cold. Heat the marmalade in a small saucepan with 15 ml (1 tbsp) water until syrupy. Brush evenly over the flapjack. Cut into 18 bars and store in an airtight container for up to 1 week.

COOK'S TIP *To weigh syrup, first measure out the sugar quantity and leave it in the scales bowl, making a small well in the centre. Add extra weights for the required quantity of syrup and spoon the syrup into the well. Both sugar and syrup will then slide cleanly into the saucepan.*

VARIATIONS

Fruit and Nut Flapjacks: Omit the orange rind, sunflower seeds and marmalade. Add 125 g (4 oz) luxury mixed dried fruit and 75 g (3 oz) chopped and toasted mixed nuts to the mixture with the oats.

Pear and Cinnamon Flapjacks: Omit the orange rind, sunflower seeds and marmalade. Add 5 ml (1 tsp) ground cinnamon with the sugar, and 150 g (5 oz) roughly chopped dried pears with the oats.

STICKY GINGERBREAD

■ 12 SLICES ■ PREPARATION 20 MINUTES, PLUS COOLING

■ COOKING 1¼-1½ HOURS ■ FREEZING SUITABLE

■ 350 CALS PER SLICE

Sticky black treacle and syrupy stem ginger make a perfect partnership in this delicious adaptation of an all-time favourite. Grated cooking apple is added for extra moisture, without detracting from the warm spiciness of the ginger. Once baked, a gloss of ginger syrup adds the finishing touch.

150 g (5 oz) preserved stem ginger in syrup, plus
45 ml (3 tbsp) syrup from jar
1 large cooking apple, about 225 g (8 oz)
15 ml (1 tbsp) lemon juice
125 g (4 oz) black treacle
125 g (4 oz) golden syrup
175 g (6 oz) molasses or dark muscovado sugar
175 g (6 oz) unsalted butter
225 g (8 oz) plain white flour
125 g (4 oz) plain wholemeal flour
5 ml (1 tsp) ground mixed spice
7.5 ml (1½ tsp) bicarbonate of soda
2 eggs

1 Grease and line a deep 18 cm (7 inch) square cake tin. Thinly slice the ginger pieces. Peel, core and quarter the apple; immerse in a bowl of water with the lemon juice added to prevent discolouration.

2 Put the treacle, syrup and molasses or muscovado sugar in a saucepan. Cut the butter into pieces and add to the pan. Place in the SIMMERING OVEN until the butter is melted; leave to cool slightly.

3 Sift the flours, mixed spice and bicarbonate of soda into a bowl. Grate three quarters of the apple into the bowl and toss lightly in the flour. Add the melted syrup mixture, eggs and three quarters of the ginger pieces. Beat well until thoroughly combined.

4 Turn the mixture into the prepared tin, spreading it into the corners. Using a potato peeler, pare the remaining apple into thin slices. Scatter the apple slices and remaining ginger over the surface of the gingerbread and press down lightly into the mixture with the tip of a knife.

5 ■■ Place on the grid shelf on the floor of the ROASTING OVEN towards the front, and slide the cold plain shelf onto the third set of runners. Bake for about 40 minutes, then slide the plain shelf onto the middle set of runners in the SIMMERING OVEN and transfer the cake to this shelf, positioning it towards the back. Bake for a further 35-40 minutes or until firm to the touch.
■■■■ Bake on the grid shelf on the fourth set of runners in the BAKING OVEN for 1½ hours, or until firm to the touch.

6 Leave to cool in the tin, then turn out onto a wire rack and drizzle the ginger syrup over the surface.

COOK'S TIPS
▶ *Gingerbread will keep well in an airtight tin for up to 1 week. It's best stored for several days before eating to allow the flavours to develop.*
▶ *For a more pronounced flavour, add 10 ml (2 tsp) ground ginger with the mixed spice.*

SHORTBREAD

■ MAKES 20 ■ PREPARATION 20 MINUTES, PLUS CHILLING
■ COOKING 15-20 MINUTES ■ FREEZING NOT SUITABLE
270-180 CALS PER SHORTBREAD

With its rich buttery flavour, this shortbread literally melts in the mouth! Make sure all of the ingredients are at room temperature before you start.

225 g (8 oz) butter
125 g (4 oz) caster sugar
225 g (8 oz) plain white flour
125 g (4 oz) ground rice or rice flour
pinch of salt
TO DECORATE
golden or coloured granulated sugar, for coating
caster sugar, for sprinkling

1 Line a baking sheet with greaseproof paper. Cream the butter and sugar together in a bowl until pale and fluffy. Sift the flour, rice flour and salt together onto the mixture; stir in, using a wooden spoon, until it resembles breadcrumbs.

2 Gather the dough together with your hand and turn onto a clean work surface. Knead lightly until it forms a ball, then lightly roll into a sausage, about 5 cm (2 inches) thick. Wrap in cling film and chill until firm.

3 Unwrap the roll and slice into discs, about 7-10 mm (⅓-½ inch) thick. Pour golden or coloured granulated sugar onto a plate and roll the edge of each disc in the sugar. Place the biscuits, cut-side up, on the baking sheet.

4 ■■ Bake on the grid shelf on the fourth set of runners in the ROASTING OVEN with the cold plain shelf on the top set of runners for 15-20 minutes depending on thickness, until very pale golden.
■■■■ Bake on the grid shelf on the fourth set of runners in the BAKING OVEN for 15-20 minutes, depending on thickness, until very pale golden.

5 Remove from the oven and sprinkle with caster sugar. Leave on the baking sheet for 10 minutes, then transfer to a wire rack to cool.

COOK'S TIPS
▶ *Never overwork shortbread or it will become tough.*
▶ *Take care to avoid overcooking too – shortbread should never really colour, just set and turn very pale.*

VARIATIONS
▶ **Spiced Shortbread:** Sift 7.5 ml (½ tsp) ground mixed spice with the flours.
▶ **Ginger Shortbread:** Sift 2.5 ml (½ tsp) ground ginger with the flours. Add 25 g (1 oz) chopped crystallised ginger to the dough.
▶ **Chocolate Chip Shortbread:** Knead 25 g (1 oz) chocolate chips into the dough.

SCONES

■ MAKES 10 ■ PREPARATION 15 MINUTES, PLUS COOLING

■ COOKING ABOUT 12 MINUTES ■ FREEZING SUITABLE

■ 240 CALS PER SCONE

450 g (1 lb) plain white flour
large pinch of salt
15 ml (1 tbsp) baking powder
75 g (3 oz) butter
25 g (1 oz) caster sugar
1 egg
200 ml (7 fl oz) milk
milk, for brushing
TO SERVE
jam
whipped or clotted cream, or butter

1 Sift the flour, salt and baking powder together into a mixing bowl. Cut the butter into cubes, add to the flour and rub in lightly, using the fingertips, until the mixture resembles fine crumbs. Stir in the caster sugar.

2 Whisk the egg and milk together. Stir the milk mixture into the dry ingredients to give a soft, slightly sticky dough; if necessary, add an extra 15-30 ml (1-2 tbsp) milk.

3 Turn out the dough onto a lightly floured surface and knead very lightly until the dough just comes together.

4 Lightly roll out to about a 2 cm (¾ inch) thickness and stamp out rounds, using a 6 cm (2½ inch) plain cutter or cut into triangles or rectangles with a knife.

5 Place on the greased plain shelf and brush the tops with milk. Immediately slide onto the third set of runners in the ROASTING OVEN. Bake for 12 minutes or until well risen and brown on top.

6 Transfer to a wire rack to cool. Serve warm, with jam and cream or butter.

COOK'S TIP *Alternatively use a food processor to prepare the scone dough. Use the pulse button when adding the liquid to ensure the dough isn't overworked.*

VARIATION

Fruit Scones: Add 125g (4 oz) raisins, sultanas or chopped dates to the mixture at the end of stage 1.

WHITE CHOCOLATE BROWNIES

■ MAKES 12 ■ PREPARATION 20 MINUTES, PLUS COOLING

■ COOKING 20-45 MINUTES ■ FREEZING SUITABLE

■ 490 CALS PER BROWNIE

Deliciously moist, laden with chocolate and crusted in a glossy coat of sugar, chocolate brownies are one of the most adorable teatime treats! This luxurious white chocolate version is packed with hazelnuts and generous chunks of creamy white chocolate.

500 g (1 lb 2 oz) white chocolate
75 g (3 oz) butter
3 eggs
175 g (6 oz) caster sugar
175 g (6 oz) self-raising white flour
pinch of salt
175 g (6 oz) shelled hazelnuts, roughly chopped
5 ml (1 tsp) vanilla essence

1 Grease and line the small Aga roasting tin.

2 Roughly chop 400 g (14 oz) of the chocolate and set aside. Break up the remaining chocolate and put into a heatproof bowl with the butter. Put in the SIMMERING OVEN for about 20 minutes (or place at the back of the Aga) until melted. Leave to cool slightly.

3 Whisk the eggs and caster sugar together in a large bowl until smooth, then gradually beat in the melted chocolate mixture.

4 Sift the flour and salt together over the mixture, then carefully fold in, together with the hazelnuts, chopped chocolate and vanilla essence.

5 Turn the mixture into the prepared tin and level the surface.
■ ■ Slide the roasting tin onto the lowest set of runners in the ROASTING OVEN, positioning it at the front, with the cold plain shelf set on the top set of runners. Bake for 25 minutes, then move the hot plain shelf to the middle of the SIMMERING OVEN and transfer the roasting tin to this shelf. Bake for a further 10-20 minutes, until the centre is just firm to the touch and the surface is crusty.

■ ■ ■ ■ Slide the roasting tin onto the top set of runners in the BAKING OVEN and bake for 20-25 minutes, turning the tin around after the first 15 minutes.

6 Leave to cool in the tin. Turn out and cut into 12 squares. Store in an airtight container for up to 1 week.

COOK'S TIP *When cooked, the mixture will still be soft under the crust; it firms up during cooling.*

VARIATIONS Use any other roughly chopped nuts instead of the hazelnuts. Almonds, walnuts, pecans, macadamia nuts and Brazil nuts are all suitable.

HONEY AND YOGURT MUFFINS

■ MAKES 12 ■ PREPARATION 15 MINUTES, PLUS COOLING
■ COOKING 15-20 MINUTES ■ FREEZING SUITABLE
■ 180 CALS PER MUFFIN

American-style muffins rise considerably during baking to produce a wonderful craggy texture and typically 'top heavy' appearance. This honey and yogurt version is light, airy and perfect served with just a dot of butter while still warm. For a sweeter variation, try the rippled chocolate and banana variation.

225 g (8 oz) plain white flour
7.5 ml (1½ tsp) baking powder
5 ml (1 tsp) bicarbonate of soda
pinch of salt
2.5 ml (½ tsp) ground mixed spice
1.25 ml (¼ tsp) ground nutmeg
50 g (2 oz) medium oatmeal
50 g (2 oz) light muscovado sugar
50 g (2 oz) butter
225 g (8 oz) Greek-style yogurt
125 ml (4 fl oz) milk
1 egg
60 ml (4 tbsp) clear honey
medium oatmeal, for dusting

1 Line 12 deep bun tins or muffin tins with paper muffin cases. Sift the flour, baking powder, bicarbonate of soda, salt, mixed spice and nutmeg into a bowl. Stir in the oatmeal and sugar.

2 Melt the butter in a heatproof bowl in the SIMMERING OVEN and leave to cool slightly. Mix the yogurt and milk together in a bowl, then beat in the egg, butter and honey.

3 Pour over the dry ingredients and stir in quickly until only just blended; do not over-mix – the dough should still be lumpy with specks of flour still visible.

4 Divide the muffin mixture equally between the paper cases and sprinkle with oatmeal. Bake on the grid shelf on the floor of the ROASTING OVEN, positioning towards the front of the oven, for 15-20 minutes until well risen and just firm to the touch.

5 Leave in the tins for 5 minutes, then transfer to a wire rack. Serve warm or cold, with a little butter if desired.

VARIATION

Chocolate Banana Muffins: Omit the honey. Mash 1 small ripe banana and mix with 125 g (4 oz) melted plain chocolate. Add to the muffin mixture at stage 2, after the liquids, blending until rippled with colour.

DOUBLE CHOCOLATE COOKIES

■ MAKES 18 ■ PREPARATION 15 MINUTES, PLUS COOLING
■ COOKING 8-10 MINUTES ■ FREEZING SUITABLE
■ 215 CALS PER BISCUIT

Chunky, crumbly and rich with chocolate, these delicious biscuits closely resemble home-baked American-style cookies.

125 g (4 oz) white chocolate
125 g (4 oz) plain dark chocolate
125 g (4 oz) unsalted butter, softened
125 g (4 oz) caster sugar
1 egg
5 ml (1 tsp) vanilla essence
125 g (4 oz) porridge oats
150 g (5 oz) plain white flour
2.5 ml (½ tsp) baking powder

1 Lightly grease two baking sheets: you will need to bake the cookies in 2 batches. Chop the white and plain chocolate into small chunks, each no larger than 1 cm (½ inch) in diameter.

2 Put the butter and sugar in a bowl and beat until creamy and paler in colour. Add the egg, vanilla essence and oats. Sift the flour and baking powder into the bowl and mix until evenly combined. Stir in the chocolate.

3 Place dessertspoonfuls of the mixture on the prepared baking sheets, spacing them well apart to allow room for spreading. Flatten slightly with the back of a fork.

4 ■■ Bake, one sheet at a time, on the grid shelf on the fourth set of runners in the ROASTING OVEN with the cold plain shelf on the top set of runners for 8 minutes or until risen and turning golden (see cook's tip).

■■■■ Bake, one sheet at a time, on the third set of runners in the BAKING OVEN for 10 minutes or until just tinged golden brown at the edges and still soft in the centre.

5 Leave on the baking sheet for 5 minutes, then transfer to a wire rack to cool. Store in an airtight tin for up to 1 week.

COOK'S TIPS

▶ *Don't position the biscuits too close to the edge of the baking sheet or they will cook unevenly.*
▶ *Remember to cool the cold shelf between baking the batches of cookies.*
▶ *Turn the baking sheet around halfway through cooking to ensure even baking.*
▶ *The cookies will only become firm as they cool. Don't be tempted to bake them until crisp. If overcooked, the dark chocolate will burn.*

VARIATIONS

▶ **Toasted Pine Nut Cookies:** Cream an extra 25 g (1 oz) sugar with the butter. Replace the chocolate with 40 g (1½ oz) toasted pine nuts. Sprinkle the tops with a further 15 g (½ oz) pine nuts.
▶ **Triple Chocolate Cookies:** Replace 15 g (½ oz) flour with cocoa powder.

ALMOND FUDGE CRUMBLES

■ MAKES 24 ■ PREPARATION 10 MINUTES, PLUS COOLING
■ COOKING 9-12 MINUTES ■ FREEZING SUITABLE
■ 130 CALS PER BISCUIT

75 g (3 oz) flaked almonds
200 g (7 oz) plain white flour
pinch of salt
2.5 ml (½ tsp) bicarbonate of soda
125 g (4 oz) unsalted butter, in small pieces
125 g (4 oz) light muscovado sugar
1 egg
5 ml (1 tsp) almond essence
50 g (2 oz) vanilla fudge, finely diced
TOPPING
25 g (1 oz) flaked almonds, lightly crushed
25 g (1 oz) vanilla fudge, chopped
icing sugar, for dusting

1 Lightly grease two baking sheets: you need to bake the biscuits in 2 batches. Break the almonds into small flakes.

2 Sift the flour, salt and bicarbonate of soda into a bowl. Add the butter and rub in, using the fingertips. Add the sugar, egg, almond essence, flaked almonds and fudge and mix to a fairly firm dough.

3 Turn the dough onto a lightly floured surface and roll into a cylinder, 23 cm (9 inches) long. Cut the dough into 24 rounds. Place 12 rounds, slightly apart, on each baking sheet (see cook's tips).

4 Scatter the crushed almonds and chopped fudge over the biscuits and press down lightly to adhere.

5 ■■ Bake, one sheet at a time, on the grid shelf on the fourth set of runners in the ROASTING OVEN with the cold plain shelf on the top set of runners for 9-10 minutes until turning golden around the edges.
■■■■ Bake, one sheet at a time, on the grid shelf on the second set of runners for 10-12 minutes, until golden around the edges.

6 Loosen the biscuits with a palette knife. Leave on the baking sheets for 5 minutes, then transfer to a wire rack to cool. Serve dusted with icing sugar.

COOK'S TIPS

▶ *Use a slab of vanilla or 'cream' fudge, or individually wrapped sweets.*
▶ *Don't position the biscuits too close to the edge of the baking sheet or they will cook unevenly.*
▶ *Remember to cool the cold shelf between baking the batches of cookies.*
▶ *Turn the baking sheet around for the last few minutes of baking to ensure even cooking.*

VARIATIONS

▶ **Coffee and Walnut Crumbles:** Add 15 ml (1 tbsp) finely ground espresso coffee to the dry ingredients and substitute finely ground walnuts for the almonds.
▶ **Apple and Raisin Crumbles:** Use raisin fudge and substitute chopped dried apples for half of the almonds.

HINNY CAKES WITH SUGARED BLUEBERRIES

■ MAKES 10 ■ PREPARATION 10 MINUTES ■ COOKING 10-13 MINUTES
■ FREEZING NOT SUITABLE ■ 190 CALS PER CAKE

Once fried, these moist spiced teatime cakes are topped
with blueberries and sugar, then lightly toasted to bring
out the full scented flavour of the berries.

175 g (6 oz) self-raising white flour
pinch of salt
5 ml (1 tsp) baking powder
1.25 ml (¼ tsp) ground mace
1.25 ml (¼ tsp) ground cloves
50 g (2 oz) unsalted butter, in small pieces
25 g (1 oz) ground rice
25 g (1 oz) caster sugar
90 ml (3 fl oz) milk
a little oil, for cooking
TO FINISH
225-350 g (8-12 oz) blueberries
40 g (1½ oz) caster sugar

1 Sift the flour, salt, baking powder, mace and cloves into a
bowl. Add the butter and rub in using the fingertips until the
mixture resembles fine breadcrumbs. Stir in the ground rice
and caster sugar. Add the milk and mix to a fairly soft
dough, using a round-bladed knife.

2 Turn the dough out onto a lightly floured surface and
knead very lightly. Cut into 10 even-sized pieces. Using
lightly floured hands, shape each piece into a flat cake.

3 Lightly oil the SIMMERING PLATE, using a piece of
kitchen paper dipped in oil. Place the cakes directly on the
SIMMERING PLATE and fry for 3 minutes until golden
underneath. Turn the cakes over and cook for a further
3 minutes or until cooked through. Transfer the hinny cakes
to the plain Aga shelf.

4 Spoon the blueberries onto the cakes, piling them up
slightly in the centre. Sprinkle with the sugar. Slide the shelf
onto the top set of runners in the ROASTING OVEN and
cook for 4-7 minutes, watching closely, until the blueberries
are bubbling and the cake edges are lightly toasted. Serve
immediately, with whipped cream, or crème fraîche.

WHOLEMEAL BREAD

■ MAKES FOUR 1 KG (2 LB) LOAVES ■ PREPARATION 30 MINUTES, PLUS RISING

■ COOKING 30-40 MINUTES ■ FREEZING SUITABLE

■ 175-150 CALS PER SLICE

To use the capacity of the Aga oven to the full, it makes sense to bake four 1 kg (2 lb) loaves at a time, freezing those you don't need to eat straight away. A large food mixer with the dough hook, or flat beater attached takes all the hard work out of kneading the dough.

For this recipe, strong, stoneground wholemeal flour is used. If you prefer a lighter loaf, use strong brown flour or replace a proportion of the wholemeal flour with strong white flour. It is possible to use less yeast; the dough will obviously take longer to rise but it will develop a superior flavour.

100g (3½ oz) fresh yeast, or 40 g (1½ oz) dried yeast
200 ml (7 fl oz) warm water
1.4 litres (2½ pints) hand-hot water (approximately)
2.25 kg (5 lb) stoneground wholemeal flour
40 g (1½ oz) salt

1 Grease four 900 g (2 lb) loaf tins.

2 In a bowl, mix the yeast with the 200 ml (7 fl oz) warm water. Leave in a warm place until the yeast has begun to froth.

3 Place the flour and salt in a very large bowl. Make a hollow in the centre and pour in the yeast liquid. Add sufficient hand-hot water to mix to a soft but not sticky dough. Turn out onto a lightly floured surface and knead in 2 or 3 batches until smooth, no longer sticky and elastic in texture.

4 Turn into a lightly floured large bowl, cover with a dry cloth and place on a folded tea-towel on top of the SIMMERING PLATE (or a WARMING PLATE of a 4-oven Aga). Leave to rise until doubled in bulk.

5 Divide the dough into four equal pieces. Shape each one into a sausage shape and place in the tins. Cover with a dry cloth and leave to rise until the dough feels spongy when touched with a finger and springs back. The dough should come to the top of the tin.

6 Bake on the grid shelf on the fourth set of runners in the ROASTING OVEN for 30 minutes. Lower the grid shelf to the floor of the oven and bake for a further 5-10 minutes if necessary until the loaves sound hollow when tapped on the base and the vibration can be felt throughout the loaf (see cook's tip).

7 Turn the loaves out of the tins and cool on a wire rack.

COOK'S TIPS

▶ *The lids of the aga plates are ideal warm spots for rising bread dough. It is important to place a folded tea-towel underneath to ensure that the dough doesn't overheat.*

▶ *For an extra crisp crust, turn the loaf out of the tin after 30 minutes and bake directly on the grid shelf for the last 5-10 minutes.*

▶ *Each loaf cuts into 10-12 slices.*

VARIATION

Assorted Wholemeal Loaves: Make up the dough to the end of stage 4, then divide into 4 equal portions and proceed as follows:

▶ Set aside one portion to make a plain loaf.

▶ Knead 25 g (1 oz) each sesame seeds, poppy seeds and sunflower seeds into one portion, reserving 10 ml (2 tsp) of the mixed seeds.

▶ Add 150 g (5 oz) rye flour and approximately 100 ml (3½ fl oz) warm water to one portion and knead to give a soft dough.

▶ Add 100 g (3½ oz) walnut pieces and 15 ml (1 tbsp) thin honey or molasses to the last portion and knead until evenly blended.

▶ Shape and prove as in step 5. When risen to the tops of the tins, brush the seeded loaf with a little milk and sprinkle with the reserved seeds. Slash the top of the rye loaf 4 or 5 times, using a sharp knife. Bake as above.

FOCACCIA

■ MAKES 2: EACH SERVES 6-8 ■ PREPARATION 30 MINUTES, PLUS RISING

■ COOKING 20-25 MINUTES ■ FREEZING SUITABLE

■ 275-210 CALS PER SERVING

This light multi-purpose bread is used to make sandwiches, and eaten as an accompaniment to soups, stews and hearty dishes throughout Italy. The secret of a truly light focaccia lies in three risings, and dimpling the dough so that it traps olive oil as it bakes; spraying the dough with water helps to keep the bread moist. You can create infinite toppings, and focaccia can be thin and crisp, or thick and soft, as you like!

25 g (1 oz) fresh yeast, or 15 ml (1 tbsp) dried yeast
pinch of sugar
450 ml (3/4 pint) warm water
700 g (1 1/2 lb) strong plain white flour
105 ml (7 tbsp) extra-virgin olive oil
coarse sea or crystal salt, for sprinkling

1 In a bowl, blend the yeast with the sugar and whisk in the warm water. Leave for 10 minutes until frothy. For other yeasts, use according to the manufacturer's instructions.

2 Sift the flour into a large bowl and make a well in the centre. Pour in the yeast mixture and 45 ml (3 tbsp) olive oil. Mix together with a round-bladed knife, then using your hands until the dough comes together.

3 With clean, dry hands, knead the dough on a floured surface for 10 minutes until smooth, elastic and quite soft. If too soft to handle, knead in a little more flour; if too dry, add 15-30 ml (1-2 tbsp) water.

4 Place in a clean oiled bowl and cover with a tea-towel. Place on a folded towel or thick tea-towel on the lid of the SIMMERING PLATE (or on the WARMING PLATE of a 4-oven cooker) and leave to rise for about 1 hour until doubled in size.

5 Lightly oil two shallow 25 cm (10 inch) metal pizza or pie plates (see cook's tip). Knock back the dough and divide in half. Shape each piece into a round ball on a floured surface and roll out to a 25 cm (10 inch) circle. Place in the oiled tins and cover with a damp tea-towel. Place on folded towels or thick tea-towels on the Aga plate lids (or WARMING PLATE of a 4-oven cooker) and leave to rise as before for 30 minutes.

6 Remove the tea-towel and, using your fingertips, make deep dimples all over the surface of the dough. Cover and leave to rise as before once more until doubled in size – about 1 hour.

7 Drizzle over the remaining oil and sprinkle generously with salt. Spray with water and bake in the ROASTING OVEN for 20-25 minutes. Spray with water twice during cooking. Transfer to a wire rack to cool. Eat the same day or freeze as soon as it is cool.

COOK'S TIP *If you do not have two large pizza plates, shape one large focaccia in the large roasting tin instead.*

VARIATIONS

▶ **Rosemary Focaccia:** Insert small sprigs of rosemary into the dough at intervals at the end of stage 6.

▶ **Sage and Onion Focaccia:** Chop 20 sage leaves. Peel and thinly slice 2 small red onions. Knead the chopped sage into the dough at stage 3. Sprinkle the dough with extra sage leaves and the onion slices at stage 7 before baking.

▶ **Olive and Sun-dried Tomato Focaccia:** Drain 50 g (2 oz) sun-dried tomatoes in oil; slice and knead into the dough at stage 3. Sprinkle the dough with 225 g (8 oz) black or green olives at stage 7, before baking.

PRESERVES

PUMPKIN, APRICOT AND ALMOND CHUTNEY

■ MAKES 1.6 KG (3½ LB) ■ PREPARATION 30 MINUTES
■ COOKING 3-3½ HOURS ■ 50 CALS PER 25 G (1 OZ)

This golden chutney must be allowed to mature and mellow for at least 1 month before using. Serve with cold meats and cheese.

450 g (1 lb) wedge of pumpkin
600 ml (1 pint) cider vinegar
450 g (1 lb) soft light brown sugar
400 g (14 oz) onions, peeled and sliced
225 g (8 oz) dried apricots (not no-need-to-soak), cut into chunks
225 g (8 oz) sultanas
finely grated rind and juice of 1 orange
30 ml (2 tbsp) salt
2.5 ml (½ tsp) turmeric
2 cardamom pods, crushed
5 ml (1 tsp) mild chilli seasoning
10 ml (2 tsp) coriander seeds
125 g (4 oz) blanched almonds

1 Remove any seeds from the pumpkin and cut off the skin. Cut the flesh into 2.5 cm (1 inch) cubes.

2 Place the vinegar and sugar in a large heavy-based saucepan, cover and bring to the boil on the BOILING PLATE. Transfer to the SIMMERING PLATE and add the pumpkin, together with all the remaining ingredients, except the almonds. Stir well, bring to the boil and let bubble for 5 minutes.

3 Cover and cook in the SIMMERING OVEN for 2½-3 hours or until all of the ingredients are very soft.

4 Return to the SIMMERING PLATE and cook, uncovered, for 15 minutes or until thick and pulpy. To test, draw a wooden spoon through the mixture – it should leave a clear trail at the bottom of the pan which fills up slowly.

5 Stir in the almonds and pack the chutney into warm sterilised jars. Seal and store in a cool dark place for at least 1 month before using.

COOK'S TIPS

▶ To blanch almonds, put into a heatproof bowl, pour on boiling water to cover, then place in the SIMMERING OVEN for 10-15 minutes. Allow to cool, then skin.
▶ If preferred, lightly crush the coriander seeds and tie with the cardamom pods in muslin. Add at stage 2; remove before potting.

CRANBERRY AND ROAST SHALLOT CHUTNEY

■ MAKES 1.2 KG (2½ LB) ■ PREPARATION 25 MINUTES
■ COOKING ABOUT 30 MINUTES ■ 45 CALS PER 25 G (1 OZ)

A dark ruby-red relish made with sharp flavourful cranberries and chunks of sweet caramelised shallots. Unlike the usual cranberry sauce, this is more versatile and a little sharper, which makes it a perfect accompaniment to farmhouse cheese, thick slices of cold ham and, of course, the cold Christmas turkey!

450 g (1 lb) shallots
45 ml (3 tbsp) olive oil
225 g (8 oz) soft brown sugar
salt and freshly ground black pepper
150 ml (¼ pint) red wine
450 g (1 lb) fresh or frozen cranberries
2.5 ml (1 inch) piece fresh root ginger, peeled and grated
15 ml (1 tbsp) mustard seeds
200 ml (7 fl oz) red wine vinegar

1 Put the shallots in a heatproof bowl, pour on boiling water to cover and leave until cool. Drain and carefully peel, leaving on a little of the root end to hold them intact.

2 Halve the shallots lengthwise and place in a roasting tin. Sprinkle with the olive oil and 45 ml (3 tbsp) of the sugar. Roast on the floor of the ROASTING OVEN for 15-20 minutes, turning from time to time. Transfer to the grid shelf

on the fourth set of runners and cook for a further
5-10 minutes until soft and caramelised, but not burnt.
Season generously with salt and pepper.

3 Lift out the shallots and set aside. Add the red wine to
the roasting tin and bring to the boil on the BOILING PLATE.
Let bubble until reduced by half.

4 Meanwhile, place the cranberries in a heavy-based
saucepan with the ginger, mustard seeds, vinegar and

reduced red wine. Bring slowly to the boil on the SIMMER-
ING PLATE. Cover and cook in the SIMMERING OVEN for
10-15 minutes until the cranberries are very soft. Add the
remaining warmed sugar, bring to the boil on the SIMMER-
ING PLATE and cook for 10-15 minutes until thick and pulpy.
Stir in the shallots.

5 Spoon the chutney into warm sterilised jars. Seal and
store in a cool dry place for up to 6 months. Once opened,
store in the refrigerator and use within 1 month.

THREE FRUIT MARMALADE

■ MAKES ABOUT 3.8 KG (8 LB) ■ PREPARATION 40 MINUTES, PLUS STANDING
■ COOKING 1½-2 HOURS ■ 35 CALS PER 15 ML (1 TBSP)

There is nothing better than the flavour of homemade marmalade – it's worth every moment of effort. Choose firm fruit with unwaxed skins.

2 medium sweet oranges, about 450 g (1 lb)
4 lemons, about 450 g (1 lb)
2 medium grapefruit, about 700 g (1½ lb)
2.5 litres (4¼ pints) water
2.6 kg (6 lb) granulated sugar, warmed

1 Scrub the fruit. Halve the oranges and lemons, squeeze the juice and strain into a preserving pan or large saucepan, reserving the pips, pith and peel. Peel the grapefruit, removing and reserving the skin with the white pith. Roughly chop the grapefruit flesh, reserving any pith and pips. Add the grapefruit flesh to the pan.

2 Using a sharp knife, shred all the orange, lemon and grapefruit peel into pieces, about 1 cm x 3 mm (½ x ⅛ inch). If the fruit is very pithy, trim to leave a 5 mm (¼ inch) thickness on the peel before shredding. Reserve any removed pith. Add the shredded peel to the pan with the water. Tie all the pips and pith in a piece of muslin and add to the pan.

3 Cover and bring to the boil on the SIMMERING PLATE. Let bubble for 5 minutes, then transfer to the SIMMERING OVEN and cook for 1-1½ hours or until the peel is very soft. Remove the muslin bag. Add the warmed sugar and heat again on the SIMMERING PLATE until dissolved. Transfer to the BOILING PLATE and boil hard for 15 minutes or until setting point is reached (see preserving tips).

4 Leave the marmalade to stand off the heat, for about 15 minutes so that it thickens slightly. (This prevents the peel from rising to the top of the jars.) Pot and cover in the usual way.

COOK'S TIP Add all pips and excess pith to the muslin bag as they contain pectin, which helps to set the marmalade.

VARIATION
Seville Orange Marmalade: Use 1.4 kg (3 lb) Seville oranges in place of the citrus fruit listed above. Add the juice of 2 lemons at the beginning of stage 3.

GENERAL PRESERVING TIPS

▶ *Use a large preserving pan or large wide saucepan to allow maximum evaporation. Stainless steel or non-stick aluminium pans are best.*

▶ *Preserving sugar gives a slightly clearer finish, but granulated sugar is fine for most preserves, including marmalade. 'Sugar with pectin' is used for jams made with fruit which is low in pectin.*

▶ *The sugar should be warmed before it is added to jams or marmalades. Simply place in a large heatproof bowl at the back of the Aga, or in the SIMMERING OVEN (or PLATE-WARMING OVEN) for about 30 minutes.*

▶ *Make sure the pan is never more than half full. If necessary, divide the mixture in half before adding the sugar and cook in two batches.*

▶ *Test jams and marmalades regularly for a set. If boiled for too long preserves darken and caramelise.*

▶ *A sugar thermometer can be used; the preserve is ready when it registers 105°C (221°F).*

▶ *For the saucer test, you will need 1 or 2 chilled saucers. Spoon a little of the jam or marmalade onto a cold saucer. Push a finger across the preserve: if the surface wrinkles and it is beginning to set, it has reached 'setting point'. If not, boil for another 5 minutes and repeat the test.*

▶ *Once setting point is reached, pour into clean, warm jars, filling them right up to the top. Cover immediately with waxed discs, wax-side down. Leave to go cold, then cover with dampened cellophane. Label the jars and store them in a cool, dry place for up to 6 months.*

STRAWBERRY JAM

■ MAKES ABOUT 1.8 KG (4 LB). ■ PREPARATION 10 MINUTES, PLUS STANDING
■ COOKING ABOUT 10 MINUTES ■ 35 CALS PER 15 ML (1 TBSP)

900 g (2 lb) strawberries, hulled
1 kg (2.2 lb) 'sugar with pectin', warmed
juice of ½ lemon

1 Put about a quarter of the strawberries in a preserving pan or large saucepan and crush with a wooden spoon. Add the warmed sugar and lemon juice. Heat gently on the SIMMERING PLATE, stirring until the sugar is dissolved. Add the rest of the strawberries.

2 Transfer to the BOILING PLATE and bring to the boil. Boil steadily for about 4 minutes or until setting point is reached.

3 Remove from the heat and remove any scum with a slotted spoon. Leave to stand for 15-20 minutes.

4 Stir the jam gently, then pot and cover in the usual way.

PLUM JAM

■ MAKES ABOUT 3.8 KG (8 LB) ■ PREPARATION 15 MINUTES
■ COOKING ABOUT 1¼-1½ HOURS ■ 75 CALS PER 15 ML (1 TBSP)

2.7 kg (6 lb) plums, washed
600 ml (1 pint) water
2.7 kg (6 lb) sugar, warmed
knob of butter

1 Put the plums in a preserving pan or large saucepan with the water. Cover and slowly bring to the boil on the SIMMERING PLATE. Let bubble for 5 minutes, then transfer to the SIMMERING OVEN and cook for 45 minutes to 1 hour, until the fruit is very soft.

2 Return to the SIMMERING PLATE and add the warmed sugar. Stir until dissolved. Add the butter.

3 Transfer to the BOILING PLATE and boil rapidly for 10-15 minutes or until setting point is reached.

4 Using a slotted spoon, remove the plum stones and any scum from the surface. Pot and cover in the usual way.

COOK'S TIP *If dessert plums are used, rather than a cooking variety, add the juice of 1 large lemon.*

LEMON CURD

■ MAKES ABOUT 700 G (1½ LB) ■ PREPARATION 20 MINUTES
■ COOKING 25-30 MINUTES ■ 55 CALS PER 15 ML (1 TBSP)

4 eggs
grated rind and juice of 4 medium ripe, juicy lemons
125 g (4 oz) butter, cut in small pieces
350 g (12 oz) caster sugar

1 Lightly whisk the eggs in a bowl, then strain into a large heatproof bowl. Add all the rest of the ingredients and stand the bowl over a pan of simmering water on the SIMMERING PLATE. Stir until the sugar has dissolved.

2 Continue to heat gently, without boiling, for 20-25 minutes or until thick enough to coat the back of the spoon.

3 Pour the lemon curd into sterilised jars. Cover in the usual way. Store in the refrigerator and use within 2-3 weeks.

COOK'S TIP *If you are feeling confident, to save time, simply place all of the ingredients in a heavy-based saucepan and cook very gently on the side of the SIMMERING PLATE, stirring continuously, for about 5 minutes until thickened. Immediately pour into a cold bowl to prevent further cooking. Pot, cover and store as above.*

VARIATION
Lime Curd: Replace the lemons with the grated rind and juice of 5 large ripe, juicy limes.

WARNING The young, elderly, pregnant women and anyone suffering from an immune deficiency disease should avoid eating homemade lemon curd, owing to the possible risk of salmonella from lightly cooked eggs.

INDEX

almond fudge crumbles, 133

apples: apple and blackberry pudding, 101

  apple and cinnamon pancakes, 109

  apple and raisin crumbles, 133

  apple and walnut cake, 120-1

  Bramley apples with ginger, 106-7

  crumbly apple and cheese cake, 126-7

  ricotta strudel, 117

  tarte Tatin, 106

apricots: pumpkin, apricot and almond chutney, 138

asparagus: asparagus and broad bean frittata, 90

  roasted asparagus salad, 22

aubergines: aubergine, red onion and mushroom pizza, 81

  baba ganoush, 18

  baked aubergines, 93

  lamb steaks with aubergine relish, 66

  moussaka, 66-7

  pasta and aubergine gratin, 80-1

  tomato, aubergine and pepper Parmigiana, 89

baba ganoush, 18

bacon: bacon and celeriac soup, 14

  bacon, potato and mushroom gratin, 90

  toasted bacon and goats' cheese salad, 17

baking oven, 10

bananas, baked with cardamom and rum, 114

beef: aromatic braised steak, 54

  chilli with potato wedges, 52

  Italian meatballs, 52-3

  meat pie with cheesy vegetable topping, 53

  mustard roast rib of beef, 50

  pan-fried steaks with Roquefort and red pepper butter, 56

  ragù alla Bolognese, 56-7

  rich beef daube, 54-5

  traditional steak and kidney pie, 57

biscuits: almond fudge crumbles, 133

  apple and raisin crumbles, 133

  coffee and walnut crumbles, 133

  double chocolate cookies, 132-3

  shortbread, 129

  toasted pine nut cookies, 133

  triple chocolate cookies, 133

black-eyed bean casserole, 72-3

boiling plate, 10

Bolognese sauce, 56-7

Bramley apples with ginger, 106-7

bread: focaccia, 137

  wholemeal bread, 136

broccoli: Calabrian pasta, 88-9

brown sugar meringues, 116

brownies, white chocolate, 130-1

bruléed lemon tartlets, 112

cake baker, 10

cakes, 10

  apple and walnut cake, 120-1

  carrot cake with mascarpone topping, 122

  chocolate pecan fudge cake, 124

  Christmas cake, 125

  crumbly apple and cheese cake, 126-7

  hinny cakes, 134

  rich chocolate cake, 121

  sticky gingerbread, 128-9

  whisked sponge with cream and strawberries, 120

  white chocolate brownies, 130-1

Calabrian pasta, 88-9

calves liver with black pudding and bacon, 70

cannelloni: crespoline, 82

caramelised rice puddings, 101

carrots: carrot and ginger soup, 12-13

  carrot cake with mascarpone topping, 122

casseroles, 10

  aromatic braised steak, 54

  baked black-eyed bean, 72-3

  chicken and pepper, 42-3

  harvest pork, 60

  Mediterranean fish, 29

  rich beef daube, 54-5

  vegetable couscous, 74

  vegetable stew with rouille, 73

celeriac: bacon and celeriac soup, 14

cheese: baked Cheddar and onion soup, 13

  crespoline, 82

  crumbly apple and cheese cake, 126-7

  melting cheese and ham parcel, 88

  ricotta strudel, 117

  toasted bacon and goats' cheese salad, 17

  tomato, aubergine and pepper Parmigiana, 89

  the ultimate cheese tart, 85

cheesecake, lemon, 110-11

cherry sauce, roast duck with, 48-9

chicken: chicken and pepper casserole, 42-3

  chicken hotpot with leeks, 38

  devilled roast chicken, 38-9

  golden chicken lasagne, 41

  lemon chicken with saffron risotto, 40

  Provençal chicken bake, 40-1

  Thai green curry, 42

  traditional roast chicken, 37

  warm chicken, cashew and noodle salad, 92

chilli: chilli with potato wedges, 52

  vegetable chilli, 76

chocolate: chocolate pecan fudge cake, 124

  chocolate, walnut and maple puddings, 104

  double chocolate cookies, 132-3

  profiteroles with chocolate sauce, 113

  rich chocolate cake, 121

  triple chocolate cookies, 133

  white chocolate brownies, 130-1

Christmas cake, 125

Christmas pudding, 105

chutneys: cranberry and roast shallot, 138-9

  pumpkin, apricot and almond, 138

cleaning the Aga, 11

coconut crème brulée, 100

cod fillet wrapped in filo pastry with rocket, 30

coffee and walnut crumbles, 133

cold plain shelf, 8, 10

conserving heat, 7

cookies see biscuits

corn salsa, 36

couscous, vegetable, 74

crab cakes, crispy, 20

cranberry and roast shallot chutney, 138-9

crème brulée, coconut, 100

crespoline, 82

croissant pudding, golden, 102
curry, Thai green, 42
custard: golden croissant pudding, 102
  vanilla custard, 104

dates: rippled date and banana loaf, 126
desserts, 100-19
devilled roast chicken, 38-9
duck: duck breasts with rösti and apple, 48
  roast duck with cherry sauce, 48-9

eggs: asparagus and broad bean frittata, 90
equipment, 10

fish and shellfish, 25-36
  fish fillets with spicy tomato sauce, 26
  Mediterranean fish casserole, 29
  roasted fish with courgettes and tomatoes, 30
  see also cod, salmon etc
flapjacks, sticky orange, 128
focaccia, 137
frittata, asparagus and broad bean, 90

game and poultry, 37-49
ginger: sticky gingerbread, 128-9
  sweet ginger dip, 20
gnocchi, potato, 78
grid shelf, 10
grill pan, 10
guinea fowl, pan-fried with red wine sauce, 46-7

ham: braised ham with spring vegetables, 61
  melting cheese and ham parcel, 88
harvest pork casserole, 60
hazelnuts: hazelnut butter, 72
  hazelnut meringue gâteau, 114-15
heat, conserving, 7
heat indicator, 8
herrings, baked with an oatmeal, mushroom and parsley stuffing, 28
hinny cakes, 134
honey and yogurt muffins, 132
hot plates, 10

Italian braised lamb shanks, 65
Italian meatballs, 52-3
Italian sausage ragù, 70-1

Jamaican jerk lamb, 68-9
jams: plum, 141
  strawberry, 141
Jerusalem artichokes: mushroom and artichoke soup, 16

koftas on green herbs, 69

lamb: Italian braised lamb shanks, 65
  Jamaican jerk lamb, 68-9
  koftas on green herbs, 69
  lamb steaks with aubergine relish, 66
  moussaka, 66-7
  rosemary and garlic-scented roast leg of lamb, 64
  tomato-crusted lamb, 68
lasagne, golden chicken, 41
leeks: chicken hotpot with, 38
  vichyssoise with lemon grass, 16-17
lemon: bruléed lemon tartlets, 112
  lemon cheesecake, 110-11
  lemon chicken with saffron risotto, 40
  lemon curd, 141
liver: calves liver with black pudding and bacon, 70

marmalade, three fruit, 140
meat dishes, 50-71
meat pie with cheesy vegetable topping, 53
meatballs, Italian, 52-3
Mediterranean fish casserole, 29
meringues, 10
  brown sugar meringues, 116
  hazelnut meringue gâteau, 114-15
mince pies, traditional, 108
minestrone alla Milanese, 12
monkfish: braised monkfish wrapped in Parma ham, 34
moussaka, 66-7
muffins, honey and yogurt, 132
mushroom and artichoke soup, 16
mussels: mussels in saffron cider broth, 25
  mussels with ginger, chilli and coriander, 20-1

oats: sticky orange flapjacks, 128
olive and sun-dried tomato focaccia, 137
onions: baked Cheddar and onion soup, 13
  onion tartlets, 18-19
  roast onions, 44
  white onion pizza, 86

oranges: sticky orange flapjacks, 128
  three fruit marmalade, 140
ovens, 6-9

pancakes, apple and cinnamon, 109
pans, 10-11
parsnip potato galette, 98
pasta: Calabrian pasta, 88-9
  pasta and aubergine gratin, 80-1
pecan fudge cake, chocolate, 124
peppers: chicken and pepper casserole, 42-3
  grilled pepper salad, 94
pheasant, traditional roast, 46
pies: crusty Mediterranean parcels, 80
  meat pie with cheesy vegetable topping, 53
  rhubarb and cinnamon cobbler, 110
  traditional mince pies, 108
  traditional steak and kidney pie, 57
  turkey and ham pot pie, 45
pine nut cookies, 133
pineapple and almond roulade, 118-19
pizzas: aubergine, red onion and mushroom, 81
  tomato, artichoke and prosciutto, 86
  white onion, 86
plate-warming oven, 10
plum jam, 141
polenta, Italian sausage ragù with, 70-1
pork: glazed spare ribs, 62
  harvest pork casserole, 60
  peppered garlic pork, 62-3
  pork medallions in a creamy sloe gin sauce, 60
  roast loin of pork with sweet-sour vinaigrette, 58-9
  roast pork with minted apple and horseradish sauce, 58
potatoes: bacon, potato and mushroom gratin, 90
  baked jacket potatoes, 84
  chicken hotpot with leeks, 38
  chilli with potato wedges, 52
  crispy potato skins, 96
  crunchy roast potatoes and shallots, 96
  potato gnocchi, 78
  potato parsnip galette, 98
  rösti, 48
poultry and game, 37-49
prawns: king prawns with a spicy tomato and pepper sauce, 21
preserves, 138-41

profiteroles with chocolate sauce, 113
Provençal chicken bake, 40-1
pumpkin: pumpkin, apricot and almond chutney, 138
 pumpkin risotto, 72

rabbit with grainy mustard, 49
ragù: Italian sausage ragù, 70-1
 ragù alla Bolognese, 56-7
raspberry sauce, brown sugar meringues with, 116
red kidney beans: chilli with potato wedges, 52
reheating food, 10
rhubarb and cinnamon cobbler, 110
rice: caramelised rice puddings, 101
 koftas on green herbs with tomato rice, 69
 see also risotto
ricotta strudel, 117
risotto: lemon chicken with saffron risotto, 40
 pumpkin risotto with hazelnut butter, 72
 seafood risotto, 25
roasting oven, 8
roasting tins, 10
root vegetables, 9
rosemary focaccia, 137
rösti, 48
roulade, pineapple and almond, 118-19

sabayon sauce, 105
saffron risotto, 40
sage and onion focaccia, 137
salads: grilled pepper, 94
 roasted asparagus, 22
 roasted tomato and shallot, 22
 toasted bacon and goats' cheese, 17
 warm chicken, cashew and noodle, 92
salmon: roast salmon in mustard butter, 33
 salmon escalopes with cucumber and dill salsa, 32
 salmon terrine, 24
 with hollandaise sauce, 32-3
sauces: ragù alla Bolognese, 56-7
 sabayon, 105
sausagemeat: Italian sausage ragù with soft polenta, 70-1
scallops: seared scallops with roasted plum tomatoes, 26
scones, 130
seafood gratin, 34-5
seafood pesto chowder, 14-15

seafood risotto, 25
shallots: cranberry and roast shallot chutney, 138-9
shellfish and fish, 25-36
shortbread, 129
simmering oven, 9
simmering plate, 10
soups, 12-17
 bacon and celeriac, 14
 baked Cheddar and onion, 13
 carrot and ginger, 12-13
 minestrone alla Milanese, 12
 mushroom and artichoke, 16
 seafood pesto chowder, 14-15
 vichyssoise with lemon grass, 16-17
spinach: crespoline, 82
splatter guard, 10
steak and kidney pie, 57
stews see casseroles and stews
stocks, 9
strawberries: strawberry jam, 141
 whisked sponge with cream and strawberries, 120
strudel, ricotta, 117
swede and carrot gratin, 97

tarts: bruléed lemon tartlets, 112
 onion tartlets, 18-19
 roasted vegetable tart, 84
 tarte Tatin, 106
 the ultimate cheese tart, 85
teabreads: rippled date and banana loaf, 126
terrine, salmon, 24
Thai green curry, 42
toaster, 10
tomatoes: crespoline, 82
 fish fillets with spicy tomato sauce, 26
 Italian meatballs in tomato sauce, 52-3
 Italian sausage ragù with soft polenta, 70-1
 koftas on green herbs with tomato rice, 69
 onion tartlets with tomato and caper salsa, 18-19
 oven-baked tomatoes, 93
 roasted tomato and shallot salad, 22
 seared scallops with roasted plum tomatoes, 26
 tomato, artichoke and prosciutto pizza, 86
 tomato, aubergine and pepper Parmigiana, 89
 tomato-crusted lamb with summer vegetables, 68

trout with almond and herb purée, 28-9
tuna: seared tuna steaks with corn salsa, 36
turkey: turkey and ham pot pie, 45
 turkey with roast onions and Madeira gravy, 44-5

vanilla custard, 104
vegetables, 9
 baked vegetable purses, 94
 braised ham with spring vegetables, 61
 crusty Mediterranean parcels, 80
 golden roast vegetables, 97
 meat pie with cheesy vegetable topping, 53
 roasted vegetable tart, 84
 stir-fried vegetables, 77
 tomato-crusted lamb with summer vegetables, 68
 vegetable chilli, 76
 vegetable couscous, 74
 vegetable pasanda, 76-7
 vegetable stew with rouille, 73
vegetarian dishes, 72-84
vichyssoise with lemon grass, 16-17

warming plate, 10
whisked sponge, 120
wholemeal bread, 136

Yorkshire pudding, 50